Eclipsed

A heartfelt story of how a kid dances his way into the Spider-Man suit,
eclipsing his 'celebrity' dad in the process.

Eclipsed

Dominic Holland

Dedication

For my family

Acknowledgements

My thanks to Martin Williams, a brilliant artist and illustrator for his work on this front cover along with Shana for her help also.

Thanks to Jon Furniss, a press photographer who I enjoy bumping in to on various carpets, most usually red, for allowing me to use one of his images in this book.

I make much mention of all my family throughout this book, which is no surprise since it is a chronicle of my entire family life; taking up from my marriage to becoming a father and watching my boys grow up. But in particular, I need to pay tribute to my wife, Nikki. This is my book. It is my story. I have written it. It was my idea. But without Nikki, there wouldn't be much of a story to tell and this becomes increasingly apparent on reading. So, from me and presumably from Tom as well – a very big thank you.

Foreword by Tom Holland

You know how your parents embarrass you with old photographs which most usually involve nudity?

Well, when my dad mentioned that he had an idea for a blog about my show-biz success against his on-going struggles I didn't give it much thought. I do remember thinking at the time that my dad was successful. He is funny (he's a comedian by the way) and at this point he had long been on the verge of making it in Hollywood as a writer. At this time, we were all in Thailand where I was making my first film, *The Impossible*, so I guess that I was already ahead of my dad's 'verge' stage and he explained that our comparative success stories in film would make a funny story.

But dad, what happens when you get your movies made? Wouldn't this make the story redundant? And it could look a little boastful as well?

Dad didn't seem too concerned by this. He even muttered something about the whole thing being fated.

Okay then, but what if *The Impossible* is the only film that I get to make? I mean, what if this is the end of my career in show business, will this be enough of a story to tell?

Dad gave this some thought as though I might have a point. He explained that this was even likely and that *The Impossible* could well be the end of my acting days. He went on to say that lots of child 'stars' see their hopes and dreams cruelly extinguished!

As my dad says in this book, he is frequently wrong and thankfully so in this instance because so far, the roles have kept on coming and this project has become even more important for my dad since his film career appears to be no longer on the verge.

Although I never said anything at the time, I did privately worry that this project could be embarrassing; if my dad is too gushing about me but also if he is too hard on himself.

Deciding to publish the book, Dad gave me permission to end the project completely when he handed me his final draft and I should never have worried because I think it is spot on.

I really enjoy the coincidences and counter-balancing between our colliding journeys and even though he is a little hard on himself, I figure that this is for comic effect and I note proudly that he is still at the coal face with his writing and his stand-up. And as much as the films I have appeared in are great reminders of my mis-spent youth, *Eclipsed* binds these experiences together; of what I expect will be the most important decade of my life and an exciting time for my whole family.

I am told by many to expect a raft of unauthorised biographies of my life; cobbled together from various sources and old pieces of journalism and usually not very real or authentic. At least with *Eclipsed*, people can share in my story and get the real answers to the question, I am most frequently asked; 'so dude, how did you become Spider-Man?'

Author's Note

This book was first published in January 2013 and titled - *how tom holland Eclipsed his dad*. At the time, this title made good sense because to my dismay (I am often dismayed) the manuscript was roundly rejected by ALL the traditional publishers and so I embraced technology and went the eBook route instead; my metaphorical middle finger to the past. Determined to prove them wrong, I was advised that my on-line book needed to be search engine friendly and it was agreed that the words, 'Tom' and 'Holland' were easily the two most attractive elements of this project and ideally should feature in the title – and so *how tom holland Eclipsed his dad* was born.

The manuscript was rejected for the most part because Tom was not really a 'star' and the story is incomplete. Other rejections were more flattering, explaining that Dominic Holland was far too successful a comedian to write such a book!

Mmm...

In the intervening years, both issues have been firmly dealt with. Tom Holland was introduced to the world as *Spider-Man* in *Captain America, Civil War* in 2016 and at the time of writing (Saturday, October 20th, 2016) this evening, I am performing stand-up comedy at a primary school in Woking as part of a fundraiser. Next year (2017) I am heading back to the Edinburgh Festival on a career rekindling mission where I will play the Free Fringe and begin each show with the words, 'Good afternoon...'

This venture began as a blog and it was always my intention to end this yarn (I promise to avoid using the word 'journey') with the release of Tom's first film, *The Impossible*.

This book, *Eclipsed* (2017) remains the original eBook - an explanation of how a 16-year-old kid should find himself on a red carpet in LA and on the long list for an Academy Award. And from this juncture, just a cursory glance on-line can establish how Tom has progressed to becoming Peter Parker and the iconic Spider-Man.

But on deciding to create a print edition and reading the eBook through after so many years, I have made some edits and some additions in the light of current developments in the diverging lives of Dom and Tom. At the end of certain chapters I have added some further observations as footnotes.

Commonly I am asked, how has my son managed to become a super-hero and less frequently, what ever happened to my own career? This book answers both questions and I hope much else besides.

October 2016

Contents

Prologue

It is the natural order of things that successive generations will achieve more than their predecessors or at least this has been the way until now. Margaret Thatcher's dad was a grocer, Jim McCartney was a professional trumpeter and had a son called Paul, and Charles Dickens's dad was a clerk in the navy pay office. It is also normal for parents to be ambitious for their children and so when a child does overtake a parent, it should engender pride rather than any sense of failure. This is good news on a practical level as well, especially if the parents are hoping that their children might care for them in their twilight years, ideally in a spare room or in the case of Mr and Mrs Bieber, in the spare wing.

But some parents of course will never be eclipsed by their children. I expect the young McEnroe children never bothered with tennis once they realised the mountain facing them. Likewise, Tiger's young son might be ill-advised to try and emulate his famous dad in either of the two fields in which he has been so dominant.

Like most parents, when my first child arrived way back in 1996, I hoped that he would achieve more than I managed for myself. I did not expect, however, that this would happen barely twelve years later and in the same profession as me, really?

I am a comedian by the way – a professional stand-up comedian – and all told, I have been pretty bloody successful. Making people laugh has been my sole source of income for well over twenty-five years and it has provided very well for me and my family, thank you very much. Self-employed, there is no such thing as sick pay in live stand-up comedy. It is a career than hinges on a very simple equation of no gigs, no income – and no laughs, no gigs.

I have four children, all boys and all of them have remained fed, watered and clothed solely from the proceeds of me being funny and making people laugh.

The Holland boys in Portugal

Tom is my eldest at sixteen (now twenty) and is the unwitting star of this rather unique family story: a story that probably began to gestate as I sat in the stalls at the Victoria Palace Theatre watching him play Billy in the hit show *Billy Elliot the Musical*. It is a rather extraordinary role, and as I watched him pirouetting about the stage, it struck me just how much he had achieved already in his short life.

The seed of this story germinated at this point and then some two years later, as I manned a BBQ on a beach in Thailand and handed a sausage to Ewan McGregor, the story was almost fully formed and one that I felt compelled to write.

This is that story.

How a kid danced his way from London's West End to Hollywood, overtaking his 'celebrity' dad along the way.

This book was (first) completed in 2013 when *The Impossible* premiered in Los Angeles. I wrote then, that as a matter of principal, I would not update the book whatever happens to either Dad or son. I did not relish the prospect of being a parent putting his family life up for scrutiny. At this juncture, reality television had emerged but the phenomenal success of reality families like the Kardashians had yet to reveal itself. And no matter how much fame they have accrued or wealth they have banked, it is even clearer now that my instincts on this were correct.

I signed off the eBook with '*readers interested to learn more about our respective careers can do so by following our on-going work in movie theatres across the world or in village halls across the UK'*. Indeed, I wrote this with a smug confidence that I would manage to get myself back on the television and, I hoped that Tom might continue as an actor of course. In these intervening years, only one of these things has happened and it makes this story even more acute. A good thing then?

The hallowed red carpet

The true-life story of the movie, *The Impossible* is a remarkable one, but what has happened to my little boy since the film's release has been just as impossible. Approaching publishers with the original book and convinced that it would be snapped up and become a bestseller - my delusions are an important spine of this book - and I have already explained why the publishers disagreed.

A perfect comic story then and even more remarkable because the whole thing has been a complete fluke. There have been no stage schools, tutors nor pushy parents involved. I hope that this story is more attractive and compelling because it has happened by chance, with its two protagonists, father and son, playing their roles perfectly. Two careers crossing to create a story with, dare I say it, the X factor? A show that I loathe, but grudgingly I accept its popularity and its place in modern culture.

To put the authorial tone of this book into context, I defer to one of our greatest writers, George Orwell:

Every life when viewed from the inside is a series of defeats.

Like most things, fame and celebrity are relative. The height of my 'celebrity' was back in the last century when I appeared on *The Royal Variety Show*, my first BBC Radio 4 series ran and I published the first of my novels. I had no idea at the time that this would be my peak. I could make people laugh and I just assumed that my success would continue. As I write this new edition now in 2016, I have not performed comedy on television for almost fifteen years; and my greatest successes in life have certainly been off-stage and in the more important parenting arena?

Recently, sitting backstage at a village hall ahead of my latest one-man show, it struck me as comic: the diverging lives of father and son. Enjoyable as these shows are, I do ponder on how things have transpired, but I also revel in the comic potential and the upside of the story that it provides me with. Every cloud... as the cliché goes.

This is a story that spans twenty odd years and seems so perfect to me now that I wonder if the whole thing has not been preordained. It is written with affection by a dad who is much prouder than he is bemused. And certainly, I am not angry. There is no disgrace in being eclipsed by a kid who counts Robert Downey Junior as a colleague. This is a story that even the comedians filling our nation's arenas could write - if of course, they were lucky enough to be Spider-Man's dad.

Stand-up comedy is not for the thin-skinned and only very few will ever truly prevail. As such, all comedians will try their hands at writing. Certainly, all comics will write a sit-com. Most will attempt a novel or a play and some, like me, will take a crack at film. Sitting on a freezing cold train in 1995, I had an epiphany and decided that I would become a screenwriter and head off to Hollywood. And why not? Films get made, right? Metaphorically, I am still on this train and my misadventures in film have become an unlikely and useful backdrop for this story.

Because whilst Hollywood was refusing to return my calls, something else was afoot without anyone realizing it, something that would result in me finally flying to Hollywood in a big seat. And no matter that this interest is not in me, but in my son and not just my eldest son either.

This is a true story of an ordinary family encountering the extraordinary. A story of good old fashioned endeavor, bound by good fortune and serendipity. No spoiler warning when I say that it has a euphoric climax.

I hope you enjoy it as much as I have enjoyed writing it and indeed living it.

Welcome to *Eclipsed*.

Author Footnote

All parents understand the essential ritual of dressing up. A rites-of-passage which all the Holland boys have been fully committed to.

In this book – without being mawkish, I account for my premature career plateau and my increasing reliance on self-help books, read most voraciously each January and usually petering out by mid-April. A central tenet of these books is the simple and powerful art of visualization. The reader is promised that if they vividly visualize whatever it is that they truly desire, then guess what happens?

Er... in my experience, nothing! But I am intrigued that for maybe five years or more, my first born, was absolutely convinced that he was Spider-Man. We have a series of birthday party photographs of Tom in various Spider-Man outfits, all in various states of disrepair. He was not Tom. He was Spider-Man which has since come to pass and so a feather in the cap of the self-help visualization fraternity?

Well, to a point. Because I know that my son is not alone in this fixation when he was growing up. At gigs the sheer number of mums and dads who explain to me that their son is Spider-Man crazy and that he dresses up at every opportunity. Practically all little boys fixate on Spider-Man and want to emulate him. Perhaps my son just visualized better and more convincingly than those other kids? Of course, I don't believe this. The stars just aligned and he was willing and able to take each opportunity that came his way. And as his dad, I find it hard to articulate how this really feels. Proud. Bemused. Stunned. Ecstatic. Fretful. Relieved. Excited. All of these and more.

And so, revisiting this book has been a useful and cathartic exercise for me to reprise my happy memories of being a young dad and 'burgeoning comedy star' and it helps me to try and figure out how and why everything has gone so wrong and so bloody well right.

The Big Apple

New York is an exciting city to visit, even without my unusual set of circumstances. I've been to the Big Apple before of course, modern man of the world as I am (albeit only for a single night, en-route to the less credible Orlando for my 'Work America' summer during my student days). This was way back in 1989, when visitors to New York did well to avoid being murdered. I'd ventured out tentatively onto the crime-ridden and gang-run streets, just long enough to gaze up at the buildings, agree that they were very tall indeed, before scarpering back inside to the relative safety of my youth hostel.

This trip to New York, precisely twenty-one years later, is in every sense a big step up. To start with, this is a business trip. I am now a dad and I am being accompanied on the trip by my eldest son, Tom, who is fourteen. More accurately, I am accompanying him because it is Tom who is on business and not me. An all-expenses-paid, week-long trip with no communal transfer buses or youth hostels in site.

We are met at JFK Airport by Charlie. I didn't catch his surname. He didn't have a sign saying Holland or even Tom Holland. He just knew who we were and introduced himself then led us to our waiting limousine. It's a Lincoln; I don't know which model, but it's gleaming black, very muscular and very big. It needs to be climbed into and from a considerable height I haul Tom in after me. Inside, it's what I expect. It has a fridge, which I don't bother with. Tom is very excited by the car and I pretend not to be. It is not something I approve of. It is an affront to the world's finite oil reserves, although I concede that it is bloody comfortable.

It is night time as we approach Manhattan, which Charlie explains really is an island. Charlie is an assistant. In the world of Hollywood, the only things more plentiful than assistants are wannabes. Charlie is the assistant for the meeting taking place here in New York. He is our point man, available to Tom for whatever he might need – and perhaps to me as well? I'm not sure and I don't like to ask.

In a half hour or so, we arrive at our hotel. I jump down from the Lincoln and manage to land safely. Our bags are swept away by two bell boys who are going to be disappointed when they realise that as yet I have no dollars. And even if I did, what is the actual value of someone opening a door for me? The hotel is the Soho Grande, which is appropriately named because as I enter its ultra-modern reception, I am feeling pretty damn grand.

It is late now, 11.00 p.m., and with the meeting scheduled for 9.00 a.m. the next morning, I'm keen for Tom to get some sleep. Charlie asks if I would like a wake-up call. There's absolutely no chance that I will sleep in and miss such an important meeting, but I agree to the alarm call anyway, just to be on the safe side. I also don't want to seem rude, and I suspect that Charlie will enjoy having something to organise.

They had offered us a hotel room each, but in the interest of currying favour with the production company behind this $50m film, I explained that we would be happy to share. Also in my thinking was that Tom probably wouldn't want to be in a room on his own. I figured he had enough on his mind already without having to worry about how to turn off all the lights in a luxury hotel room.

The Soho Grande is a fusion of modern urban chic and old industrial, the sort of place that only advertising executives could ever consider normal. It's a brand-new building, fitted out to look like a reclaimed warehouse: exposed brickwork, wrought iron and stone, minimalism that speaks volumes. The whole place aches under the strain to appear cool, an effort which is readily taken up by the androgynous and beautiful staff, who are more aloof than impolite. I expect that their demeanour is deliberate. It allows the celebs who choose the Grande a chance to relax amongst people almost as cool as themselves.

The man guarding the bar area has long blonde hair and full make-up. He reminds me of Marilyn, the bloke who used to hang out with/of Boy George. He is wearing a skirt and has a neck full of tattoos leading to his face of ultra-indifference. Nothing could impress or turn this guy's head. If there was a fire, this guy would take his chances and stroll to the exit. Naturally, Tom is curious. I explain that he is definitely a man and I tell him not to stare. No one stares at anyone in the Soho Grande. In the Grande, we are all celebs. I decide that the Marilyn lookalike is opportune and I explain to Tom that because the film he is about to star in is going to be shot largely in Thailand, he needs to get used to seeing 'is-she-isn't-he' types. I say this with absolutely no experience of Thailand whatsoever.

What with the time difference, the next morning we are awake before the larks at 5.00 a.m., and we wait an hour to be the very first in the dining room. We sit in comfortable chairs and I glance at the menu. The prices are hilarious and I wonder if we might be the only takers for breakfast, although I suspect not. I have a bowl of warm granola with fresh fruits of the forest, and Tom plumps for pancakes which he can't finish. I have a thing about waste in general and particularly food waste and this would have irked me, especially if I had been paying. Tom does the best he can and we are ready for a brisk walk in Manhattan ahead of the meeting. This will clear our jet-lagged heads and is also a useful way to avoid any awkward moments at the hotel by bumping into the people we are due to meet.

It is July and as we exit the hotel, we are enveloped in warm sunshine that helps us both relax a little. Immediately, I feel somewhat lied to all these years because I realise that New York is not in fact the 'city that never sleeps'. The city of New York has indeed been asleep and is just waking up. Men in overalls are hosing down pavements, cafes are taking deliveries, putting out tables, and various trucks and cleaning crews are busy getting their city ready for just another day.

To be fair, there are a lot of water hoses; even Tom noticed it. On every street corner, there is a man with a hose and I could be forgiven for making an observation later in the day that will draw odd looks from everyone, and that I will be reminded of and embarrassed by several times in the months ahead.

New York's grid system might not allow for quirkiness, but it does mean that even the most directionally challenged can avoid getting lost. Still, I was taking no chances. I kept a rigid handle on exactly where we had come from and how we would get back to the Grande. If I had a ball of wool I would have used it. The meeting place was room 412 of our hotel. They'd flown us across an ocean and hired us a room in the same venue as the meeting. There was no way on earth we could be late. Our commute was exactly one flight of stairs. There could be no excuses.

In my family, because of what I do for a living, I tend to assume complete authority on all matters of Tom's career and on show business in general. I speak with misguided confidence, often about things I have absolutely no experience of at all. And even though I am proved flat wrong time and again, my family still kindly defer to me and allow me to prattle on, albeit with eyebrows raised on an increasingly frequent basis. And being a showbiz person, naturally, Tom depends on me to explain what might lie ahead. On this morning, however, I haven't got a clue. How could I? This meeting is a complete first for me as well. I don't admit this of course. I'm his dad and dads are supposed to be heroic and strong and know the answer to everything. So, I lie. I tell him what I think he can expect but I phrase it definitively and he doesn't question me. Why would he? I'm his dad.

In my defence, these are white lies at worst because I am also a filmmaker. I wrote and sold my first screenplay before Tom was even born. I've sold the film rights to my first novel more times than I care to admit. I had sold my latest film project just a year ago. My scripts have taken me to LA. I've done the meetings. I've signed on the dotted line but crucially, I am still waiting to hear that seductive word – action. And this status remains unchanged, four years on in 2016.

I glance at my watch and carefully subtract five hours. Just over an hour to go. Tom asks me again what he might be asked in the meeting. I wish I knew. I think about asking Charlie, but I decide not to. I want him to think that this trip is routine for me and in fact, with my hectic schedule, even a little inconvenient.

Tom has been cast in this film though. I run the phone conversation through in my mind. Yes, no question, he has already landed the role. But then I panic momentarily because as yet nothing has been signed. Unhelpful theories bombard me; namely that this whole New York trip is just another audition, to get the approval of the actual movie stars who will be carrying this film. So, what if the meeting goes badly for Tom and they want another kid? This would be very bad indeed and I put it out of my mind.

My best guess is that the meeting is just a get-together: a chance for the director to meet his main cast and for Tom to establish a rapport with his co-stars. Co-stars? I do not refer to them as Tom's co-stars because this would imply that Tom is also a star. Tom is not a star. He's my little boy, albeit my eldest with three brothers back home, no doubt running their mum ragged. This reminds me that I need to call my wife, Nikki, and play down the opulence of the hotel. 'Yeah, you know, it's okay...'

What Tom really wants to know is whether I am going to sit in on the meeting with him. As a 'filmmaker' myself, out of curiosity, naturally I would like to attend. My instincts though tell me that this is unlikely to happen. The director might not like it. But at only fourteen, surely Tom's needs are greater than a director's sensitivity, and if Tom wants me to stay then I will. He says that he does and so it is settled. I am going to the meeting as well, and Tom relaxes by the same amount that I tense.

We get back to our room at 8.30 a.m. Under our door is a note from Charlie, reminding Tom that he has a meeting. Er, yeah, thanks, Charlie, because, do you know, I had clean forgotten. I also make a note that the note states that Tom has a meeting. It is singular and not plural and I wonder if Charlie is making a point?

I have never been a cool person. I am not trendy. I have nothing pierced. The only metal in my face are my fillings. I have no tattoos. I've never dyed my hair. Apart from some low-grade marijuana, I've never done drugs. I've never dropped an E and nor an H for that matter, unless I have a workman to the house. I've never been to Glastonbury. I've never woken up in the wrong bed or with the wrong person. The only time I've ever worn a hat is on a golf course. I play golf. And the only time I have ever been late for anything, was when I was born and only by a day.

Being late can be considered chic but this is a mistake. Being late is always rude. But what is chic, however, is being allowed to be late. Being forgiven for keeping everyone waiting denotes status. And the higher your status, the later one can be and with no apology required either. This is not where I live. I am always early and true to form, Tom and I are outside room 412 with a full ten minutes to spare.

I sense that nobody has arrived yet, but I knock on the door anyway and we begin an awkward wait. Awkward because we are in a narrow, dimly-lit corridor with nowhere to sit or anything to do. This isn't a meeting room but a bedroom, just like ours on the floor below.

Suddenly, along the hall, the elevator pings and we quickly straighten. Three people emerge into the gloom but I can't make them out. Why are 'cool' hotels so impossibly dim? The people don't have luggage, just briefcases, and they're moving in our direction. From their body language alone I can sense that they are equally apprehensive: two men and a woman. I don't recognize any of them so they are not the actors. The men are both very small.

At one of Tom's auditions in London, my wife, Nikki, had met the director and she remarked how young he looked. This irked me. A watershed moment in any career is when the people making decisions are suddenly younger than you are. My wife adds that he is also tiny, even smaller than me! This cheers me a little but not completely.

I can see the lady now: a glamorous and attractive woman who I recognize from a meeting in London. The third bloke I don't recognize but it doesn't matter because Tom now recognizes the director. This is a Spanish film production and this is the Spanish contingent: the film's director, producer and I suspect, the writer.

There follow some stilted and cursory introductions, and factoring in their accents and the circumstances, none of their names stick with me at all. In my head, they remain the attractive lady, the director and the other bloke.

A rather strained silence descends as the lady fumbles with the key card to get room 412 open. A red light now in the door mechanism will be a disaster. All of us need to get out of the claustrophobic corridor before the real stars arrive.

The writer and director follow their producer colleague into the room and I trail in after Tom with a growing sense of awkwardness which I try to ignore. I shut the door behind me as a signal of my intent to stay. This is what Tom wants and Tom gets what Tom wants. Doesn't he? Being honest, as much as I want to support Tom and be 'there' for him, I am equally keen to meet his fellow actors.

As I expect, the room is just another bedroom but with the double bed replaced with a central table and chairs. It's a little cramped which adds to the strain, and no one takes a seat. There are some pastries and a pot of coffee already in situ with bottles of water, sparkling and still. The refreshments are a welcome distraction as strained conversations continue about flights and how high the buildings are in New York. On the table is a pile of scripts. All we need now are Tom's on-screen parents.

There is a knock at the door which focuses everyone's attention. Charlie appears, followed by Naomi Watts. I've been looking forward to meeting Ms Watts. Do I call her Naomi? I'm not sure. Damn, I should have checked. The first thing I notice is the dog under her arm. It's a Yorkshire terrier wearing a body brace and the lower half of its tiny frame is shaven.

Naomi says a general hello but she is clearly under some strain herself but I suspect not for the same reasons. I shake her hand and she tells me that she is Naomi. I know this already of course but I appreciate it nonetheless. I fight the urge to say something stupid like loved you in *King Kong* or even worse, fancied your pants off in *Mulholland Drive*. As it turns out, the dog's presence is a good thing. It has a broken back which Naomi explains happened when she tripped whilst carrying him up the stairs to her Manhattan roof terrace. As well as breaking the dog's back, it breaks the ice at the meeting. I wonder if I should risk a joke. I'm professionally funny after all, but I decide against it. This is a good decision, but I will shortly take the plunge and get it very wrong.

As we all fuss over the dog, we establish that he is called Bob and I offer up that Tom has a granddad called Bob. It doesn't get a laugh; why would it? It's not even a joke, it's a fact. It's just a coincidence and not even a very good one because Bob is a common name. Rumpelstiltskin would have been funny. Bob wasn't, and luckily it was quickly lost with another knock at the door. Same drill, only this time it is Charlie with Ewan McGregor.

He doesn't look much like a star, dressed scruffily in jeans and T-shirt.

He is bloody handsome though, which I'm curious about because I never really had him pegged as a looker. In the flesh though, I can see it. And now I understand some of the frankly hysterical reactions of various female friends when we explained who would be playing Tom's dad.

He has great hair. I rarely notice hair on a person but I certainly notice his. A deep red chestnut I'd say, and he has loads of it. More than is needed by any one person and far too much for a man of his age. He could harvest and sell it if the roles ever dry up. He's very warm and at ease, making eye contact with his firm handshake. He smiles broadly which is when I notice his teeth. He has magnificent teeth. I have reasonably good teeth myself. My teeth are arguably my best feature, but they are nothing like Ewan's.

He is already much cooler than me because he's a film star, but he also has a large tattoo on his upper arm and this puts him firmly in the trendy bracket as well. In so many ways then, he is nothing like me and yet he is being asked to pretend to be the father of my son. To do so, he is going to have to act his socks off.

Ewan and Naomi greet each other warmly and clearly already know each other. He calls her darling and they kiss. This might just be a celebrity thing of course; whereby famous people have a kind of special affinity with each other. Ewan fusses over the dog much more than I did and I worry a little because it does have a broken bloody back. Either he really loves dogs or he's a very fine actor indeed. Everyone is still standing although some people have pulled out chairs or have claimed spots with a draped jacket in readiness for the meeting, which can now begin. Everyone is present and yet everything is not correct. Screen mum and dad and screen son are all present. The process of bonding can begin and they will go on to become a handsome family.

Tom with his pretend parents

But for now, though, one person is still present who is surplus to requirements and it isn't Charlie. He left sharpish, the moment he had delivered Mr McGregor in good health.

I was the elephant in the room. Later, even Tom would agree that I had to leave. Momentarily, I had sat down but it felt so wrong that I leapt up again as if the chair was wet. It was apparent that I needed to leave but no one was going to ask me to do so. This would have been humiliating for me and embarrassing for Tom and so I did the right thing and put everyone out of their misery.

So, shall I leave then?

The relief was palpable and the communal sighs were almost strong enough to blow me out of the room. In their jet stream, I stole a furtive glance at Tom, offered him a quick thumbs-up and he nodded back his assurances. I turned the handle and was jettisoned from the room. I felt like the cowboy who flies out of the saloon bar with the stable doors flapping, landing in a heap and scrabbling for his hat. Metaphorically, I dusted myself down, stared briefly at the bedroom door and thought of the illustrious people inside, with my son.

Then it dawned on me. I mean, it really dawned on me. Of course, I already knew that it was Tom who had been cast in the leading role of a film called *The Impossible*, to be directed by J.A. Bayona and co-starring Naomi Watts and Ewan McGregor. And that the meeting in New York was for Tom and not for me. I was delivering him, nothing more. My work was done in making the child, along with his mum of course; whom I called the moment I got back to my room.

Nikki would have been delighted to fulfil the legally required role of chaperoning Tom to New York without the remotest worry of her ego being bruised, and so she was hardly sympathetic to my situation as I explained it over the phone. And I can understand why. She was stuck in London with our three other boys. The last time she was in New York was en route to Orlando way back in 1989 with a potential suitor who was slowly wearing her resistance down. And that suitor was now in Manhattan with her first born. Go out and enjoy yourself was her thrust and let Tom get on with becoming a movie star. She was right of course, and I pulled my socks up, literally, and hit the streets of New York, again.

I am in the most exciting city in the world with nothing to do and no kids. Every dad's dream, surely, but a nightmare for me as well with the realization that my eldest son is on a path that will see him eclipsing his old man. And this path is now complete.

A Night to Remember

Wednesday May 5th, 2010 was a big night for me and as ever, I was nervous. The theatre was packed which was unusual. Even a sold-out show has the odd empty seat dotted about the place, but tonight there was none, not even up amongst the Gods or the few 'restricted view' seats behind pillars or facing the wrong way. This was a special night and a palpable excitement hung in the air with expectations high. It would certainly rank as one of my biggest nights ever in a theatre, on a par with my appearance at The Dominion in *The Royal Variety Show* in 2000, or my appearance at Her Majesty's Theatre after my nomination for the Perrier Award in 1996. Going back even further, to 1993 for my first ever solo show at the sixty-seat Hen and Chickens Theatre on Highbury Corner, adrenalin coursing through my frantic body, it was much like this evening, only the pressure tonight felt very different and even worse. I checked my watch again, something I always do before a show, a literal nervous tick of mine.

I grab for Nikki's hand and squeeze. We assure each other that everything is going to be fine. The audience will love it; why wouldn't they? They will laugh, some might cry and at the end, they will cheer, clap and roar their approval. This was practically an invited audience of already fully signed up fans: a partisan home crowd if ever there was one. I check my watch again and reassure myself that pre-show doubts are quite normal, helpful even because they bring out the best in the performer. This might well be true, but my pre-show nerves are highly developed and they never feel very helpful or constructive to me as I pace back and forth. Some comedians go quiet before a gig, others like to pace. I do both as I try to convince myself that I am a funny man in between sips from my always-to-hand bottle of water. Comics live in dread of the dry mouth. No comedian can ever fully recover from the moment when his tongue sticks to the roof of his mouth, especially since the sound is so helpfully amplified for the audience to hear.

Tonight, the stalls are even noisier than usual. People are chatting loudly without a care in the world, not even the price of the tickets and the goodies they've just bought. Coats off, bags tucked away and drinks safely to hand, with one eye on the stage to check their prospective view. I am always struck by and a little resentful of just how relaxed an audience is ahead of a show, in stark contrast to the performer backstage. I check my watch again. Almost show time. This is the most nervous I have been for some time. I know the reason why and this irritates me even more. He probably won't even show up and so what if he does? He's no different from anyone else. He's just an ordinary bloke like you and me. I say this to myself but I don't really believe it. He might have the same appendages as the rest of us, but he isn't ordinary, not really. And I wonder what this must feel like, to have such a hold over people, to have a whole theatre waiting and hoping for a glimpse of you. I wonder if he is even aware of this. Of course, he is. An ego like his? He's worked hard for it though and he certainly deserves it and I bet he bloody well loves it. Who wouldn't?

Who was I kidding? Normal? He certainly isn't normal, not since he stopped calling himself Reg Dwight anyway. Bloody hell, Elton John is rumoured to be coming to see my son in *Billy Elliot the Musical*. Pardon me, *Sir* Elton John.

It's a long time since Elton and I have seen each other. Actually, we haven't seen each other since we worked together on the Brit Awards in 1994, some nineteen years ago, so we have so much to catch up on. Since then we've both been very busy. Elton is now a sir and I have made four boys, the eldest of whom, Tom, at thirteen years of age, is playing Billy in tonight's performance at the Victoria Palace Theatre in London's West End. It is now 7.35 p.m., already five minutes late and with kids in the show, *Billy Elliot* never goes up late. I nudge my Nikki and state with absolute conviction that this means that His Majesty is attending.

The London Billy in New York

As I have explained already, on all matters show-business, I am the oracle. Nikki allows me to witter on. It doesn't do any harm and it makes me feel important.

7.40 p.m. and now I'm fed up, worried sick for Tom and a little scornful that the singing maestro should be keeping me and so many others waiting. It's typical Elton, I say. And I should know because I know him!

Tonight, is a special performance because it is the show's fifth anniversary. Over two thousand performances of *Billy Elliot* in London alone and the show has since opened in New York and elsewhere to equal acclaim, harvesting a raft of awards. A hit musical is a cash cow that needs milking and the more teats the better.

I don't know this yet - but scroll forward a couple of months and I will visit New York with Tom (on his ticket) and we will catch the Broadway show.

The mantra goes that 'the show must go on' and it really must, at least eight times a week: two matinees, six evenings and Sundays off. The role of Billy is played by a boy between the age of eleven and fifteen and the eight performances each week are usually shared between four boys who are cast at any one time. At this point, Tom has played Billy for almost two years and Nikki and I have decided it's time for him to hang up his leotard and leave the show. Fortunately, Tom agrees. We had tried to get him out of the show a couple of times already, but Tom had been reluctant and the producers were keen for him to stay. My most recent attempt was abandoned when the carrot of the fifth anniversary and the probable attendance of you-know-who, was dangled before us and we all relented.

The anniversary show would be one of Tom's last, concluding an extraordinary period that had begun some four years earlier. Our reasoning for Tom to stop pirouetting was that we were both keen for him to get back

to school and to a more normal teenage life. We hadn't sought the role for him; it happened completely by chance with Tom being talent spotted, and although it had been a remarkable experience and a great success, I explained with my usual aplomb and authority that there was no certainty of a career ahead in the world of entertainment. On this, Nikki readily agreed based on how things had panned ou for the comedian who was officially crowned 'The UK's Best New Comedian' at the Edinburgh fringe in 1993'.

The trophy I still have, but I gave this watch to Tom for his 18th

The whole family was looking forward to having Tom home again. His brothers missed him and I was secretly pleased to be resuming my role as the most successful show business personality in the Holland family. I couldn't really compete when my son *is* Billy Elliot but I figured I could emerge from his shadow when my son *was* Billy Elliot. It was time for Tom to step out of the limelight.

The story for this book had now taken root and the timing was precise and felt fateful. This is because Tom's time on the West End stage occurred at a point in my comedy career that a PR 'professional' would describe as a plateau.

Back stage at the Royal Variety Show after chatting with the heir to the throne of England, if a seer had appeared and explained that within a decade I would be doing a national tour of village halls then I would most likely have burst in to tears or not believed it. Only it turned out to be true.

Rural Arts, as the name suggests, provides arts to the rural masses, away from the cities with their theatres and large populations who take their cultural provision for granted. Rural Arts is culture aimed at a much more local level in areas where live entertainment is largely still confined to lambing. Simply put, it was taking my comedy to villages, where the venues commonly have a badminton court on the floor and there are no velour seats. Even with a packed house, village halls are not venues that lend themselves to a live DVD. These are venues often without a stage, let alone a stage door, and a nursery store room/cupboard that doubles as my dressing room. I am not a tall man but even for me, a chair designed for a five-year-old is not a comfortable way to prepare for a show. My cramped back might heal reasonably quickly but the damage done to my ego would take longer and might even be irreparable.

And it is comic that these village hall gigs coincided with the time that Tom was playing in the West End. Like two ships passing in the night: one headed for the Seychelles and another bound for Mogadishu.

But these shows in villages had an enchantment to them. When I would arrive, I would be met by the key members of the 'committee', who were often quite worried and even more nervous than me because I was usually the very first comedian they had ever booked. Often, the evening would include some kind of meal for the audience, in the interval or at the end, and usually would be referred to as supper. Sometimes, the food would be made on site and sometimes everyone would bring a plate of something with a central coordinator to ensure there wasn't surplus quiche and too little salmon. It was all very civilised and impossibly uncool, especially if the buffet was laid out on a trestle table in front of the stage as was the case in this photograph.

Showtime!

This particular venue was Whitchurch in Hampshire where I played twice!

There would always be a raffle with prizes nobody really wanted and mostly things that had probably already been won before and handed back in. And I could face some unnerving questions as well when I arrived, which never augured well. You didn't want a microphone, did you? Can you do any tricks because we have lots of children coming and they love magic?

When I toured the UK with Eddie Izzard I was frequently told, almost nightly in fact, that I would soon be playing Eddie's venues on my own. I was always very flattered by this but always slightly disbelieving. And this is my problem in life and certainly in show-business; I have a restricting imagination whereby I didn't believe this would ever happen and if the self-help brigade is to be believed, this might have been my biggest mistake.

Something to ponder then as I sit in my makeshift dressing room with Child-line posters on the wall and boxes of soft play toys. How did I ever arrive here, I wonder during every interval? Ready for the second half and there's a knock at my door? 'We seem to have too much quiche; would you like a slice?'

Not that the gigs were not successful, though. Using a Dunkirk spirit, the shows were often wonderful and I expect that they are still talked about in certain villages about the land – the night the funny man came from London. I used to take great delight in telling my audiences about Tom's exploits as Billy. Looking at my watch, I would explain that at that precise time, Tom was on stage in the West End in front of two thousand people, and then just a look from me at my surroundings was all that was needed.

Backstage cum dressing room!

Our different venues could not have been starker and it was always funny. (To me at least.)

These shows tended to be full because the villagers were so happy to have something to attend and playing on that situation was usually where I would start each show. I would note that the shows were not terribly economic for me. 'Not exactly an earner,' was how I put it, but I would then explain that I could make ends meet because the houses in the village would be empty during the show and I was accompanied by an empty van and a couple of burglars. Then I would normally pick out a bloke near to the front and add that his wardrobe was safe. They would laugh and I would be away.

Now, though, Tom's run in *Billy Elliot* was coming to an end and he was returning to a more normal childhood. Naturally, there is a lot of press in the build-up to the anniversary of such a show. Something was planned for the finale involving all the nineteen boys who had previously played Billy, but whatever these young maestros could conjure up between them, still the hope remained that Watford's most famous son would grace us with his presence. When Tom was told that he had been chosen to play Billy on the night, he was delighted but nervous also, and he came to me for advice, naturally. Where else would he go?

Just ahead of the show, Tom explained that he was backstage in his shared dressing room, which was affectionately referred to as 'the Billy room'. He was preparing in his usual manner because this was just 'a show like all the others that had gone before it, with the same script, the same dances and the same songs, and he needn't treat it any differently'. So, he was probably surprised when Nick Evans, the resident director of the show, was at the door beckoning him because there was someone he wanted Tom to meet. En route, Nick explained that he was taking Tom to meet the man behind the music of the show and Tom ran through in his mind what he might say. Thanking him would be a good place to start, for helping to create a show that had changed his life and quite possibly might breathe some new life into his old man's as well.

Tom with Nick and Fox Jackson Keane

Nick led Tom to a room in the theatre that he had never been to before and didn't even know existed. It was plush and comfortable and unlike the rest of the old building. It is a room that I imagine all London's theatres would have had when they first opened, when theatres were the principal form of entertainment and royalty and other aristocrats would frequently attend and need a place to separate themselves from the great unwashed. And so it remains today, when an illustrious individual or a genuine VIP fancies seeing a show, because pre-show and interval drinks for Tom Cruise or Beyoncé would cause pandemonium.

Over the years, many hundreds of luminaries must have used this room at the Victoria Palace, like Michael Jackson when he famously attended *Billy Elliot* some years back. And I can add another showbiz name to this list, of less status and one who wouldn't normally warrant a mention if it didn't complete this story so nicely. It is, of course, yours truly.

It was way back in 1996 at a performance of *Jolson*, starring Brian Conley. I met Brian when we were both guests on *Des O'Connor Tonight*, and he kindly invited Nikki and me along to see the show, after which we were ushered backstage and shown to the room. It was the same room where Brian had previously entertained Tom Cruise and Nicole Kidman, so it must have been something of a comedown for him but it was a step up for us.

Now, though, just ahead of the fifth anniversary performance of *Billy Elliot*, this same room is the private office of Sir Elton John and naturally he wants to meet the star of his musical.

We had discussed how Tom should address him and I plumped for plain old Elton. Mr John felt wrong and having seen *The Apprentice* and noting the saccharine and embarrassing way the hopefuls address 'Sir Alan' and then 'Lord Sugar', I advised against Sir Elton. Just call him Elton and don't stare at his hair. And if you get a chance, tell him your dad and he once worked together and that I have a film script which might be of interest to his company, Rocket Pictures. Don't stress about this Tom, but you know, '...just if the opportunity presents itself!'

As it turns out, I didn't prep Tom very well because I made one silly assumption; namely that Tom would recognise the knight of the realm if not from his frequent TV appearances, then at least from his picture in the sodding show programme. This was a big mistake because with the occasion and the stress, when Tom entered the room, he didn't have a clue who was who. It didn't help that there were three or four men in the room. Elton's partner and now husband, David Furnish, and at least two others, security I suppose. This was enough to confuse Tom who was starting to panic. His unusual name didn't help matters either, not following the convention of having a Christian name followed by a surname, like Michael Brown or for that matter, Reg Dwight. Sir Elton John has two Christian names. Is he John or is he Elton?

As Nick steered Tom in the right direction, it became clear who was who, but still Tom wrestled with the name. Then at the very last moment, Tom decided against using his first name altogether and opted for the safer and more respectful Mister and surname, but unable to square the name John with being a surname, in his panic, he plumped for 'Hello, Mr Elton' instead. Elton just smiled. Given that so many people were waiting for them both, they spoke for a few moments before Tom was backstage again and ready for the show.

Back in the auditorium, without any announcement, Stephen Daldry suddenly took to the stage. He is tall and urbane, and he must have enjoyed the instant recognition and spontaneous applause that spread from the stalls back and upwards, and then it built considerably when the audience clapped eyes on Lee Hall, the writer of the show, followed by Sir Elton himself.

So, I was right all along; Elton John is here, but I don't have time to congratulate myself. Stephen speaks for a few moments about the 'journey' and the 'joy' and what a humbling experience this musical has been, without mentioning what an astonishing earner it has been as well and then hands over to Elton. He's probably more comfortable sitting behind a piano and banging out 'Rocket Man', but nonetheless he is a man at ease on stage. He speaks easily to his rapt audience and yet I can't hear much of what he says and not because I can't hear. As well as being worried for Tom at this precise moment, I am completely transfixed by how ill-fitting Elton's suit is.

John, Daldry and Hall

This is a man known as much for his flamboyance and panache as for his talent. His appreciation of the finer things in life is well documented. And not short of funds, surely his clothes are made for him? And if so, then perhaps there was a mix up at his tailor and Elton picked up a suit for Stephen Fry by mistake. At this point, the audience would have erupted if a white piano was suddenly wheeled onto the stage but Elton would have struggled to get a tune out of it because we could barely see his hands. The speeches were gracious, and then quickly the stage cleared so that the show could begin and – darling, let me tell you – what a show it was.

It is safe to assume that most people attending the show will know the story; that against the terrible backdrop of the miner's strike, a young boy defies his dad to learn ballet and quickly becomes a maestro. And as such, the audience are all expecting to see a young kid who can dance his socks off. It's why audiences have flocked to see the show the world over.

The show begins with the entire cast on stage and the first time I saw it, I was excited to establish which of the many kids was Billy. Billy joins the first scene some way in, pushed on stage by his gruff father, but he isn't revealed to the audience until the stage clears, leaving just two young boys on view: Billy and his friend Michael. And even then, it is only when Billy delivers his first line – 'Focked if I know' – that he is finally revealed.

I saw the show many times and Tom's first appearance on stage was always exciting for me and never normal. Living away from home as he did in a chaperoned 'Billy' house, it was just nice to see my little boy again even withstanding the unusual setting. On this night though, something occurred which only happened twice in the two hundred-odd shows that Tom completed. Namely, the audience spontaneously applauded when 'Billy' entered the fray. This would happen again when Tom made his very last appearance a few weeks later. On this occasion, once again, Nikki was clutching my hand even tighter than she had done the moment she squeezed the little boy into the world.

The finale to this show was very special for us and indeed, for all the people present in the theatre that night. Mr. Elton would later describe is as 'unbelievable' and it was. All nineteen former and current Billy's somersaulted and pirouetted about the stage as the audience screamed their approval.

All the Billy's

This amazing sequence began with the curtain rising to reveal the three original Billy Elliots standing on the stage. The three boys who had kicked the whole thing off five years go.

It was a privilege to witness and odd to see that they were now young adults and salutary too to be reminded of just how quickly time passes. I haven't the skill as a writer to explain how exciting this was to watch. Better that I rely on technology and provide a link for those of you so inclined. http://www.youtube. com/watch?v=ZE43cwH5LhM This is a fabulous short film that captures the evening and the event brilliantly.

At the stage door, afterwards a huge throng gathered, fans and press alike, eager for a glimpse of Elton. The street running alongside the theatre had been cordoned off to cars for some time for subterranean work, but of course, Sir Elton's gleaming Porsche was allowed through and was purring patiently in the middle of the road. It was quickly enveloped by the crowd, such that Moses would be needed to create a passageway when its owner finally emerged.

I joined the melee but I wasn't waiting to see Elton. I was waiting to retrieve Tom and take him around to the bar at the front of the theatre where a party until the small hours was about to get started. During Tom's time playing Billy, I was always struck by his anonymity after the show. As masses of people left the theatre and headed for Victoria Station, Tom could easily join the crowd without being recognised by people who had just watched the show and cheered his every gyration. Even on the train, we could sit amongst people with their programmes, discussing the show and they would have no idea that 'Billy' was sitting opposite them. And so, it was tonight when Tom emerged through the Stage Door. A few heads turned, but most stayed trained on the door.

The party after the show was so busy and loud that it was impossible to have any meaningful conversation with Tom, save to congratulate him. I did manage to establish that he had met with Elton privately and a thought immediately occurred to me, which is unique to all performers. I wondered if my name had come up in their conversation. Ludicrous I know, but there we are.

The next morning, I found out that it hadn't. And it didn't dent my mood at all, thank God, as my phone almost melted with the number of texts I received from friends, all drawing my attention to a news item on the television, which seemed to sum up this story.

All morning on breakfast television, a hastily grabbed, backstage interview with Elton John was being played every thirty minutes on the news loop. In the interview, a teary Elton talked about the show and how much it means to him emotionally, and in doing so he described the boy who had played Billy as 'astonishing'. I waited patiently for the item to appear on television before I remembered this new thing called the internet and a website called YouTube. And sure enough, there it was: Sir Elton John with a tear in his eye, which he couldn't wipe away as his sleeves were too long, gushing on about how astonishing my little boy was – a pinch-me moment of my life as a parent if ever there was one. Nikki and I watched it over and over. The clip made me smile broadly because I expect that Elton would have been interviewed backstage after the Brit Awards in 1994. I didn't see this interview, but no matter because I am certain that he wouldn't have lavished such praise on the warm-up man from that night at the Ali Pali.

Author Footnote

At the time of writing, Tom is 20 years old and has just been nominated for a BAFTA. Much is made of the fact that Tom has had no formal acting training. No drama school or lessons. Tom's first ever speaking part in a play was his role in Billy Elliot. And given how many of our current crop of 'star' actors hail from the most esteemed private schools, I consider Tom's good fortune that he went to a comprehensive school. And good fortune because this was a practical decision on our part and not an ideological one. I just wasn't funny enough to extend my boys private education beyond primary school.

But it is a little disingenuous to claim that Tom has had no training and therefore that he must be a shear natural. Nick Evans had an enormous bearing on Tom. They spent hour's together working on Tom's performance as Billy. Stephen Daldry might well have spotted the kid, but it was Nick Evans who trained him. And in a similar vein, now is a good time to introduce a chap called Ben Perkins, Tom's acting coach on The Impossible.

Tom with Ben Perkins, his acting coach on The Impossible

Tom's role in the film was crucial and as inexperienced as he was, the producers were taking a considerable risk. Ben too was a little green at the time but they became firm friends and the resulting film was so positive for them both with Ben about to start work as a coach on the forthcoming instalment of Jurassic World.

Nick and Ben have both had a great influence on Tom for which Nikki and I are very grateful. And if Tom wins this gong in February, there will be many people he will feel a need to thank, but right up there in the pecking order should be these two.

Have You Met Elton?

'Have you met Elton?'

This is one of the most ridiculous questions I have ever been asked, right up there with when British Gas first phoned me to ask if they could supply my electricity: a question that inspired one of my most successful stand-up routines ever.

Over the course of my still 'on-going' career I have met and worked with many celebrities. I even count some as my friends, but my reach in the world of celebrity has never really stretched to rock stars; although I did once turn down a night out with Robbie Williams. We met on the set of *Shooting Stars* a little after he had left Take That and after the recording, a boozed-up Robbie asked if I fancied a night out in town. But alas, I had a young baby at home (Tom) and I wanted to get home. Doh!

Human beings have had the Iron Age and the Stone Age and we are currently living through what will be known in years to come as the Celebrity Age. And in centuries to come, historians will have more than the odd cave drawing and lump of iron to hypothesise with. Back catalogues of *Hello!* alone will prove that we were transfixed by the lives of certain people and their immaculately presented houses.

This isn't terribly new. Fame has always obsessed us, but Warhol was right with his fifteen-minute prediction. With the advent of the reality 'star', becoming famous is now a genuine career option and for too many, even a rite of passage.

Even though I have always wanted to be a comedian, it was not because I wanted to be famous. I just knew that I could make people laugh and I enjoyed the feeling that came with it.

But still this explosion of celebrity doesn't really dent or dilute the notion of the real star, the A-lister as we know them, of which there can be no doubt that Elton John is a member. Internationally recognised and admired. An individual who can only appear in public behind red ropes and accompanied by men in dark glasses and furthermore, Elton is a member of a small band of individuals who can go by one name only. Madonna and Elvis. Liberace. Freddie. Brad. Pele. Marlon. Diego. Boris. Roger? Ali and Tiger. Jude perhaps and even Sienna?

And how about Dominic? No, certainly not. We are relatively few but there are still enough of us and no Dominic has yet done enough to make the name their own. Unlike Elton, which is why I was asked, 'Do you know Elton?'

'No, of course I don't, you idiot. How the hell would I know Elton John?' is what I wanted to reply. He plays arenas and I play pubs. But this response would have been rude and so I just said, 'No.'

The man asking was the producer of the Brit Awards. The year was

1994 and I was hot. In fact, I was officially the hottest new comedian in Britain. The Brit Awards wanted me as their warm-up act during the 'as live' recording. I was flattered, but three thousand people at the Alexander Palace, on and off stage up to ten times, following the likes of Meatloaf and Take That, I didn't take long to decide. No. Definitely not. Not interested. Altogether too terrifying. Find some other mug.

But then they offered me £1,000 and immediately my position shifted. I had never earned anything like £1,000 before for a single gig. I was getting married later in the year and my fiancée had let it slip that she fancied a Maldivian honeymoon. A grand for a night's work? Yes, okay, go on then.

My manager at the time was Pete Harris. Pete is adamant now that he was my manager and not my agent, but I can't see that there is any difference. A comedian tries to be as funny as he can be and the agent (manager) earns 15% of how much money the comedian can sell his jokes for. I opted for Pete because at the time he had a very exclusive stable. Just three acts in fact: myself, John Hegley and some bloke called Eddie Izzard, which was how I got to tour with the great man. Naturally, Eddie absorbed most of Pete's attention and so his assistant, David, got involved in the increasingly bizarre offer from the Brit Awards.

David called me again and I worried that the gig was off, but it was no such bad news. David was perplexed and even a little embarrassed when he explained that the man from the Brits had upped his offer from £1,000 to £1,250. Upped his offer? But hadn't I already accepted £1,000? David thought so, but wires had obviously got crossed and the offer now stood at £1,250. This was great news. The Maldives were looking like a real possibility and I might even be able to afford air conditioning. I said yes. Again.

Then David phoned again and this time he was laughing. They were counter offering once more and the fee now stood at a handsome £1,500. As I write this now, I realise that I should have held out for the inevitable further offers, but I was thrilled with the fee and it was inked in the diary. The island of Bandos, Maldives, here we come.

With the deal done, the producers wanted to meet me at their offices in Chiswick and it was here that I was asked the 'Elton' question because that year, he was hosting the awards.

We are all familiar with name-dropping and fame by association. It bolsters our place in the world and I tend to exaggerate my dealings with the famous people I have encountered over the years, something which my family delights in maligning me for. An example is when my boys discovered the film *Get Smart* and were particularly smitten with the smoldering and curvy Anne Hathaway. I enjoyed seeing their looks of awe when I explained that I had met Anne and in Los Angeles no less. This is not true. For the record, I have never met Anne Hathaway. However, it *was* in LA that I 'didn't' meet her. That bit is true. I was in LA for some disastrous film meetings, increasingly forlorn and by chance, I hooked up with a British producer who was really a wannabe much like myself. He had read my script, *Only in America*, and liked it enough to allow me to tag along with him for a day. This association would last for five years and with some highs, most notably attaching Bette Midler to the project. He optioned the script with a view to producing, but then bailed when money was due to the writer. Who'd be in film? Anyway, in LA, he was polite and kind. I was desperate and so we fitted perfectly. He was having lunch at The Four Seasons with the head of publicity from DreamWorks and a producer from Overture Films, and would I like to join them? I checked my schedule. Clear. Anne (Hathaway) was in the hotel bar with some friends and was so incognito that she needed to be pointed out to me. I don't mean literally pointed at. In LA, only the people on the wrong side of the ropes point and stare. People on the inside are not supposed to be impressed by movie stars.

I am slightly embarrassed now to admit that this is the end of this anecdote. So, I didn't meet her at all. I just happened to be in the same bar as her and nothing more. But my boys were all incredibly impressed by my silly claim that I had met the beautiful actress. Tom even suggested that I text Anne to say hi and that Get Smart is 'awesome'. Painted into a corner now, the truth finally emerged and I might have dropped a few notches in Tom's celebrity estimation, but hopefully I rose a few in his affections as well.

I've claimed similar meetings with other stars as well, where our paths have converged but never really crossed. Robert Redford springs immediately to mind, which is understandable because his is a heavy name to drop, but also, for some reason, Martine McCutcheon, which is more difficult to explain.

The man from the Brits ran me through the running order for the evening: Meatloaf, Take That, Stereo MCs, Bon Jovi and Van Morrison, amongst others, all interspersed with some light-hearted observational comedy from the UK's best new comedian, Dominic Holland. As I sat there, the reality dawned on me: I should have held out for more money.

Van Morrison was topping the bill and receiving the top-secret award for outstanding contribution to music. The man from the Brits explained to me that Van could be tricky, which I might know about already? Er, no, I didn't know that. How would I? And then as casually as you like, he asked me if I knew Van. I worried now that he had me confused with my namesake, Jools. We both have high-pitched voices and dark hair and I feared that he might expect me to bang out a tune on the piano for Van to sing along to.

I was told that Mr Morrison did not like to be addressed by his name. In fact, I was told not to address Mr Morrison at all and if I did need to speak to him, then I would need to go through his people first. I just shrugged. Van the Man had nothing to worry about. I gave my assurances that I wouldn't even make eye contact and I dropped any plans for comedy material about tiny Irishmen with magic hats.

On the day, I was needed at the Alexandra Palace early in the afternoon for a rehearsal. Ever punctual, I arrived at 3.00 p.m. on the dot for my allocated slot, only to find that Meatloaf was thrashing about the stage like a spoilt brat and I didn't have the confidence to interrupt him. 'Oi, Loaf! Fuck off! This is my slot!' Instead, I found myself an empty seat, which wasn't difficult as there were three thousand to choose from, and quietly started to allow a seizing sense of panic take hold of me.

Meatloaf finally finished and I stood up for my rehearsal but deferred quickly as the Take That boys emerged. I waved them on, not that anyone noticed. I had things to do anyway, namely continuing to work myself in to a full-blown panic whilst castigating myself for chasing the money. Ultimately, it was my fiancée's fault with her lofty sights on the Indian Ocean.

As it transpired, I never did get a chance to do a sound check, which didn't help my nerves very much. I had calculated that I would be needed on stage on fifteen different occasions and so I broke my act into fifteen parts in descending order of funny. On paper at least, it was hopeless and I knew it. I'm an anecdotal comedian. Each routine feeds and lives off what went before. A greater sum than their constituent parts, they don't stand up so well on their own. They are not self-contained jokes. I was going to be humiliated in front of thousands of people, including Nikki, the woman I was expecting to marry. She was coming along with my sister, Sarah, and it struck me that if things went badly, then I might end up in Bandos on my own, a first in the history of Maldivian tourism.

I was too nervous and resentful backstage to be star-struck. Jon Bon Jovi was horsing around far too much for my liking. I've never been much of a stadium rock fan myself and his greatest hit, 'Living on a Prayer', grated on me almost as much as his stupid bloody name. Speaking of stupid names, Meatloaf's ubiquitous presence was almost too much to bear. He and BJ were aping about the place like kids without a care in the world, as if the gig was no big deal and I suppose it wasn't. After all, they only needed to sing one of their saccharine ballads each. I had to go on fifteen bloody times and make the audience laugh, not swoon. Fucking laugh!

I now hated the man from the Brits as well. At the 'Do you know Elton?' meeting, he had been charming and attentive, but now on the day, he was dismissive and remiss. Apparently, he had more important things to deal with, like where the hell had Van Morrison got to and which idiot had had the temerity to look at him?

By now I would gladly waive my fee altogether and just go home. They didn't need a warm-up man anyway. A comedian who soaks up any audience lethargy and cajoles them into a good mood so their reaction plays well to the viewers at home is entirely needed for a naff studio sit-com, but this was a rock gig. Surely, they don't need geeing up?

Backstage at the Brit Awards, I felt both helpless and ridiculous. I felt more like a boxer than a comic, bouncing from foot to foot ahead of the biggest fight of my life. Whatever lay ahead this evening, I assured myself that I would technically survive and live out the rest of my life, and hopefully with Nikki.

A phrase I coined about stand-up comedy, which is particularly relevant here is: 'There is nothing quite as loud as the silence when a comedian is on stage.'

Comics commonly refer to this experience as dying on stage. Not wishing to sound defeatist, but I knew that I was going to die at the Brit Awards. And so, back-stage, as I continued to bob up and down and sip my water, I suddenly became aware of someone who had come up and was standing right next to me. I usually like to avoid people just ahead of going on stage: a chance to gather my thoughts and run some links and focus. This person was standing altogether too close and it wasn't just the proximity that struck me; it was his odd shoes. Red, I think, with large bows or a buckle, the kind that Dick Whittington might wear, especially since they were accompanied by tights and not trousers. The feet were wide and the calves were powerful. This was definitely a man. Eddie Izzard perhaps, who had come to take my place and rescue his young charge? No such luck. It wasn't Eddie but Elton.

This felt decidedly odd and I took a moment to consider my reality. I was standing next to Elton John ahead of the biggest show of my life. Naturally, I wanted to speak to him but I couldn't think of anything to say other than I was here for the money because I was getting married and *she* wanted a fancy honeymoon. I stole a quick glance at him and I was staggered to see just how nervous and vulnerable he looked as well. If anything, he looked more nervous than me and there was no solace in this for me. If the man who plays stadiums for a living looks terrified, then how the hell should I be feeling?

We made brief eye contact and acknowledged each other and somehow, it seemed that he was looking to me for some assurance that he was going to be okay. And as such, something extraordinary occurred between us. I looked him in the eye, nodded and said, 'You'll be fine.' And remarkably, he seemed to take comfort from this and looked even grateful.

And I was right. He was fine. The audience screamed their approval and hung on his every word, whether spoken or sung. I fared less well. My opening gambit was a mistake: a routine about the London Tube. It was fine for The Comedy Store but it didn't resonate quite as well with an audience of record executives who probably don't struggle on and off the tube like normal Londoners.

On stage at The Comedy Store, London.
The best comedy club in the world

I was largely ignored. It certainly wasn't a pleasant experience, but I did survive and I didn't do so badly that Nikki called off the wedding. And aside from the Maldives, I am pleased that I did this gig because of how the lives of singer and comedian were set to converge again in the years ahead.

Amongst other achievements in his illustrious life, Elton would go on to write the score for a musical that would become a worldwide smash hit and yet, interestingly, this musical has certainly had a greater impact on my life than his. Because no matter how many awards that *Billy* collects, such accolades must eventually lose their allure and the extra noughts on his bank balance must blur also. But Tom being cast as Billy has changed his life as well as mine, and I wonder if Sir Elton remembers the Brit Awards like I do and the moment that passed between us? And for this moment of kinship between two performers and for the kindness that I showed to him that night, I could even argue that Sir Elton John owes me. At the time perhaps, but not anymore, however. After *Billy Elliot*, I owe Mr Elton John big time and I suspect a free copy of this book is not going to be enough.

Author Footnote

Today is 9th November 2016 – a seismic date in the world calendar because it is the day that Mr Trump prevailed and much soul searching is underway and in earnest? I am no political analyst but I make the following observation that might have contributed to how Donald became the Top Trump – it was the celebrities who won it for him! The point being that Trump did not have any celebrity endorsements while Hilary Clinton had A-listers all over her.

What is generally agreed is that this election was won by a disenfranchised body of voters who felt isolated from those people who govern them. These voters were rather crudely categorized as uneducated, white working class but if this is indeed correct, then I am dubious whether it was a good play by Hilary Clinton to use her 'celeb' mates. Because presumably disconnected voters are unlikely to feel much association with Madonna, Bruce Springsteen, Beyoncé or Leonardo Di Caprio with their gilded lives of private jets and homes across the world. *I can't make enough money to pay my bills and a rock star with his own island is telling me what I need to do?* There are not many things more grating than this. In this chapter, I called this the age of celebrity, but in this instance, the chic and the stardust of the celebrity became toxic and their endorsement might have misfired?

I do not manage Tom, another question I am frequently asked. Tom has his 'people' and they do their thing. However, I do advise him as and when and he is free to heed or to ignore what I say. But an area and a stance that I am keen on, is that Tom should remain apolitical. When I was twenty years old, I did not have even an inkling about the world and how things worked. But this didn't matter because nobody asked me nor cared about what I thought or said. But this is not the case for Tom. Understandably, people are desperate to speak with him and to find out what makes him tick and get his take on various issues. So, when being interviewed, my advice is always the same; be polite, engaging, enthusiastic, amusing (if possible) and never be political, at least for the time-being anyway. And for how long is up to him but my advice is for a good while yet. I like the idea of four decades to be safe, or possibly five and even then, only with extreme caution.

Me and Janet Jackson

I don't know anyone who doesn't enjoy basking in a bit of reflected glory. I went to Cardinal Vaughan School, a Catholic comprehensive in Shepherds Bush. This was the 1970s and 80s, a time when the sport of boxing meant something to the nation, when our world champions like Alan Minter and Charlie Magri were as famous as any football player of the day. The meek Barry McGuigan had the nation enthralled with his impeccable manners, thanking anyone and everyone over and over. In 1985, Barry won his world title at Loftus Road, home to Queens Park Rangers Football Club, on a night when the whole of Kilburn decamped to Shepherds Bush to see their man beat the great Eusebio Pedroza of Panama. My school was overcome with excitement to the point that at least four boys I knew of were claiming Barry as their first cousin. In a fashion, like how most men of a certain age from London's East End claim to have personally known the infamous and incredibly popular Kray twins.

Over the years, I have often told people that I went to school with the famous football player Dennis Wise. This is complete and utter nonsense. Dennis Wise went to a nearby school called Sir Christopher Wren, who we played each season. Such were his talents, if Dennis lined up against us then we could expect to lose by anything up to five goals, and if he was injured or elsewhere, we had a chance of a draw.

In this frank admission, I have just been deliberately misleading again, because I used the phrase 'we had a chance' to imply that I was in the team against the boy who would go on to bag himself over twenty England caps. This is not true. I was never in the team. By 'we' I refer to our school team, but not to my inclusion in its team. I was in the B team (Captain!).

But isn't this normal? Don't we all embellish and exaggerate our connections and anecdotes to attract as much attention as possible and to prolong our airtime? The facts in this case were largely intact; I just altered them a little, which seems agreeable enough, in my world at least. Had I said that I was at school with Diego Maradona and kept him out of the team until I got injured in suspicious circumstances, then I would be delusional and a cause for concern.

But my anecdotes are all rooted in some reality: a combination of my energetic imagination and an innate need to impress. And over the years, my go-to anecdotes have flourished with incremental embellishments and harmless exaggerations. You will recall my encounter with the Hollywood actress, Anne Hathaway. If I hadn't nipped this one in the bud then, who knows, by now our fictional liaison might have developed into a full-blown affair with perhaps a love child called Lettuce or Pineapple?

I maintain that moderate delusions of grandeur are healthy, but for the purposes of this book, however, I can stick rigidly to the facts as they are. No exaggerations about Tom's career or mine are really needed.

I relished the time when Tom was finally cast and offered the role of Billy. It came after eighteen months of solid training and not knowing, but also a series of odd events and occurrences that conspired to make this happen. It wasn't something we sought for Tom and was in fact a complete fluke, thanks in part to Des O'Connor and Janet Jackson.

As soon as Tom was cast, quickly I realised that I enjoyed a very special kind of reflected glory in his success because people immediately made two assumptions: because I am a performer myself, that I must be responsible for his talent and that I had been useful to him because of my lofty connections in show business.

I need to dispel both theories immediately. Obviously, I have had a large hand in his upbringing, but his natural ability withstanding, which could have come from either of his parents, I have had nothing to do with Tom being cast as Billy Elliot. In fact, had it been left to me, I wouldn't be writing this book at all because Tom would now be a regular kid at school worrying about his future and his chances of getting a girlfriend. As I write, he is back at school and I suspect he worries about his future and the whole girlfriend thing much less than I did.

I can write *Eclipsed* because of his mum and what Nikki did for him, not to mention Tom's own determination and good sense to seize every opportunity that presented itself.

Another thing that I can be clear on is that my place in the show business world has not helped Tom one single jot. Nepotism is a rather unpleasant fact of life, as much a reality as gravity and the passing of time. It proves the maxim that it really is *who* and not *what* we know. In show business, nepotism reigns supreme. A famous forebear trumps ability pretty much all the time. And whilst I find nepotism irksome, my attitude to it is completely hypocritical. Had my dad been a movie director or an actor then I would have been delighted for his guiding hand and helpful introductions. As it was, he was a teacher and my mum was a nurse, and neither profession appealed very much. I apply a similar approach to my kids. Where I can pull strings for them, I will yank as hard as I can, but in the case of Tom and whether he was helped by having a 'famous' dad? If only.

The people behind the film and the musical *Billy Elliot* are Working Title, Britain's foremost film company. I first started talking to Working Title about my various film projects way back in 1996 and have received some interest over the years, but no deals and certainly, no cash. So, I can't see how they might look particularly favourably on my son, unless they felt sorry for him of course? But this is not how show business works. It is a business without sentiment. It is a business about selling product, like any other.

To this end, when Tom was finally cast and put onto the Working Title pay role, we started to receive a pay-slip in the post each week and Nikki would joke that it was nice for the Holland family to finally get some money out of Working Title. A little cruel perhaps, but certainly true and if Nikki hadn't cracked the joke, then I would have done so myself.

And since this is a book about parenthood as much as anything else, for the record, I would like to note that all monies that Tom has accrued in his career to date can be forensically accounted for. It has all been invested and can be liquidated and handed over to him when he reaches an appropriate age. I should also add that Tom hasn't a clue what this figure is and I am conscious that this could present me with an opportunity if my finances ever go completely soft. It is also up to me to decide when I consider Tom is old enough to take control of his money, and if need be I could opt for an age beyond the generally accepted twenty-one. Obviously, I hope that neither of these situations ever occurs. It will be a terrible day when I must sit Tom down on his fiftieth birthday and explain the importance of family before handing over what little is left.

So, his balanced and compact golf swing aside, most of Tom's achievements to date are down to his mum. And playing Billy has been the key to it all. It landed him the role in *The Impossible* and if his mum hadn't noticed that he could dance, then none of this would have happened. For this, he has his mum to thank and for that matter, so do I. Oh, and Des O'Connor as well.

Live at the Apollo is the show to be on nowadays and to some extent, *Des O'Connor Tonight* in the 1990s was a similar vehicle, albeit with fewer miles per gallon because there wasn't YouTube and anytime television schedules that that we now have. But Des's show was a big coup for an up and coming comedian and I was delighted to be booked.

Des is an affable type who arguably extended his career by not taking himself too seriously and welcoming the affectionate derision that Eric and Ernie heaped upon him. As such, he doesn't suffer from the jealousies and ladder-pulling-up tendencies that afflict too many celebrities. Like the late Bob Monkhouse, Des was happier embracing the crop of new comedians sprouting up on his patch, or sofa, where every comedian worth his salt could expect to sit comfortably and wait for Des to tee up their routines for them.

'So, Jack, tell me, what's getting on your nerves at the moment?'

And as Jack Dee would oblige with a beautifully honed routine, Des would dutifully play his part by slapping his thigh and wiping away the odd tear. Lee Evans, Eddie Izzard and Frank Skinner all made bum dents in Des's sofa and even though they were all destined to make it anyway, *Des O'Connor Tonight* certainly helped them on their way.

Married now, I had long been promising Nikki (and myself) that I was going to become a famous comedian. This sounds arrogant but there we are; it's how I felt. Crucially though, my sense of destiny was never really matched with corresponding levels of confidence and this was without the burden of the diversity laws which would arrive and wreak havoc with many a career in the arts. But whatever the cause, what is without doubt, is that too early in to my career, I started to plateau and not from a sustainable height to last a whole career, and certainly not for a dad with four bellies to fill. Village halls awaited me although I didn't know it at the time.

I had been feted in Edinburgh already and called a star of tomorrow.

'Making it' felt like a formality: a matter of *when* rather than *if*. So, when the call came from *Des O'Connor Tonight*, it wasn't that much of a surprise.

It was just the start of things to come, right?

All of us need to rein in our horizons from time to time. Nothing ever goes entirely to plan for anyone, even the most successful people. Need I remind anyone of the Orwell quote earlier in this book? My saving grace is that from such high expectations and hitting the ground with such a bump on my village hall tour, I am lucky that I have been disappointed without becoming terribly angry. And when I am angry from time to time, it is most usually at myself rather than the industry or other people. I say lucky because Louis CK and Bill Burr aside, rancour is usually the enemy of creativity and all but the death knell of successful comedy.

And who knows? Maybe this is because I still believe that my time is yet to come – 'life is a journey and not a destination!' – and if not as a comedian then as a writer and the success of this record-breaking book is a great place to start!

Saying such a thing is obviously a folly, setting myself up beautifully for a bloody nose, but I confess that I always imagine such lofty outcomes for all of my ventures. Otherwise, I don't think I would ever begin anything new and I probably wouldn't finish anything either.

Des O'Connor Tonight did, however, change my life. In fact, it probably had a greater impact on my life than it did on any of the other comedians who have since gone on to become national treasures. But it changed my life in a way that I could never have planned for, and its impact on my family wouldn't become apparent until almost ten years after my last appearance on the show. It was a chain of events that stemmed from when Janet Jackson appeared on *Des*, combined with the vision of a doting mum and abetted by a healthy dollop of good fortune – surely the secret and intangible ingredient to every successful career?

I had appeared as a comedian on the show twice already when the producers called again, but this time they wanted me as a writer and I probably heard a distant siren signalling that I was reaching the plateau to which I have already referred.

My employment as a writer on the show lasted for only one series and was largely a miserable experience. In fairness to Des, it wouldn't have been his idea to hire me, but that of the producer who probably realised that the series was ailing, and some new writing blood was his attempt to reinvigorate things and stave off the inevitable cancellation that came anyway.

Des had a long-term writer who had written for *The Two Ronnies* and everyone in between. He'd been delighted to hold my hand when I had appeared on the show as a comedian, but he was much less excited at having me on board as a writer, and who can blame him? Des was his payday and my sudden appearance must have been unsettling. As things transpired, he needn't have worried. The show carried on just as before. The producer was happy because I was in place and it looked like he had tried, and I was reasonably happy because I was being well paid to sit around and do nothing.

This certainly wasn't the writing that I had in mind though, and having already completed my first screenplay, which was set to become a worldwide hit (you see?), in no time I expected to be back on the show, but on the sofa in the studio and not on the sofa in Des's dressing room. I had even scripted the introduction that Des would give for me.

'Now my next guest is a funny man. A friend of the show, he's been on twice before as a comic but he's here tonight as a movie maker, his first film opening to huge box office success around the world. Please give a big hand to...'

In every show, Des would feature a musical act, ranging from the current UK chart topper trying to make some hay to the occasional American superstar passing through. One such act was Janet Jackson, who I was certainly looking forward to meeting. Sure, it wasn't her brother Michael, but it wasn't LaToya either and Janet would rank very high in my list of famous people that I have met/worked with, no matter how tenuously.

Janet Jackson arrived at the studios in Teddington, complete with her dance troupe and her 'people', and shortly afterwards she was on the studio floor blocking out her routine for her new single, 'Together Again'. The auditorium was empty apart from one bored writer with nothing to do. The backing track started up and quickly Janet and her dancers got to work for what felt like my personal concert. The song was catchy, the dancing was magnificent and I was spell-bound. At the end of the song, a couple of her assistants set about trying to justify their Transatlantic air fare, fussing with Janet's hair and make-up, as the studio floor manager was muttering with the director through his headset. We were all waiting for a 'clear', whereby the director is happy and Miss Jackson can retire to her boudoir. I was hoping that the director, like me, might like to see the routine again and he duly obliged. The floor manager politely asked whether Ms Jackson wouldn't mind shaking her booty once more. Janet took up her position, I remained in mine and I had to remind myself that I was being paid to be there.

Afterwards, Janet was lovely and kind. She gave me a copy of her CD and I regret now not getting her to sign it. This last part didn't happen, but I figure (hope) that you have worked this out for yourself already. Just like I didn't go to school with Dennis Wise and nor did I ever play football against him.

I have no idea if Janet Jackson was nice or not and she certainly did not give me a copy of her CD. Ms Jackson was collected from the studio floor by her security guards and led away to her dressing room, which was probably two rooms knocked through into one especially for her. I never saw her again until I watched the show on television along with millions of others. We didn't speak to each other. Not a word. Not even a hello, although I did smile in her direction, but I don't think she saw and if she did, then she certainly didn't return it.

Technically though, Janet and I did work together. Des might have asked her a question based on something that I had said to him on the day of the recording. I don't think this happened, but no matter; I worked with JJ and in a way much more significant than the popcorn salesman at the Super Bowl during her infamous appearance. Our professional paths had crossed, but not so that Janet would remember. She might like to know, however, that her appearance on the show left an indelible mark on me and on my family. (Memo to self: another free copy of *Eclipsed* to Ms Jackson.)

Parents are hopelessly deluded when it comes to their own children and particularly so, their first born. Most parent's think that their child is the most beautiful, brilliant and special baby that has ever been born and on balance, this is a good thing. It makes it much more likely that the child will be cherished; the worry being when the parents realise their error? But hopefully, this realisation is like a slow puncture and happens over sufficient time for a bond to form.

The competitive instincts (delusions) of new parents are heightened if they have attended a course like the National Childbirth Trust (NCT). Such classes are heavily female skewed where men are tolerated but not encouraged. These classes provide Mum with masses of information about 'baby' and five or six brand new friends who each have babies to be compared against in the only race that lasts a lifetime – the human race.

Whether dads or modern society like it or not, the mother is always the key parent and even more so in the very early stages of a child's life. By virtue of nurturing and growing the child within, giving birth and then feeding the child, a greater connection between mother and child is inevitable and as such, mums are more disposed to noticing features and facets about 'baby' than dads. Certainly, Tom's reaction to seeing Janet Jackson on *Des O'Connor Tonight* passed me by completely, but fortunately it wasn't lost on his mum.

Having seen the rehearsals in the studio, I flagged up Janet's forthcoming appearance on the show and made a point of us sitting down to catch the transmission. Never mind that I thought Nikki would enjoy Janet's performance and routine; I had promised Janet that I would watch it as we chilled out together in her dressing room after the recording and blocked out some new dance moves together.

Whenever we extol the virtues of something, we put ourselves under some pressure in the hope that the other person will share our enthusiasm. As such, I was glued to the screen as Janet strutted her stuff and I missed baby Tom's reaction completely. Nikki, in complete contrast, was glued to Tom and missed Janet entirely. And in a rare moment of organisation in my life, I had thought to record the show. If I hadn't then things might have all been very different.

I pushed 'play' and once again marvelled at the dancing on the screen, but Nikki was still more interested on the effect it was having on her son.

'Look, Tom can dance.'

This was less apparent to me and I would never have spotted it myself. But on the third or fourth play, I could sort of see it, possibly.

'I'm telling you, Dom, he can dance.'

He couldn't yet walk and spent most of his time in what are known as bouncers: a padded sling with two leg holes and an elastic cord, which suspends the child just off the ground and usually in a door frame. I expect they are now banned. Tom was a frenetic baby.

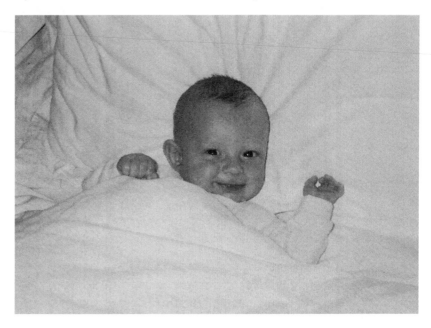

Tom as a baby - looking tired!

He slept fitfully, never stayed still for long and demanded to be held facing outwards so that he could see everything around him. He liked to be carried about the house as if he was valuing the property that one day he would inherit, or at least part thereof, and so the bouncer was welcome respite for his rapidly tiring parents. We certainly got our use out of it and it might have even helped to exaggerate his reaction to Jackson's performance, because he was in the bouncer when he first heard the song and he did literally freak out.

Quickly, this became funny. We could put the music on without telling him and as soon as he heard it, wherever he was in the house, he would drop whatever he was doing and crawl to the lounge, and in sheer delight he would start to dance feverishly. It wasn't really dancing though. Keep in mind that he couldn't yet walk or stand up, so it was just movements, which according to his mum, were completely in time. 'Dom, I am telling you. Tom can dance..'

We tried other disco staples and floor fillers of the time: Donna Summer, Chic, Kool and the Gang... Not even Earth, Wind and Fire could interest him. It was most peculiar, like a synapse in his brain was either created or bridged by my dear old mate Janet.

Tom in the bouncer! Obvious dancing talents only to a doting first-time mum?

I don't wish to come over as aloof here and disinterested in my only child. I can recall being absolutely delighted at this discovery as well. It was certainly endearing but what really interested me was the prospect of wearing the little dynamo out. With all this 'dancing', as his mum insisted on calling it, I figured he might start to sleep for the odd hour and give his parents the chance to do the same and possibly even make him a sibling to play with. With three boys to come, this obviously worked, but it is where his dancing would lead that is as exciting. So, this passage of the book can serve as a thank you to Janet Jackson on two levels: for the sleep in my thirties and for the excitement and the hope in my forties.

Our VHS recorder couldn't really keep pace with the incessant demand for 'Together Again' and I was dispatched to buy the CD from Our Price, as I recall. It was the very least Janet deserved. Quickly, it became our party piece, and Tom never failed to perform no matter how many visitors we sought to impress with our little dancing boy. We wanted people to watch him dance and had no idea that within eleven years, people would pay do so, although not in a bouncer.

I was less interested in the actual assertion that he could dance. I suspected that this was a classic case of MIM (Motherhood Infatuation Myopia), but even if Nikki was right and the kid could dance, so what? Carlos Acosta, Darcey Bussell, Margot Fonteyn, Rudolph Nureyev and Wayne Sleep, after which I was completely out of dancers, so what future was there in dance? Obviously, this was before Louie Spence burst in to our lives but being honest, even Louie wouldn't have persuaded me that dance was the way I wanted my little boy to go. Dance is a nice life skill, sure, but mainly confined to the school disco, where his experience would certainly be very different from mine. He wouldn't need to feign tiredness and sit out the last dance like I had done for years until I managed to grab a flat-footed straggler at Leeds University who I haven't let go of since. Dancing was fun, but not much of a future, and I smiled at my doe-eyed wife and hoped my little boy might get his golf handicap down to single figures.

After all, when it comes to boys, dads know best, right?

Author Footnote

Reading this chapter now in 2016 evokes a lot of memories and certainly makes me smile but also it reminds me of how finite everything is. Teddington Studios are no more and I would wager has been replaced with 'luxury' flats? Same fate for Our Price Records in Kingston which I expect now is a shop that sells coffee with too much milk. VHS had barely fifteen minutes of limelight before being cast aside by DVDs, then Blue Rays and now somehow, we watch stuff from clouds. And poor old Janet as well, usurped by Adele and Beyoncé and numerous other divas who probably had her posters on their bedroom walls. And let's not forget Des O'Connor of course, who I expect still sits on a sofa but in slippers now and most likely in a conservatory and with a cup of something warm?

And as for dancers, let me quickly share a lovely encounter I had just the other day. Sitting in Wagamamas just off the Strand and behind Covent Garden; I was on my own and waiting to attend the press night of David Baddiel's one-man-show at the Vaudeville Theatre. A story of family life albeit this is no ordinary family. With searing honesty, David delivered a remarkable show as hilarious as it is tragic and heart wrenching.

Anyway, I've had my noodles and I am about to pay my bill when a man enters the restaurant and is seated on the same bench as me as is the way in this restaurant chain with their refectory style seating. The man doesn't look like a normal patron and immediately he catches my eye. He is notably handsome. He has far too much hair and is conspicuously healthy looking. With his lithe frame, he could have chosen the chili squid starter without a flicker of guilt or worry. He looks like an athlete. A Brazilian football player perhaps? He is certainly familiar and I chance another furtive glance. His demeanour alters and I sense that he knows that he has been spotted. I now know that he is indeed famous as he begins emitting 'I just want to be left alone' signals. All famous people know how to do this. Even me, albeit rarely these days.

And then I make the connection and I know who exactly who he is. I smile broadly as I start to approach him with my out-stretched hand. I can see that this is disappointing for him; the price of fame? He must have this the world over and so the excitement of being recognized quickly wears thin. No doubt, he is hoping that I am just a fan who wants a quick 'selfie' and will be on my way before the interest of other diners' is piqued.

It is Carlos Acosta, the Rudolf Nureyev of his day and I am delighted to shake his hand. Quickly I explain that my son played 'Billy' and Carlos immediately relaxes. I am not a freak who is going to ask him to sign my chest. Carlos has seen the show and we know lots of mutual people and he is pleased to hear that Tom admires him so much. And knowing how impossibly hard ballet is, I have a little insight in to what a remarkable man it is who I am meeting and I am proud to share with him my connection to his world.

So, I leave the restaurant and head to the Vaudeville with an added spring in my step. I FaceTime Tom on the Strand. He is in America making a movie called *Homecoming*, his first stand-alone Spider-Man movie. Normally I call in just to see if he is okay but today I am excited to share with him my meeting Carlos Acosta.

And to finish, I would like to make clear that I did not bother Carlos for a 'selfie'. This is what fans do. Sure, I've been eclipsed by my son but I am still in the game and players don't get star-struck. On the set of Homecoming in July this year, I met Michael Keaton. By this, I do not mean that I met 'with' him. Like a scheduled meeting? We didn't sit down together and have coffee. It was more that we bumped in to one another on set; Mr Keaton knew who I was and we chatted, briefly. Not for very long either but long enough for me to learn that he drives a Tesla which can get up to 60mph in 3 seconds and I chose not to share that I drive a Honda FRV which has three seats in the front.

Again, no selfie with Mr Keaton. The day that I start asking for such things will be the day that I start writing my final book entitled something like, 'Ah, Bollocks, what is the point. I give up.'

Which I hope is never.

Child Benefit

The two things in life at which I have been most successful, are being a dad and being funny, and it is interesting that these two things have dovetailed and almost become mutually dependent. I use my comedy to look after my kids and I use my kids to inspire much of my comedy.

My children started to arrive in 1996 and I was quickly laden with four boys.

The boys in France trying out for a GAP ad?

I always knew that I would become a comedian and I always hoped that I would be a dad. I can recall walking my dog as a young boy, being around ten years old and performing monologues to myself. They probably made little sense at the time, but no matter because I felt sure that one day I would make similar speeches for audiences. So, when I finally pinched my nose and took the plunge into the waters of mirth, everything had a feeling of fate to it. And I hadn't been on stage for very long before I acquired Eddie Izzard as my agent-cum-manager.

This was something of a fluke. Eddie was working with a comedy club promoter called Pete Harris and they formed the imaginatively titled H & I Management. Pete had already spotted my fledgling talents and singled me out as a potential client of H & I, but Eddie would need to agree. And for this, he would need to see me at work. Gulp! He came along to see me perform at the Cartoon Comedy Club in the Plough Pub, alongside Clapham Common Station in London. It is a pub and a venue long since lost to comedy, which is a shame because it worked brilliantly as a gig, despite it being an unlikely room. I loved playing the place and looking in my diary, it was the best upcoming gig to display my skills for Eddie to judge. I was closing the show, with Sean Locke in the 'easy' middle slot, so I felt some added pressure, given that the evening felt very much like an audition. Eddie turned up fashionably late, of course. He was already a massive name in comedy and the talk of London's comedy circuit, and although he stayed at the rear of the room, his presence somehow percolated through. Heads turned and news spread, and so maybe the audience sensed the reason for his presence because they duly gave me an encore and when I finally floated off the stage for a private audience with the hallowed one, a rather remarkable conversation took place. Eddie was pleased for me. He had seen me doing short spots before, but never an entire set, never closing a show and never with an encore. So, I was a shoe-in, surely? Not quite. Not yet. Eddie wanted to know whether I thought of myself as a world class comedian? Er... no, but I didn't say this. I didn't say anything, so Eddie clarified himself. Did I think that I could become a comedian playing theatres all over the world? I didn't imagine this at all but it seemed to be very important to him. 'Dom, do you see yourself as world class comic? Can you become an international force in comedy?' It was a straight 'yes or no' question and so naturally, I plumped for yes. In effect, I lied and I happened to be correct because this was what Eddie wanted to hear. He smiled and shook my hand. Welcome to H & I. If planet earth ever needed a comedy team then Eddie Izzard and Dominic Holland would be on the team-sheet. H & I disbanded a year later and that was it. Eddie did go on to become a world comedian and probably has no idea that some comedians now do shows in village halls.

As well as his unbounded talent, a key factor accounting for Eddie's unrelenting rise to the top of the comedy world was his complete and unstinting sense of confidence and self-belief. After my triumphant Edinburgh debut, I returned the next year as a real contender with a must-see show. But quickly the wheels wobbled and signs appeared that I was unlikely to go on and represent earth as a funny man. On the first Monday of the festival, two terrible reviews ran in the local press. *The Scotsman* went with, 'middle class...and bland' and *The Glasgow Herald* was 'hugely disappointed', and so was I. My confidence was already fragile but these reviews stripped me bare and I am embarrassed now that they affected me so adversely. Al Murray was kind. He was greatly aggrieved on my behalf and told me to ignore the reviews, which I couldn't and I focused more on what Alan Davies advised me to do, which was to write funnier jokes. I realise now that I should have reacted differently. I don't blame the two journalists either, although their names are still crystal clear to me, which is a worry, given how little I can recall these days. But such notices are part of the job and other comedians have coped with far worse. Waldemar Januszczak, twice the UK arts critic of the year, famously described Eddie Izzard in *The Guardian* as 'bilge' and at a time when Eddie was at the very height of his powers. If poor notices hurt Eddie then it never showed and they certainly couldn't deflect him from his pre-ordained path.

Similarly, Harry Hill, who in 1994 had found himself a rich vein of comedy which he continues to mine to this day and I am pleased to say that we have remained friends.

Dom and Harry, Old friends

Towards the end of our very contrasting Edinburgh festivals in 1994, Harry and I sat in the Pleasance courtyard discussing life and its greater meaning, although at the time there wasn't much beyond comedy for us both. This was not quite true in my case because I was about to get married and Harry was aghast, arguing that I was far too young for something so grown up. This worried me because until this point, Harry had been right about everything else. He was a unanimous five-star act and a doctor to boot. So, he was probably right about my impending marriage, but it was too late to do anything about it now. The date was set. The wedding was only two weeks off and I could hardly cancel. Nikki would surely have already booked things and incurred costs and no doubt, bought a dress as well? Plus, we were heading to the Maldives afterwards, a holiday I had literally died on stage for to afford. So, I got married on September 10th, 1994. It was a frenzied two weeks from the festival ending to the big day with other people encouraging me to cancel the wedding as well.

At the time, Chris Evans was leaving *The Big Breakfast* and my screen test to replace him had gone very well indeed. So well in fact, that Charlie Parsons, the executive in charge, called me in and offered me the job. Blimey! Perhaps I was going to surprise myself and become world famous after all. In the upcoming week, Charlie wanted me to do some live pieces on the show as well as some 'as-live' screen tests with Gaby Roslin, only I couldn't because I was getting married. 'You're doing what?' Charlie asked. It reminded me of Harry's reaction and I worried again. He let the offer hang; for me to see reason and cancel my nuptials. Well? He prompted. But I reasoned that this woman is out of my league and I never really believed that the sea is teeming with plenty more fish.

So, now then, everything in my life was big: the big day, *The Big Breakfast* and the BIG showbiz break all coming to a head to create a very big call. Delay the wedding, cancel the wedding or make them wait two weeks. But surely two weeks wouldn't be a problem? I'll be the same person, only married, plus I'll be tanned. What's the difference? I chose Nikki and I spurned Charlie. I need not explain that my honeymoon cost me dearly because I never did replace Chris Evans. It seemed the Maldivian holiday was set to cost much more money than I could ever have budgeted for. Whether things might have been different had I not gone, I don't know and I don't care. I am still married, very happily - and *The Big Breakfast* is now toast.

And my marriage has been creative and productive in so many ways: not least because fatherhood has been the spine of my stand-up comedy. Child benefit then, as this chapter is called?

Every year, one of the national newspapers will run a feature on the cost of raising a child with a headline figure that is eye-popping and entirely unaffordable for the ordinary family: a figure so huge that if it was taken literally then it would threaten the very future of mankind. Thankfully though, human urges trump financial prudence every time and we humans live on. Certainly, in my case, with regards to family planning, there was absolutely no planning at all and this might explain how I now have four children when realistically I can afford only three. But how to decide which one must go? Not Tom, obviously!

It is true enough that children do come with enormous price tags or at least they do with certain life choices. In monetary terms, I would categorise my children as middling but we are an unusual family because my children have already fully contributed to the Holland family income. Indeed, it could even be argued that my kids have even been an earner.

Over the years, my 'Dad' material has allowed me to carry on gigging and crucially, invoicing. Tom was particularly inspirational because he was my first child. All parents complain about their lack of sleep, but Tom was a particularly awake child. I likened him to a mobile phone; he didn't sleep, he recharged, and this inspired one of my better-known and much-relied-upon routines. The exact wording of the routine went as follows:

...he doesn't sleep, he recharges. He's like a mobile phone. You plug him in for an hour; he's good for the whole day. I'll be in the lounge and I'll be knackered. And I'll say, 'Listen... Nokia, I'm exhausted. I just want to sit down and relax. How about that, if dad sits down for ten minutes or so?'

'Yeah, sure, Dad. No problem. You put your feet up and read the newspaper, but while you're doing that, I tell you what, I'm going to get up and run around - and do you see this sharp edge, this one here at head height? I tell ya what, I'm going to head butt it? How does that sound to you?'

And now we've got the twins as well – Motorola and Ericsson. Trying to feed them at the same time, in one arm I've got Motorola and in the other arm I've got Ericsson. Luckily, Nokia is hands-free now...

Me holding Motorola and Ericsson

I don't know how funny this reads now, but at the time it always brought the house down and got me out of a few holes. And so, I went on developing such routines as my boys got older – taking kids swimming, the cost of nappies, pram etiquette, dog poo and shoes with commando treads and more latterly, dashing from a village hall in Hampshire to pick up Nokia from the Victoria Palace Theatre. Thankfully audiences have kept on laughing. And to be fair, the lion share of my income has been spent on my kids, so it's a perfect symbiotic relationship then. My career and family are intertwined. My boys are much of my inspiration and much of my motivation to succeed. I want to provide for them, but I also want to make them proud of me.

And so, it is with this story, *Eclipsed*: an opportunity to validate my often-hilarious experiences in the film world over the last fifteen years, which appropriately enough, mirrors the time that I have been a dad. And as such, I wonder if *Eclipsed* isn't perhaps my harvest from all this effort, as if soil and water has been dropped onto the stony path on which I have been haplessly been sewing my filmic seeds for the past decade.

Albeit inadvertently, my kids just keep on giving and whilst I am excited by the prospect of *Eclipsed*, whether it is a success or not, it has already served one very important function of being a heartfelt thank you to my wife and to our boys.

Dad, seriously, it's full of Girls...

These dates are a little hazy, but Tom's first experience of a formal dance lesson was when he was five. Nikki had enrolled him in our local branch of Stagecoach, which exposes kids to all the performing arts, but it was dance that he liked and he quickly lost interest in all the acting nonsense, so Nikki kept an eye out for a suitable dance class.

A friend told her about a local tap and ballet class at a nearby church hall and we all pitched up one weekday night to observe. Exclusively female was my immediate observation, which could go either way. A good thing or a bad thing, I didn't really know yet. Tom completed the class and promptly announced that he wanted to continue.

'You're sure? You really want to do this?'

I must have played The Comedy Store that weekend. I know this because my wallet was stuffed with cash and only The Comedy Store pays such amounts in cash, with an invoice I might add. Now though, my bulging wallet was rapidly emptied to pay for the lessons themselves and he would need tap and ballet shoes of course.

'You're sure about this, Tom?'

He nodded again.

'A leotard... Really?'

Despite his assurances, he only lasted a further two classes before announcing that it wasn't for him. 'Dad, it's full of girls'. Most parents will experience something like this. Music lessons are a major culprit of parents wasting money they can ill afford. I put the almost-pristine tap and ballet shoes into our loft on the unlikely basis that one day we might have a girl.

Tom still wanted to dance though, but it needed to be 'cool' dancing, like 'what black people do'. Nikki kept her eyes open for a class and I wondered whether I should address the delicate subject of racial stereotyping. A little later, perhaps six months, Nikki spotted an advert in a local newspaper for a dance class called Nifty Feet. Unbeknownst to us, it would have a seismic effect on my entire family.

The lady who ran the dance class was called Lynne Page. Lynne is well known in the dancing world and so was completely unknown to me. She had choreographed West End shows but her dance school was hardly grandiose. Held at a council leisure centre close to where we live, it ran for a couple of hours on a Saturday afternoon and Tom loved it immediately.

A black guy called Winston was Tom's first teacher. No hair, built like a sprinter, he had danced on *Top of the Pops* and he was way cooler than me. Tom thought he was awesome and he was hooked; and his twin brothers, Sam and Harry, would later join also. A highlight of my week was to get to the class a little before it ended so that I could watch whatever routine they had put together. And then in the evening, I would drive to a comedy club to do routines of my own.

Tom with the twins at a Billy After-show

Until my twins joined, (seen here with Tom on his last night playing Billy), Tom was only one of three boys in the class and by some distance; he was the third best male dancer. A boy called Robbie was a year older and was simply magnificent. He would go on to dance for Zoo Nation, and there was a good-looking lad called Kyle who had already modelled and appeared in various TV adverts.

And so, it went on for a few years with all three Holland boys funking out on their Saturday afternoon. Tom would have been nine or so at the time and the twins, seven. They enjoyed it and so did we. By now, their baby brother, Patrick, had arrived and Saturday afternoons were almost peaceful with the three brothers learning how to catch prey at future school discos.

We knew that Lynne had an association with *Billy Elliott the Musical*, but we didn't know what and we never thought to ask. The leaping image of Billy Elliot that you see on buses had featured on the original advert for the dance class and was what caught Nikki's eye, so maybe it was fated all along? Here is Tom in a similar pose on a digital campaign that made escalator rides on the London Underground never long enough.

Lynne worked with the choreographers on the show and helped to organise the training schedule for the many boys going through the long auditioning process for the role of Billy. And knowing the arduous nature of this process and the role itself, Lynne was protective of her Nifty Feet students. She never linked Tom with the role and neither did we.

At Easter each year, we all gathered at White Lodge in Richmond Park, home of the Royal Ballet School, a fitting setting for what was about to unfurl. 'Rich Dance' was a chance for all the local dance classes in the area to prepare a routine to impress their parents and grandparents. Nifty Feet took part each year.

To be honest, the show was largely a torturous watch with parents and extended families gathered to see their own children perform and nobody else's. It is one of life's impossibilities to be truly objective when one's children are concerned. 2006 was a particularly special 'Rich Dance' for the Holland family because for the first time, three of my boys, Tom, Sam and Harry, would all be dancing.

Naturally, Nifty Feet were stunning, the best by far, and my boys were particularly magnificent! At the time, I knew that Kyle had recently auditioned for *Billy Elliot*. He hadn't been successful, but I was still very impressed that he had been considered and I had to fight my urge to tell those people sitting around me that he might have been Billy. At this stage, I still hadn't seen the musical but like all Londoners, it was impossible to miss the posters all over town. It was a show receiving huge attention, much like the film had done when it was released five years earlier.

I was first made aware of the show by the *Evening Standard*. Most Londoners will have a few *Evening Standard* moments, on their way home from work when they discover a story or an event. I have three 'Standard' moments relevant to this story:

John Inverdale, the sports broadcaster, is a friend of mine and my regular golf opponent. Playing rugby one day, he had his forehead gashed open.

His horribly bruised face stared out at me from the newspaper as I sat on the train. Immediately, I reached for my phone as I read the inevitable section about how he was lucky not to lose an eye. John isn't terribly good with his phone. He rarely answers, but on this occasion, he did. He assured me that he wasn't going to die, but he couldn't talk because he was about to go in to see *Billy Elliot the Musical*. Quickly, I ended the call. This was a time when *Billy* tickets were like gold-dust and I figured that John's ticket was probably some kind of celebrity freebie thing. He would later tell me that the show was possibly the most fun that he had ever had in a theatre. High praise indeed, although I should add a caveat that John enjoyed the film *Wimbledon* and even saw it twice.

Another 'Standard' moment also involved *Billy Elliot* when the original boys were cast. The front page carried a photograph of three boys wearing big white T-shirts emblazoned with 'BILLY' across their chests, leaping from the steps of Eros in Piccadilly Circus. Their names were Liam Mower, James Lomas and George Maguire, their beaming faces a stark contrast to the tired faces of the commuters making their way home that night. I read the article out of general interest and I smile wryly now when I recall my reaction. Firstly, because of how the show would affect our family, but more so because, at the time, I just couldn't see how *Billy Elliot the Musical* would work. This is typical of me, to call something so wrong. I did the same with *Little Britain* and *Father Ted* – a matter of taste which is always subjective – but not seeing the appeal of *Billy Elliot the Musical* is particularly worrying because it is so bloody obvious. It was a hit film and it features a kid who wants to dance. What other ingredients of a hit musical are missing? None. Which makes me an idiot.

I felt happy for these three boys. Each of them looked delighted and why not? They were undoubtedly talented kids who had emerged from hundreds of hopefuls, possibly even thousands. And even though all my boys danced at the time, it never occurred to me for a single second that any of them could ever be as lucky as these three lads. Not that I didn't rate my boys; it was just that this kind of good fortune happens to other people's families, not mine.

A few days after 'Rich Dance', we received a phone call from Lynne, which was a little odd. Immediately, I could sense awkwardness in her voice. Was she going to ask me to join her class? It had been ages since I had danced, but I was nimble back in the day. Plus, I have always looked young for my age but a teenager still, really? But then she got to the point. Apparently, a member of the Royal Ballet School had been at the 'Rich Dance' event and he wanted to know why Tom hadn't been put forward to audition for Billy. Lynne explained that there was an audition in London in a couple of weeks' time. Would Nikki and I discuss it and get back to her?

I put the phone down and laughed. I found Nikki before speaking to Tom and she was equally dumbfounded and laughed as well. We told Tom. Ditto. Might be fun to go along though, eh?

We decided that it was a good idea if we knew what exactly Tom was going for and with my thirty-ninth birthday coming up, it was a good excuse to splash some cash and catch a show. We didn't tell Tom where we were going, but kept it as a surprise. I had meetings in town and I had arranged to meet Nikki and Tom at Victoria Station. Ever early, I went upstairs and stood outside on the mezzanine balcony with a view over the concourse. It was packed, heaving with people, charging home and praying for a seat on their train or at least something to lean on. Then I spotted Nikki and Tom. He looked tiny holding his mum's hand and I smiled at the idea that we were heading off to a show for which this tiny little boy was auditioning to play the title role.

Under these circumstances then, our anticipation for the show was heightened and as the show unfolded before us, what struck me was just how long Billy remains on stage. He practically never leaves as he dances and sings and acts repeatedly.

During the interval, none of us said very much other than what an amazing kid the boy playing Billy was. His name was Liam Mower, the very first boy ever to play the role. I can remember wondering how puffed up his parents must have been. I imagined that they must see most of his performances and therefore, there was every chance that they were in the theatre that very evening. They must have been in the stalls and as we had a box, I reasoned that they would have been easy enough to identify: two people swollen with pride. I scanned the stalls and quickly drew a blank. Must be in the bar. I would have loved to meet them, to congratulate them, but also to ask what it feels like to watch their son do such a thing: a question that cannot really be answered as I would come to discover.

After the final curtain and on the way out of the theatre, all three of us were laughing again, chuckling to ourselves as we all agreed that Tom was never going to play Billy. There was just no way. No chance. Ballet, tap, singing, acting; Tom had never done any of these things. He had never even been cast in any of his school plays. We discussed cancelling the audition, but decided that it might be a good experience anyway. It was flattering to be asked along and I reasoned that life is a factor of how we can cope with disappointment and rejection. And for this reason, it would be a worthwhile life lesson if nothing else.

Go along, Tom, be polite, do your best and just see what happens.

The Star Signs are Not Good

I don't think this book would work if I was, say, Richard Curtis or Michael McIntyre.

'Hey, I made it and guess what? So, did my son! Here's how...'

I am always embarrassed when I am described as a celebrity and even more so, a star. I certainly don't live in the world that we associate with 'stars'. I worry about my income. I live in a house with a number and not a name. I do have an ISA but I can rarely add to it and never with the amount my government permits me to. We have one car and it's a Fiat - now a Honda. When I was young I imagined driving a Ferrari but when I was able to afford one (second/third hand?), I had lots of children and my priorities had changed. But I do have a very cool job, which I sometimes need to be reminded of.

I made a speech one year at my boys' annual school dinner dance. It went down very well, particularly so for one parent who didn't know who I was. He thought I was just a regular dad who had drawn a very short straw. He was a lawyer and when someone explained that I was a pro comic he was incredibly excited. He bounded up to me and told me something that has always stuck with me; that I had the coolest job in the world. And I guess I do. Making a living by thinking of funny things to say is damn cool.

Getting invited to the annual BBC 'Party of the Stars' back in 2000 was pretty damn exciting and the closest I ever came to feeling like a genuine star. This was my zenith you may recall. The invitation came hard off the back of my spot on *The Royal Variety Show*, my BBC Radio 4 series and my appearing regularly on *The Clive Anderson Now* Series. Suddenly, I had done enough and I was on the list. Blimey!

It is an event where the great and the good from the world of show business get together to congratulate themselves. A little like an awards ceremony, only without any awards. I am not sure whether the Party of the Stars still runs, from which you can draw your own conclusions.

It wasn't much of a venue, just a studio at BBC Centre where I had recorded both my sets for *The Stand-Up Show* on BBC1 with the mighty Barry Cryer at the helm. But it was the company that made it all so exciting and how I was treated as well. Ben Elton had hosted my recent *Royal Variety Show* and he sidled up to me and explained that I was set for great things. I need to contextualize this a little. Back in 1985, I was a student at Leeds University. Ben Elton came to Leeds on his tour, resplendent in his sparkly suit, and he quite literally blew my world apart. It was like how people reminisce about seeing Zeppelin or The Stones. Incidentally, I have seen neither of these iconic bands, but I did once see Kool and the Gang at the Hammersmith Apollo. Ben ended the first half of his brilliant show in his best 'mockney' accent, 'Ladies and gentlemen, that was an hour of stand-up comedy. Let's come back in half an hour and we'll do another hour of stand-up comedy.' I was spellbound. I don't know how many people were at the gig; a thousand? But he rocked the place and I was in complete awe that one man could have such an effect on so many people. My ambitions to be a comedian had nagged at me for years but now they crystallized completely. I now had a hero and something to aim for. So you will understand a little better now that Ben's words at the stars party pretty much rocked my world.

At the time, I was still doing the warm-up for *Have I Got News for you* and Angus took me to one side and explained that my warm-up days were over and that my time had come.

On the way to the toilets, Alan Yentob emerged and high fived me. He even called me Dom. And now I really started to believe and I didn't care if the creative director of the BBC (Yentob) had washed his hands or not. But the greatest accolade of the evening and my whole career was yet to come. The great and the good of British comedy were present, including a man I admired most of all, Ronnie Barker. My dad is heavily responsible for this because as a small boy, I was fascinated that Barker could make my dad laugh so much. Whether it was *Porridge* or *The Two Ronnies*, my dad loved Barker and therefore, so did I, even before I understood why he was such a giant amongst comedians.

Any exponent of comedy will tell you just how rare it is for such a funny writer to be equally blessed as a performer. Barker was both and having watched and admired him for so long, understandably, I was nervous about meeting him. Ronnie Corbett had done the *Royal Variety Show* as well and he was very happy to introduce me. As I approached him, I fretted about what I might say and settled on the bland, what an honour... But as it turned out, I couldn't say much at all because Ronnie Barker looked up and said, 'Hello, Dominic...' This threw me completely. How the hell does he know who I am? Had he been at the Cartoon Comedy Club as well? It turned out that Ronnie Barker was a fan of my radio 4 series and he went on to tell me how much he liked my comedy. He liked my comedy? So, flattered and overwhelmed, I could barely reply and I hope that I didn't disappoint him.

The comedy world is very much like a club. Firstly, there is one big club to which all stand-up comedians automatically belong: all comedians together, big and small, from the arena stars all the way down to the struggling pub turns and open spots. Writers are excluded. Writing funny is important. It is difficult and more people do it badly than well but it ain't the same as performing and it never will be. Stand-up comedy is the most exposing of all the art-forms and the constant threat of death makes this club exclusive to those stupid enough to do it. But within this big unwieldy club is a clearly delineated hierarchy and narrowing until a hallowed inner sanctum of the 'in' comedians is reached: a rarefied private members club, but with a very public and apparent membership. Just turn on the television to see who is a member and who isn't.

All comedians apply to this club but only a tiny few will ever be accepted. I had a few interviews over the years, but that night at the star's party, everything aligned and finally it felt as though I was in. I was disappointed that Nikki wasn't with me. She had been invited but was too exhausted and so I rushed home early with my exciting news that my application had been approved. I was in. I was famous. It was late and Nikki was fast asleep, but she would want to be woken, surely? Like when I got home from the Comedy Store on the night that Princess Diana died and I woke her. This news was even bigger. She roused reluctantly and did her best to sound excited, but at the time we had three kids under the age of three and getting back to sleep appealed much more.

Despite such excitement heralding from the Stars Party, it seemed that my membership was quickly revoked. The *Clive Anderson Series* was cancelled and marked practically my last appearance on mainstream evening television, aside from one difficult appearance on *They Think It's All Over* the following year. I had sent Jonathan Ross a loose manuscript of my first novel, *Only in America*, and then again when the publisher made some bound proofs. It wasn't exactly an unsolicited thing. I had been Jonathan's warm-up act in the past and I was friends with his brother, which was how I came by his address. During rehearsals for the TV show in the late afternoon, the panelists block out the show in the studio. I was on Gary Lineker's team and took my seat. The auditorium was empty apart from a gaggle of crew and crucially, the show's writers. I wanted to catch Jonathan's eye to say hello because I felt awkward at having sent him my novel twice.

Writers are most vulnerable when they have submitted their work and the worst possible response is to hear nothing. I wanted to nod a 'hello' to Jonathan in a 'no problem' kind of way and let's have a good show. But before I could get to this, Jonathan called out loudly across the studio, 'Will you stop sending me your fucking book?' I was mortified. It might have been a marker down to the comic on his show or more likely it was just blokey banter and I should have laughed along with the delighted writers in the stalls. But I couldn't. I felt humiliated. My confidence evaporated and the show was torturous.

I was lucky then that I had a two-book deal from a publisher and my anxiety about performing live stand-up could be circumvented because I was going to become a famous comic novelist. And furthermore, the film rights would be snapped up and provide me with my passage to Hollywood and complete the Holland master plan.

In general, comedians depend on the club circuit for their stage time and income until such time that they can fill venues on their own, in arts centres, theatres and occasionally, arenas. The comedy circuit becomes too small to contain them and off they fly. This was not how I left the comedy circuit. I left because the corporate circuit opened to me. Fewer gigs for much higher fees and this was not the only attraction to me. There is no kudos in corporate entertainment and certainly no career path. Almost all comedians do them, although some are at great pains to conceal it. Ben Elton was once asked, what luxury do you allow yourself and he answered, 'Not doing corporate gigs.' Good answer. But Ben is rare and can afford to take such a stand. Not me, though. And they suited me perfectly. I became good at them and they allowed me to write my novels and films. And crucially, because such gigs are not open to the ticket-buying public, my comedy felt less scrutinized. In effect, corporate gigs allowed me to hide as a stand-up and I dropped off the comedy radar altogether, just ahead of the renaissance in TV comedy. All comedians need good timing. On this decision, mine was terrible, only it didn't feel like I had much of a choice. But no matter; I'm heading to Hollywood, remember?

Speaking of timing, when I was on television a lot, my kids were too young to understand and, dare I say it, appreciate it. Now though, my boys are watching shows like *Mock the Week* and naturally they ask why I am not on. For the same reason that I don't take tea with the Queen; I am not invited, and the truth is that I wouldn't like to either, because I don't think I would fare too well: fighting other comics for screen time and laughs. It is hard enough to get laughs, but much harder to appear happy for one's fellow comedians when their laughs are louder than your own. Too often, it is not the comedy on *Mock the Week* that is to be admired. It is the acting.

Children will always need and seek their parents' approval, something which I don't think ever really ends. But the converse of this is true also, with parents needing their kids' approval. Need I remind you of my dalliance with Anne Hathaway?

I recall with fondness doing a pretty ropey gig in Swansea one night. It was just me and a support act. It was sparsely attended, neither of us had done particularly well and during the long drive home, my support act and I discussed our similar ambitions in film. I wanted to be a writer and he wanted to be an actor. He was certainly no looker and I liked my chances much better than his. Scroll forward then fifteen years or so to Christmas 2011. Nikki was away somewhere with our youngest, Paddy, leaving me with my three other boys to have a boys'-own day. It began with a four-ball for nine holes. We took in some of the world darts at a mate's house because he had Sky, and before heading for a pizza, we caught the rather magnificent *Mission Impossible: Ghost Protocol* at our local cinema. We all loved it and I had to smile to myself because my support act all those years ago was Simon Pegg, now on the silver screen, ably supporting Mr Tom Cruise. On the way home I told my boys and they were mightily impressed, but I should have seen the question coming.

'Dad, why don't you act in films with Tom Cruise?'

Where to begin with that one? And talking of stardom, back in the day, I was once asked to feature in an *Evening Standard* column called 'Star of the Future'. But having agreed, things suddenly went quiet and the journalist was eventually embarrassed to explain that I had been dropped from the column because according to her editor, I was already a star. Really? I was dubious and this remains my most flattering rejection ever and I have had many. At the time, I certainly didn't feel like a star and naturally, I was keen to see which wannabe had replaced me. It turned out to be an actor I had never heard of. A young guy from Scotland who was apparently turning heads, mostly female I guessed and I wished him well. No hard feelings, mate. Ewan McGregor was his name. So if the editor responsible ever reads this book then all I can say is - good call mate. On both counts.

It was not long before *Trainspotting* exploded and made him a global star. And had someone told me at the time that he would play the dad to my son in the most successful Spanish film of all time, then I would not have believed it. At this time, I didn't even have a son and if I did, then there was no chance he would be anything as tawdry as a child actor. No way.

Author Footnote

Reading this chapter now in 2016 I am reminded of a conversation I had a few years back with my agent at the time. Along with a bunch of other comedians of a certain age, being able to rock a comedy club these days' counts for little when it comes to being chosen to appear on television. And starting to panic because corporate gigs are borne out of TV appearances, I suggested to my agent that I might go back to doing television warm ups again. Without question, a backwards step but better than doing nothing and after all, I had once been the go-to-comic for studio warm-ups. Angus Deaton had been wrong it seems. My warm-up days were about to start back up again.

Some months went by and having heard nothing nor secured any bookings I pushed my agent for any news. He was sheepish explaining that warm-up gigs are not so easily secured these days. In other words, I can't even do warm-ups? Oh, my God, are you kidding me?

It seemed that Angus Deaton was correct after all. And with this my sense of panic increased. But no matter, I assured myself, because the book I had started to write about being eclipsed by my son was set to become a worldwide best-seller...

Luck of the Irish

It would need to be strong roots if Tom's good fortune can be attributed to his Irish lineage, two generations away as they are. But, to be sure, the little man has been bloody lucky, all right.

Gary Player famously said that the more he practiced, the luckier he became, and Malcolm Gladwell explains that it is circumstance and practice that make perfect and not innate ability. So presumably we could all become virtuoso violinists or champion golfers then? No, not really but circumstance and good fortune do play a heavy hand in every successful career.

If nothing else happens from hereon in, Tom has already had an extraordinary life. Ahead of his fifteenth birthday he has played the title role in a West End Musical, a leading role in an animated feature film and a leading role in a theatrical feature film and all without a stage school or even a drama lesson in sight.

Not that Tom has not worked incredibly hard; he has and his efforts warrant a single chapter on their own. But he has also been bloody lucky too. By chance, his mum noticed that he could dance before he could even walk. He was spotted and invited to audition for *Billy Elliot the Musical* completely by chance. But his real piece of good fortune came when Tom first auditioned for the role of Billy. The show hadn't long opened and was already a huge hit and the must-have ticket in London.

Stephen Daldry, the director of the film and now the stage play, had been all over the press and the television, talking largely about the exhaustive process of casting and training the boys to play Billy. Thousands of kids had been considered to find the three original boys, but of course the casting process is a continual one because adolescent kids quickly grow themselves out of the role. But now that the show had opened, the reviews were in and the tickets were like gold dust, Stephen Daldry could be forgiven for delegating the onerous task of locating the next tranche of Billy's to his underlings. His opinion would be sought at the sharp end again when the field had narrowed, but he certainly would not need to attend open auditions anymore and not one on a wet Sunday morning at a dance studio along from Borough Market. We learnt afterwards that Stephen Daldry was not meant to be at Tom's first audition and as things transpired, thank God, he was. Without being melodramatic, it changed Tom's life.

Even though Tom had been invited to this audition, I hadn't realized that it was in fact just an open audition to which anyone could respond to an advert and attend. As such, there were hundreds of boys attending from all over the United Kingdom. A long queue of boys and their parents snaked down the wet road: a long queue of hope, of which Tom joined the end. He was with my mum, Granny Tess, because neither Nikki nor I could take him. You might note from this picture why Nikki and my mum are often mistaken for mother and daughter.

The two redheads in my life

I expect my mum was foreboding at the length of the queue and cursing her second son (me) because I had explained with my customary confidence that Tom would be perhaps one of a dozen kids.

I assumed that Tom would need to dance for them and that this would be a problem because at the time Tom couldn't really dance. Not really. He just did a bit of disco dancing and nothing else, and certainly nothing formal. Tom was a very young-looking ten-year-old and no matter that his dyslexia had now been officially diagnosed; at this stage of his life he would have more chance of spelling pirouette than doing one.

His granny's mood darkened further when they finally got inside the building to see so many boys wearing leotards and waiting to be seen in the splits position with toes pointed. Tom was wearing football shorts and sat down cross-legged. The only thing pointing in Team Holland was my mum's eyebrows. It didn't augur well. But it didn't really matter because Tom wasn't there to get the part. In truth, he was there for the rejection. Something about the experience of an audition and learning a useful life lesson that in life we don't always get what we want.

I can't report very accurately here what went on at the audition because they always take place behind closed doors, away from prying and partisan eyes. Along with some other boys, Tom was observed dancing. Presumably, just freestyle. He had been asked to bring along his own music and it was most likely something by a Jackson, possibly Janet but nothing by Tchaikovsky.

The dancing over, Tom was asked some questions about dance and I told him to be honest and tell them that he had no formal training at all. And then they did some acting role play and that was it, and his group of boys left. A brief con-flab then ensued amongst the 'creatives' and it was generally agreed that Tom looked the part all right and so it was a shame that he couldn't dance. NEXT!

Fortunately, though, Stephen Daldry is a director and not a dancer and so Tom's lack of dance experience was of less concern to him. Ever honest, Tom explained that he had no acting experience either. Still at primary school, he had been up for every school play, every year and had never secured a speaking part. And yet Daldry was still undeterred. He saw something in Tom that he liked. He would later tell me that he could see that Tom could act and even more crucially, that he could take direction. I felt ambivalent on hearing this. Pleased that my son could take direction but bemused that he rarely did anything I ever suggested to him.

'But, Stephen, he can't dance.' The show's choreographer said.

'Fine, then teach him,' Daldry responded.

And they did. Tom was through to the next round, to 'boot camp' to use the modern vernacular, and the rest would be up to him. And over the next eighteen months, to see him go from a flat start to the West End was as beguiling as it was interesting, and it is a journey I will gladly recount here in these pages and attempt to do justice to.

I don't suppose Stephen Daldry needs any more plaudits. He is a man with three Academy Award nominations to his name, plus a raft of other wins and I assume much booty, but he can add the following citation to his Curriculum Vitae if he wishes:

'Daldry is blessed with truly great vision.' Dominic Holland, 2012

Or, in more plain English, 'God bless you and thank you, sir, Mr Daldry, sir.'

Too much?

Sure, but you see my point...

From Stockton-On-Tees to
Hollywood by Train

'Ahrm... er, ahrm sorry, Dom, but ya see, ahr cannae pay y'us for tha gig, man...'

This is supposed to read as a Geordie accent and so in translation – 'I am sorry, Dom, but I cannot pay you for the gig that you've just done for me this evening.'

This was said to me way back in 1995. It ranks fourth on the list of things that a comedian never wants to hear, after 'get off, you're shit', 'tell us a joke' and 'when's the comedian coming on?'

It was said by a promoter in Stockton-On-Tees called Bobby. I had compered his gig in a cavernous and cold room with too few people to create any atmosphere and more importantly, not enough money to salve any of the comedian's bruises. I liked Bobby and probably didn't believe that a cheque would follow me to London, but I gave him my address anyway. But never mind, as things turned out I have much to thank Bobby for, especially if this book is a success. To date, it hasn't been!

The Bed & Breakfast in Stockton had made the gig even more uneconomic, not to mention the cost of the train home, complete with its broken heating system. The freezing journey provided me with ample time for career reflection and suddenly, in an instant, it all became clear to me, that I should write a film. Before me I saw a yellow brick road that would bypass sit-coms altogether and lead all the way to Hollywood. I kicked my freezing cold heels together and set off on a journey I am still on now.

By the time my train pulled in to Kings Cross I was mildly hypothermic but had managed to stay alive on the passion that came from my new mission in life. I had already panned out a story and I even had a title, The Faldovian Club. It would be a modern Ealing comedy featuring a disillusioned everyman who is catapulted into a maelstrom of excitement by the loss of a cunning elderly relative who has planned everything and controls proceedings from the grave. Brilliant!

Excitedly, I told Nikki that I was going to make a movie and she was delighted. We were a year married and we were young and fearless. Make a movie? Sure, why not? I hadn't got paid for last night's gig and froze my nuts off for the effort. Without realizing it, this would become a perfect metaphor for my foray in to film. A never-ending journey for no pay...

But my experiences with The Faldovian Club would directly inspire a story that would become my first published novel, *Only in America*, and this book would indeed take me to LA and is the spine of this story - Eclipsed - and so well worth it then? Without doubt, because writing Eclipsed has been a cathartic delight for me and is the single piece of work in a thirty-year career of which I am most proud.

The Faldovian Club was written quickly and naively and in its early stages, it was wildly exciting for Nikki and me until it finally keeled over and died completely some four years later.

The second act of *Billy Elliot* opens with a miner hosting a Christmas party, complete with microphone and lead. This role was played by an actor called Trevor Fox, a naturally funny man, and this part of the show allowed him free rein, which he appeared to relish. It was during this small scene that Trevor would often ad-lib a line of his own that always made me laugh. Stepping momentarily out of character, Trevor would fix an audience member with a stare, mimic their sense of despondency and say in his genuine and thick Geordie accent, 'All reet! All reet! Be patient there will ya pal and the little dancing lad will be back on stage in no time.'

Because of course it was Billy that the audience had come to see and I so, I will only give a potted history of The Faldovian Club before getting back to Tom. The first draft came in at two hundred and seventy-seven pages long. This will mean nothing to most readers until I explain that ideally a screenplay should come in at around the hundred-page mark: one-fifteen, one-twenty, but never two hundred and seventy-something. Based on a minute of screen time per page, I was proposing to make a light-hearted comedy film that would run close to four and a half hours and so it was remarkable then that my big-hitting agent at the time bothered to wade his way through it. He had Hugh Grant and Chris Evans in his stable of thoroughbreds and I was his new stable boy. He had seen my show in Edinburgh in 1994 and signed me on the spot.

But I was a quick learner and this was just my first draft with as many as a hundred to come. Each one was better and shorter than the last, and each time I would finally write 'FADE TO BLACK' and imagine my Oscar speech! No one does enthusiasm and delusion quite like me.

Even more remarkably, there was immediate interest in my film, an epic comedy set to run for an hour longer than *Gandhi*. Nikki had married well; her funny little husband was on his way to Hollywood.

The producer in question was a lady called Eileen Maisel and to me she was the real deal. She was American. She was Jewish and she wanted to meet me for breakfast. At this point in my life, the only people I had ever met for breakfast were my family. Plus, she wanted to have breakfast with me at Claridges no less. At the time, I was more of a Sausage McMuffin kind of guy.

Way before the luxury of Google images, when I arrived, I had no idea who Eileen was, but I still picked her out instinctively. She reminded me of Rhea Pearlman of *Cheers* fame, barking orders at the hotel staff fluttering about her. She recognised me, which shouldn't have surprised me as much as it did. After all, I had been the Edinburgh Best Newcomer only two summers before. My screenplay (tome) was on the table in front of her as I sat down and we exchanged a quick hello. The sofa was too deep and sitting back, I practically lay flat on my back which was not a great start. She was tiny, much smaller than me, but being a Claridge's regular, she knew and was perched on the edge of the sofa. I dragged myself upright and noticed that she now had an air of seriousness about her. And then she said the following words, and I quote, 'Great story, but why the fuck is it so long?'

I floundered a little and said something about knowing that edits would be needed. You know, no big deal, just a few trims here and there. I just need to cut out the odd three hours. If my acknowledgement appeased her then she didn't show it as a waiter hovered nervously. This being a breakfast meeting, clearly, we needed to order breakfast. Ms Maisel was having her usual, so the waiter was just waiting on me. I cast my eye across the menu. What happened next is something I am struggling to explain, but I need to recount accurately because it gives an insight into my odd world and offers some texture for this story.

The menu was standard stuff – fresh fruits and posh muesli, onto pastries and from here, up to the usual cooked fare: bacon, eggs and various other options and accompaniments – but in my panic, I plumped for kippers. Nothing remarkable about this, I suppose. I like kippers but this is not why I chose them. I chose the smoked herrings because they are not easy to eat and I thought that ordering them might demonstrate my sense of composure and confidence. I genuinely thought that ordering kippers would impress Eileen. Sure, I could have gone safe and just had a Danish. But no! I went for a dish that is difficult to eat and carries a reasonable level of danger also and because of this, I reasoned that this meant Eileen would take me seriously. Here is a man so assured that he has time to bone a fish in the most important meeting of his life: a man who is surely on his way to becoming a film maker.

His script is way too long and it probably doesn't really have legs, but you know, there's just something about this writer... He ordered kippers at breakfast. I mean, who fucking does that?

This is all completely ridiculous, I know, but there we are. It is all true. Welcome to my harmless but peculiar inner workings.

Unsurprisingly, the kipper ploy failed because, despite my drastic culling and rewrites, Eileen's interest quickly waned. But there was still life in the Faldovian Club yet, because after Eileen came Jan.

Jan was very different from Eileen. Firstly, he was male and Dutch. He was at Ginger Productions and charged with firing up their film division. Chris Evans owned Ginger. He was King Midas at the time and it made sense that he wanted to touch anything and everything. The film slate at Ginger was clean and The Faldovian Club hit Jan's desk at just the right time and now it was a lean one hundred and ten pages long and fighting fit. Jan loved it and called me in immediately. Like most Dutchmen, he was almost seven feet tall and yet we still saw eye to eye. He was buying an option in my film and he was going to produce it. I have had more important meetings since but I am wiser now and more understanding of film and so I know not to get excited anymore, ever. But back then when I met Jan, I was still Dom from Kansas on the yellow brick road and I cannot remember ever being quite as excited in my life.

I literally flew out of the Ginger offices in Golden Square and called Nikki immediately with my extraordinary news. 'Quick, phone an estate agent, we're moving to Notting Hill'. I bounded and bounced the couple of miles to the London Studios on the Embankment. My exuberance was infectious and even passers-by seemed to enjoy the energy I was emitting. I was booked to do the audience warm-up for *The Clive James Show*. Full of adrenalin, I burst into the production office determined to tell anyone who would listen that my days of being a warm-up man were over. (Given the footnote to a previous chapter, feel and enjoy the extra poignancy of this last sentence!) Everyone congratulated me warmly. Hollywood, Dom, that's great news. Well done you. Clive, though, was much more circumspect. He explained that an option means bugger all and it certainly didn't mean that my script was getting made. He added that over the years, he had made a fortune from various options, but this didn't sweeten his message very much and so I decided to ignore it. What the hell does Clive James know anyway? We're talking about the arts and he's a bloody Australian, mate.

Two years since the train journey from Stockton and it was about to pay off. If Bobby's cheque had arrived that day then I wouldn't have cashed it. I didn't need his money. I hugged Nikki and then she wanted to show me something that our little boy could do. She was still going on about his dancing – can you believe that? It was lovely, of course, don't get me wrong. Sure, everyone likes to see kids dancing. But a dancing baby wasn't going to pay the mortgage and I had another redraft of my future hit film to get on with.

Author Footnote

The gig in Stockton all those years ago has taken on even more significance in the intervening years because appearing on the bill with me that night was a comic called Dave Johns. Dave has a special place in my comedy heart because along with his fellow Geordie, Mickey Hutton, they were the first comics to see my very first comedy set. Ten minutes at the Comedy Cafe on Rivington Street in London and I died very badly indeed. Lovely blokes both of them, but I am not expecting m/any of you to know who either of them are. Mickey had some TV success as a quiz host and compere playing The Comedy Store and Dave had some successful plays in Edinburgh but as a comedian could best be described as a solid squad member and little more. Never appearing on television, nor ever troubling any awards panels in Edinburgh. The last gig that Dave and I did together is poignant and memorable for all the wrong reasons. In an enormous pub in Bromley, I arrive mid-show and Dave is on stage and having a tough set. Some of the audience are engaged, too many of them are not and as I am closing the show, I watch from the back with curiosity and some degree of increasing trepidation. Towards the end of Dave's twenty minutes, he is looking to get off stage but unfortunately, he has become embroiled with a boisterous party at the front of the room. They clearly don't like Dave's set and the feeling is mutual especially when an audience member chucked his pint at Dave. Gig over. Dave leaves the stage. The punter is kicked out and I hurry back stage to console my old mate.

As disgusting as it was, I reasoned that Dave, being an old and experienced pro, that he would just shrug it off. But who was I kidding? Any comic would be ashen at such an experience and Dave was no different. He was gutted and there was very little any of us could say to console him.

And my reason for sharing this rather sad anecdote is because it has a wonderful conclusion. If Michael McIntyre goes on to break America, too many comedians will be resentful but not very many comedians will be all that surprised.

But no one could ever have predicted what was going to unfurl for Dave Johns. Ken Loach, the film-maker of *Kes* and many other films including the rather wonderful *Raining Stones* and *Looking for Eric* cast Dave as the lead in his most recent film, *I, Daniel Blake* and last night (17th October), this film premiered in London's Leicester Square complete with red carpet. I saw Dave on Facebook yesterday messaging a fellow comedian, Ben Norris who was appearing last night in the Cutting Edge Show at the London Comedy Store in Piccadilly Circus. A message to the effect - 'Hey Ben, get the whole Cutting Edge team to come out mid-show and cheer me on the red carpet at my film premiere.'

Brilliant stuff.

And why this business of being a comedian is so intoxicating. It's a nice thing to be able to do anyway. To walk on stage and make the whole room full of people laugh. But as well as this, to have the dream of where it might lead. That maybe the big break is still out there!

All comics, at least, set out with such a plan. I certainly did as I have already mentioned. And sure, it diminishes and dulls over time but it never goes out - not completely – just so long as the comic keeps treading the boards.

One final word on not giving up. Last evening, (Jan 12th, 2017), like the dutiful husband I am, I went along with Nikki to watch *La La Land*, surely, the seminal movie about hope and endeavour. In the film, Emma Stone plays a wannabe actress hoping for her big LA break and predictably enough the pain of rejection becomes overwhelming and she is ready to quit. Over the years, I would reason that I have had my ample share of rejection, but unlike an impotent actor waiting for a role, my rejection has always been softened by being able to do gigs and make people laugh. As I have said already, stand-up comedy is about making people laugh out loud and without the thousands of gigs that I have done, most which have been solid home wins, I expect that I would not have had the fortitude to carry on with my various aspirations in entertainment.

Becoming Billy

I had absolutely no expectations that the *Billy Elliot* people would want to see Tom again, especially considering how many boys had queued in the rain and from all over Britain. I explained to Nikki with certainty that they would phone in a week or so to explain that Tom was a nice kid but that he wasn't quite right. Or more likely, that they wouldn't even bother to phone at all. The adage goes that 'no news is good news', but not in the case of the wannabe actor or writer.

But the phone did ring and just two days after the audition. It was Lynne and she began by explaining that they thought Tom was a lovely kid. To this I nodded sagely because I recognized the soft let-down a mile off and I waited for the pivotal 'but' that has punctuated my career. Only, it didn't come.

'...and they would like Tom to start having ballet and tap lessons right away.'

So, I was completely wrong and delighted to be so. What an opportunity, I thought, being taught to dance by experts. And at the time, this was the extent of my thinking because it still never occurred to me that my little boy might one day land the role. Lynne was mindful to manage our expectations down, which was easy enough because we didn't have any, not really. It was all very early days. Tom was only ten years old, but the company was offering to pay for his dance lessons although this did sound like he was being trained by the people behind Billy Elliot to become Billy Elliot. Tom was thrilled and we started to look for classes locally that might be suitable.

We revisited the class that Tom had briefly attended before, which was still exclusively female. This is a photograph of Tom at his final night playing Billy with his very first ballet teacher, Louise Jefferson. I notice now just how bloody exhausted he looks.

Tom post-show, with Louise, one of his first ballet coaches

For a few weeks, Tom took Louise's ballet class and as I watched, it wasn't lost on me that I was exactly like the sceptical dad in the film *Billy Elliot*. Watching Tom leap about the place, the whole thing seemed futile and frankly ridiculous. At this time, there were two schools of thought about my son: the choreographer's school and the thinking of Stephen Daldry. And love my son as much as I do, at this point, I was with the choreographers.

I feel a need to qualify this by including a quick line or two about ballet. For most people, ballet is simply impossible. Ballet defies normal physicality, a little like when we see gymnastics on the television, because what these gymnasts can do seems completely illogical to us. But we know that it is not camera trickery and that these feats are real, but we just accept that these people are special or incredibly dedicated and we can only watch and admire. It is the same with ballet, one of the hardest feats that humans have conceived for ourselves. It requires extraordinary strength and balance. Every ligament and muscle is called upon and even the most basic ballet move is all but impossible to the untrained. Therefore the beginner to ballet always looks so completely hapless, Tom Holland most definitely included. Like a fish flapping on the river bank, he looked completely out of place in a ballet studio and all because Stephen Daldry saw something in him.

Over the next few months, Nikki or I would ferry Tom about London to various classes including a Russian ballet school. The teacher there was very serious about her craft and was appalled by the prospect of *Billy Elliot*. After just one lesson, she took me aside and urged me to drop all this nonsense. My son could be brilliant she explained. He could even become a professional ballet dancer. Instantly, I recoiled. I didn't want him to be a ballet dancer, although by now I did quite like the idea of him becoming Billy Elliot. We left the Russian class and never returned. Far too heavy.

Another audition came and went and was followed by a phone call instructing Tom to 'carry on stretching and spinning'. Tom was progressing well and his training now included a regular class with the vaunted ballet teacher, Anna Du Boisson. Anna is a sixty-something-year-old ballet matriarch. Everything about her is from the ballet text book: the poise, the voice, even the French name. Anna's class took place at a studio called Dance Works just off Oxford Street and near to Selfridges in London. It would become a second home to Tom. And this being a Du Boisson class, it was packed. Tom was one of only four boys, including Fox Jackson Keane who Nikki had met at a previous audition and his name at least had stayed with her. Nikki chatted with his dad, Kevin. She congratulated young Fox (or Cub?) on getting through the auditions so far and they shared their experiences to date. Fox was already a brilliant gymnast who had competed at a very high level, but like Tom he was new to ballet and looking at them both through the viewing window, they were both the very weak links in the chain. Odd then that they would both go on to play Billy.

We were soon given notice of Tom's next audition. It was still another open audition with hundreds of hopefuls, but by now Tom was a known quantity and was greeted as such, which must have worried other parents there for the first time. From there, further training was scheduled and by now, even I had started to believe.

To be included in his training schedule now were immediate tap lessons and if possible, at our home. I laid a wooden floor in our garage, stuck some mirrors onto the wall and made an appointment to see Tom's headmaster. They wanted to start sending a ballet teacher to his school during his lunch hour. To me, anyway, it was starting to look serious.

Tom in his school gym having an early ballet lesson

This is a very young Tom, having an early ballet class at school and one of my very favourite photographs.

Another few auditions came and went with the result always the same.

Tom was doing well and his aim should be inclusion in the Billy Elliot Summer School. Run throughout the summer holidays, it is a five-week, five-day week, intensive dance training course at Dance Works in London, and an audition would determine which boys would be included in the programme. This was June 2007 and the audition took place in a beautiful mews studio in Clapham. By now, I was fully on side and hopeful for Tom. So, my spirits sank when I saw just how many boys were there that day and still being considered: as many as thirty, all being trained by the company for the elusive role. It might have been an exclusive stable by now but the odds were still fairly long. Fox was among them and Tom was pleased to see a friendly face, albeit one that was after the same thing.

The parents watched their little hopefuls disappear, looked at each other awkwardly and then shuffled off in different directions to wait and fret. I found a café, fired up my laptop and pretended to be important, but I couldn't really concentrate and waited impatiently to retrieve my son. It was a Sunday and after the audition we were on our way to Stonyhurst, a beautiful boarding school in Lancashire. I had established a golf club at Tom's school and our boys were playing in a tournament starting on Monday. It was a five-hour drive but it would feel even longer if the audition went badly.

As a kid, I had a tendency to think that all of my public exams had gone brilliantly, only for my results to surprise me. I apply a similar approach to my current projects, this one included. I mention this because Tom beamed at me as he emerged from the audition. Whether he had been successful or not, he had certainly enjoyed himself, but I worried if the outcome didn't bear out his excitement. My fears abated a little, however, when I saw the casting director. I'm no mystic but her body language was unmistakable: Tom had done well and my money was on his success. The lady proceeded to give a cursory talk to all the hopeful parents gathered, thanking them for coming and explaining that all the boys had done very well and that the decision would be made in the week to come.

Casting a show as big as *Billy Elliot*, which probably has as many as fifty children in the show at any one time, is a feat in-itself. A continual process, hundreds of children are always being considered. Some are given good news but most are not and with so much disappointment to dispense, I expect the casting staff have developed techniques to soften the blow. But on this day, however, both the casting director and her colleague got it very wrong.

After the speech, I was corralled to one side by them both as other parents glanced over and made inevitable conclusions; namely, one less space for their kid. It was unlikely that I was being singled out with bad news, that my son had been particularly poor and that his training and their money had been wasted.

I felt even more uncomfortable because of who I was. I hoped that the other parents hadn't recognised me and if they had, then I worried that they might think I was being given special treatment or even worse, that Tom was.

The director said that Tom had been successful and I was able to contain my excitement. Tom, however, was not and his clenched fist and 'Yes!'

and no doubt ruined the journey home for other hopefuls. Our journey, though, was fantastic. We were in a hire car, so we had a decent stereo for a change and we rocked up to Stonyhurst to meet up with Tom's school mates and to share his good news. Tom was in to the summer school.

He was joined by four boys in the summer school – Lewis Cope, from Darlington and one of fourteen children; Bradley Wilson from Doncaster, son of a butcher and a dentist; Fox Jackson Keane, a tiny pocket dynamo from London; and Tom. The school was an amazing opportunity for these boys whether or not they ended up in the show. I fight a constant battle with my boys to get them away from anything with a screen. To get children, and especially boys, to read, draw, sing, dance, swim or just play with a ball is an increasing challenge and so the prospect of my son dancing all summer was a happy one indeed.

It was made clear that all four boys could be cast as Billy, but it still felt that they were competing against each other and a hierarchy quickly established itself. Of the four, Tom had the least dance experience and his ballet was still well short of the others. Brad had been dancing for years already. Lewis was an all-rounder and probably the most likely Billy of them all. Fox's gymnastics probably made him a shoe-in. But Tom had shear bloody mindedness and determination in his armoury and was completely unfazed by the ground he had to make up.

The summer school ended with all four boys being retained in training, but with no one cast yet and no decisions made. Lewis needed to remain in London for a further ten weeks intensive training, so we figured that he was still first in the barrel.

September, and Tom now left the security of his primary school for 'big' school, a stressful time for most kids. His new school was understanding and happy to release him for his on-going training in London and willing to accommodate on-site ballet lessons during lunch, but these did not last very long. Previously, Tom had been the oldest kid in a primary school, which felt more like a big family than a school, and now he was the youngest kid in a London comprehensive. Ballet lessons were somewhat exposing and we quickly ditched them.

This meant more time was required in London and away from school, and more time for Nikki or me hanging about while Tom learned to pirouette. I spent a lot of time in coffee shops with a notebook, hoping for inspiration, or else mooching in Selfridges, looking at stuff I couldn't afford and wouldn't buy even if I could.

It felt like the role was close now and failure at this point would have been awful. Tom knew all the staff on the show and the 'creatives' as they are called. Tom was popular but there would be no sentiment in their decision making. Tom would be cast only if he made the grade and at a time when the show needed a new Billy. Every hoop that they held in the air for him, Tom had leapt through and so did we. But there were still more to come and none of us ever took any of them for granted.

It's a Wonderful Life

Starring Jimmy Stewart, *It's a Wonderful Life* is one of Hollywood's most cherished and popular films; up there with *The Wizard of Oz* and *Gone with the Wind*, which should not be confused with *Gone in 60 seconds* starring Vin Diesel. And given how considered it is now, it is most interesting that, just like *The Wizard of Oz* and more recently, *The Shawshank Redemption*, it was not an immediate success. I like this fact. In my film exploits, this is something that I rather cling to.

I had not seen *It's a Wonderful Life* when it was first brought to my attention by a lady called Norma Heyman of Pagoda Films. Norma replaced Jan in the faltering life of The Faldovian Club and is the matriarch of a formidable film producing family, responsible for *Star Trek, Dangerous Liaisons, Greystoke* and more recently the entire *Harry Potter* franchise. And it was Norma who became the first film producer to stump up and buy my first script. This was a few years since 'kippergate' and a year on from Clive James and by now I was ready to prove a growing list of people wrong.

Obviously, I was nervous meeting Norma. Her office was at the top of the Twentieth Century Fox building on the corner of Soho Square, adding to the glamour and sense of occasion. It wasn't exactly my first film meeting, but I wasn't very practiced either and the stakes were high. Norma is tiny and immaculately presented. To me, she was the real deal. Expensively preserved, she is Jewish and impossible to date. She has big hair and an expensive suit. Rail thin, she greeted me like a lost son, hugging me tightly. This was a great start to a meeting and my confidence soared. At this rate, if we went out for lunch, I might have ordered crab in its shell with fresh garden peas.

By now, I have new agents. Curtis Brown no less, one of London's premier homes for those of a flouncy persuasion, and it appears that I am a good signing because a film deal is immediately forthcoming. Being honest, I really bagged the services of Curtis Brown by default. Ginger Productions were about to buy the rights to The Faldovian Club and this deal pending secured my berth at Curtis Brown. They aren't fools. But no sooner had I signed, Ginger bailed but no matter because Norma screamed into view and I was back in play. Norma gushed about the script. What a beautiful woman and perfect timing too. A protracted start in film but finally I was under way.

Now though, I can't wait for the meeting to end so that I can telephone Nikki, yet again. By now, I suspect that my wife was losing confidence in my chances of taming Hollywood, but finally I had great and tangible news to share with her.

I would like to thank the academy...

Norma likened my script to the hallowed Frank Capra and I duly thanked her. Frank Capra, such praise? Those readers not familiar with Frank Capra should spare a thought for me because at the time I didn't either. He directed *It's a Wonderful Life* and luckily, I didn't say Frank who?

I have watched it many times since and I can see why the comparison was made. As a writer, I certainly gravitate towards fairy tales. I prefer an affirming story, I'm a sucker for a happy ending and I don't care how unfashionable this might be with critics and awards panels alike.

A similar approach applies to this book, my first work of non-fiction. It has a euphoric ending too and one that I could never have made up myself. But, alas, there was no such happy ending for The Faldovian Club. Clive James was proved right all along and by the time Norma's option expired, four years had elapsed. It hadn't been an earner, but it had been great fun and it came with the unexpected bonus of inspiring a story rattling around my head that would become *Only in America*. It is a story about a writer with a wonderful script who is unable to make any progress in film. Ring any bells? The key move is to get any script on to the desk of a player: a suit with his fat paw on the switch of a green light. And I imagined what would happen if such an executive were to come across a script inadvertently or even by error. A manic hunt for the writer would ensue without even the writer's knowledge.

What a great story and I excitedly explained it to Nikki. She listened and agreed that it was enchanting and compelling, but she wasn't overwhelmed at the prospect of my writing another film. Equally, she said that the story had holes as well. A lack of romance to begin with and warming to her theme, she announced that my writer needed to be female. The audience will root more for a woman and furthermore, the American studio executive charged with finding this writer could be the love interest that underpins the story. *Four Weddings* had been massive and *Notting Hill* was about to be released. I could see Nikki's reasoning and not being overburdened with pride, I gave in completely. I was going to write a romantic comedy and it was going to be massive. Richard Curtis is so yesterday.

I wrote a treatment and quickly, film companies were interested. I met with Working Title, who were riding high on a film called *Billy Elliot* at the time. Can you see lines crossing and why I felt that I just had to write this story? The producers behind the hit comedy, *Waking Ned* were interested also and why not? My film had a strong story. It had a genuine transatlantic setting. It had a cute meet, a funny denouement and a romantic and funny resolution. What's not to like? Not much it seemed, but neither company felt inclined to pay for a script from an untested writer. You're a stand-up comic, not a writer. Come back to us when you have a script. I fired up my PC and began tapping away. Nikki rolled her eyes and probably tutted as well.

'Dom, wouldn't it be safer and more likely to happen if you wrote it as a novel instead?' Nikki suggested. I liked this idea straight away.

In around 2000, the timing was perfect and the prospect of getting off the boards and into my slippers at home with a PC was incredibly attractive. Plus, isn't a novel always followed by the film adaptation? I'll write the novel, sell the film rights and then make the movie. Perfect.

Now, my radio 4 series had been broadcast to great acclaim and I had an idea that it would make an excellent non-fiction book in the way that Jerry Seinfeld and made so much hay. My theatrical agent had already set up a meeting with the publishers Hodder and Stoughton to discuss this non-fiction book. Another meeting then and a new project and I readied myself.

But at the meeting, the two women from Hodder were immediately cool about the prospect of my coffee table book of the musings on life. 'Any other ideas?' they asked, which is never a good sign and did I have any ideas for a novel? I did and I launched into an impromptu but impassioned pitch of *Only in America* and lied that I had always wanted to write a novel.

I could sense immediately that the story chimed with them both. They particularly liked the romantic angle of the story and I smiled ruefully. Thank God, I didn't listen to Harry Hill and went ahead with my wedding. Busy spotting that our son could dance and then setting him on the path to Hollywood, and now she was doing the same for her husband. The non-fiction book was quickly forgotten. One of them announced that *Only in America* would make a great film and I feigned my surprise brilliantly. Really, do you think so? As the saying goes, 'we all have a novel in us', and mine was now bursting to get out.

An offer followed shortly after this meeting and with perfect timing too. A two-book deal; I was incredibly excited and started writing immediately for what would become the worst experience of my professional life.

Author Footnote

What I really like about being a comedian is how tangible it is. Comedy is subjective to a point but being able to make an audience laugh out loud is an obvious skill. A skill that does not need any context nor explaining. Just give the comic a microphone and let him get on with it. However, comics are further qualified if they are clever which might explain why an Oxbridge degree can be so invaluable to a comedian and why I have always been haunted by my education – or lack of.

I was not a bright boy at school; not managing a single grade A in any public examination. Solid middle set, I fared only reasonably. A summer baby plus being very late developing put me at a further disadvantage; the hairiest kids mostly making the sports teams and scoring the best grades it seemed? But I only figured this out later in life and probably too late for my lack of confidence not to take hold and have such a bearing on me.

A-levels were a struggle and ending up with a grade B and two D's my options for university were not broad. But I wanted to go. My older brother was at Birmingham studying law and would go on to become a senior partner in the City and who now lives in the sort of house that features in Hello magazine.

So, I headed to Leeds University to study Textile Management and no matter that I got a II(i), I have been embarrassed by my degree ever since and having always dreaded the inevitable question at various social gatherings, '... and what did you read?'

Textile Management? I didn't read anything mate, I knitted. Having dinner one night with Harry Hill, the ex-doctor and now multi-millionaire comedian, the subject of university came up and Harry was aghast. Textiles? 'But Dom, I always had you down as being very bright?'

This year, (2016) I was very excited to have my availability checked to appear on a celebrity edition of the ITV quiz show, 'The Chase'. Scheduled to broadcast on a Saturday evening at 7pm, this was a significant coup for me and one which I didn't expect to come off. Only it did. I was booked. Typically, I decided that this was because I happened to be Spider-Man's dad – a celebrity via my progeny with the thinking being that Tom's fans might watch the show. But who cares I reasoned. I'm booked and that's it. Take one's chances...

Now, appearing on national television on a popular quiz has its many perils and chief amongst them is appearing to be bloody thick. But my even greater concern was appearing as a 'celebrity' and the idea that the show's host, Bradley Walsh would interview me as such. I had done a stand-up show on television with Bradley many moons ago but being largely unknown to the studio audience I worried what he might ask me. 'So, Dom, you've not been on telly for years' man; so, what the hell have you been doing?'

And figuring that I had been booked because of Tom, I reasoned that most of the chat would be taken up with Spider-Man questions which I am becoming accustomed to. And that said, I should be flattered then that Tom was never even mentioned.

Bradley and I talked generally about comedy. We chatted about our stand-up gig together and then he intimated that I would be a strong player at the game because I was a university type?

'You did go to University, didn't you?'

'Yes, I did.' I answered hesitantly.

'Which one? Which university did you go to?'

Fuck sake Bradley, where is this going? Of all the lines of questioning you could take up with me? My son is Spider-Man for fuck sake.

'And what did you study?'

My eyes widened. I could not believe what I was being asked and on national bloody television as well and I now had a decision to make. I very much wanted to do well on the quiz. To win as much money for my chosen charity, DEBRA, (well worth a google when you have some spare time and cash). Plus, I wanted (needed) to remain in the game and therefore ON the bloody television for as long as possible not-to-mention the other trifling matter of not appearing to be thick.

And so, I lied.

I said, 'management studies' instead of Textile Management which is pathetic I know and odd as well that I should confess this here now. Odd because there is every chance that my little white lie might not even make the edit? But if it does, then so-be-it and I fess up here now. No doubt, people who know the truth will laugh at me but so what, because Nikki will support me, I know she will. She knows that I might not be an academic but that I have other skills to offer. And besides, she also understands that textiles is one of the great world industries and that there is no shame in studying it whatsoever. Fashion, clothes, filtration fabrics, sails, medical fabrics, industrial fabrics... I ask you; just where the hell would the human race be without bloody textiles?

In case you haven't figured it out already, Nikki did Textile Management as well. It's how we met.

I am Billy Elliot

Tom's training for *Billy* must have been very disruptive to our normal family life. In and out of London at least three times a week and then again, every Sunday and sometimes Saturday as well, but at the time the whole thing was so exciting, we didn't seem to notice and when we did, we didn't mind.

I particularly enjoyed taking Tom to Dance Works. Anyone in their forties will have fond memories of the American TV show *Fame*, with Leroy, the cool black dancer, and that geeky guy on the piano who somehow the girls liked. As a boy with a mass of curly hair, his was a character I clung on to and I even briefly flirted with learning the piano. If only it wasn't so difficult with so many keys. And pedals too!

Dance Works is exactly like Fame, The New York Academy of Performing Arts. It is full of young aspiring Leroy's – beautiful young men and women with toned bodies – and rather appropriately the place stinks of perspiration and hope. The building is grimy. Studios of differing sizes are all packed with dancers, some professional but mostly enthusiastic amateurs, and every piece of floor outside each studio is filled with students stretching hamstrings and other muscles I don't know the names of.

Visiting Dance Works reminded me of my time as a young comic working on the comedy circuit as an open spot in the early 90s, going from gig to gig full of enthusiasm for all things funny. Not that comedians are anything near as lithe and beautiful as wannabe dancers, but they can be known to sweat, particularly during a bad gig.

Tom's training continued throughout the autumn and on into Christmas and beyond. Sure enough, Lewis was the first to be cast, but as Michael and not as Billy because he had an issue with his timing, a kind of rhythm dyslexia but the disappointment was short-lived as his opening night as Michael beckoned. Then, early into the New Year, we got an abrupt email explaining that Tom's training was to stop and naturally we were distraught. They assured us that this was nothing to worry about, but we did anyway, a lot. They were forgetting that I know show business as well as I do and I concluded that this was not good news at all. It was most likely that they were letting Tom go, but I didn't tell him this of course. He knew that something was up though because suddenly his training diary was empty. He had no classes to attend. Each week, we would receive an email listing where and when Tom needed to be and we would plan our weeks ahead, childcare and various work commitments around it. And suddenly, there was nothing. But then, as quickly as things had been cancelled, a week later, it was all back on again. And now Tom was to start training with the boys who were currently playing Billy in the show. This felt like a big step up, particularly since these classes were scheduled to take place at the Sylvia Young Theatre School, creating another link between father and son.

I was no star pupil at school and although I worked hard, I was also a clown in class and probably not a very popular child in the staffroom. In my fourth year at school, our English teacher, Mr Sunters, explained to his class that a very important lady would be visiting our school. She was a casting director on the lookout for actors for a television film. The lady was called Joyce Gallie. It was a television film written by the late Jack Rosenthal called *First Love – P'tang, Yang, Kipperbang,* to be directed by Michael Apted who would go on to direct a Bond movie and much else besides. This was going to be the very first film to be shown on a new channel called Channel Four. So even though Jack Dee was the first comic to be launched by the Channel and duly went on to national stardom, I was in fact the first stand-up comic ever to appear on Channel Four. A good potential quiz question for any quiz nuts albeit not an entirely fair one?

Our school was chosen, simply because it was close to Joyce Gallie's house in the salubrious neighbourhood of Holland Park. Given that she was looking for fourteen year olds, she was put in touch with Mr Sunters and to refine her search, she asked him to single out the boys with a creative bent and flare. Mr Sunters read out his list of boys with 'talent' and I was not among them. I felt a little aggrieved and so I went along anyway. This is not something that I would never do now and I rue having lost the abandonment that comes with youth.

Ms Gallie's assistant couldn't find my name on any of her lists and she smiled when I explained that Mr Sunters couldn't be trusted. She sent me on through and maybe even asterisked my name. Cocky, worth looking at? Word quickly came back that I was being considered for one of the main roles and I allowed myself to dream. I'm going to be an actor. A further audition was planned but this time at Ms Gallie's house, no less.

I practised the lines at home, in front of the mirror, over and over, but I couldn't shake my nerves. As I knocked on her expensive door, I felt like the kid who had smashed her stained-glass window and was asking for my cricket ball back. It is said that performers need to feel nervous to perform, but this is only useful to a point. There does come a point where anxiety becomes counter-productive and my nerves overcame me completely. I was offered the part of an extra along with a bunch of other boys from my school for what would become the best Easter holidays of our lives. I did have one line in the film but it never survived the edit, which I guess is perfect for this story.

At similar stages of life, I was an extra in a film for television. Tom had just finished *Billy* in the West End and was about to play the lead in a Hollywood movie. Without even knowing it, the story of *Eclipsed* had already begun.

A great number of the kids in Rosenthal's film came from the Sylvia Young Stage School, including all the female extras and what a formative role these girls played in the lives of the boys from an all-boys Catholic comprehensive. The film itself was a coming of age story centering heavily on masturbation, which ironically, I had yet to discover at the time. Abigail Cruttenden played the lead and I instantly fell in love with her. Likewise, Frances Ruffelle, who played Eunice, and Jenna Russell and Kathy Lester, who were extras. In fact, at some point, I fell in love with all the girls involved in the film, including Alison Steadman, who was playing my teacher.

Abigail's younger brother is Hal, a tremendous stand-up comedian who you might have seen live or on various TV shows of late. Hal has just bagged himself a Radio 4 series of his own, imaginatively titled, Hal which I incidentally have co-written with him.

If the boys from my school looked a little out of place on the film set then it was nothing compared to how awkward we felt at the parties that were held at the weekends towards the end of the shoot. Trendier clothes aside, what really set us apart was that these stage-school kids could all dance. Some of the kids from our school studied Latin and most likely could have lost their stage school counterparts academically. However, at a party for adolescents, conjugating verbs are never as cool as being able to body pop and so we mostly sat out the dancing and just stared. So, thirty years later, it felt odd to sit in the same dance studio that these kids would have learnt to dance in, and there I was watching my son being trained for the West End.

The full cast of P'tang Yang Kipperbang

Tom's training now had much more purpose and urgency to it. It felt to me that he had been cast already but we were just waiting for the official nod. It was certainly a big step up, spending time with the real-life Billy's. Looking back now, it seems slightly ridiculous to be so reverent towards such young kids, but having seen the show and been through the past eighteen months of auditions and classes, I was a little star-struck when I first met them. And I've been on *The Royal Variety Show* for heaven's sake.

Fox was the next boy to be cast, this time as Billy, and I am not sure what made me prouder: the fact that Fox had been successful or how Tom reacted to the news, because he was delighted for him. By now they were firm friends and it was always high on our wish list that Tom and Fox would get cast and live in the Billy house together. They even got to perform together with Tom filling in as Michael one night to Fox's Billy. Fox is a truly lovely kid and I am pleased so say that he and Tom remain good friends and keep in touch.

Lewis was already playing Michael, his disappointment well behind him. This just left Tom and Brad to carry on getting through the hoops.

Billy Elliot is a musical like no other – and I say this as a man with no experience of musicals whatsoever – but even so, it is easy to work out why. It is almost completely dependent on its child actors. Other musicals feature children of course, but Billy is such a central role and the demands made on the kid make the role unique and special.

The call finally came and we were told that Tom was now officially cast with a September start date. We all went out to celebrate and we recalled how we had all reacted when we first saw the show with Liam Moyer. How we had laughed at the prospect of Tom ever doing such a thing and now it was going to happen.

I've often heard people say that the role of Michael is a better role than Billy. Billy is an angry young boy who rages at the world, the police and his family, but Michael is funny and adds the levity that all musicals need. Michael has a fraction of Billy's stage time, but he gets one particularly big number, called 'Express', which involves him dressing up himself and Billy in women's clothes and tapping their little backsides off. Tom was asked to play Michael a couple of times before his September debut as Billy.

I expect it is the same for all children who appear in a big show that a legion of friends and family will want to see the first performance and at sixty-odd quid a pop, and Tom having two debuts as Michael and Billy, much money was shelled out by friends and family.

When we took our seats in the stalls in July 2008 for Tom's debut as Michael, I felt almost sick with worry. It was worse than my own stage nerves because I felt impotent and unable to do anything about it. I spoke to him beforehand and he seemed fine and said that he was looking forward to it. But I knew he was lying and I told his mum as much. He was my son and he was bloody terrified and was trying to appear brave. He hid it well, though, I'll give him that. He didn't look nervous at all. A fine piece of acting, I thought. Maybe he really had a future as an actor. Either that or he just wasn't nervous?

At the start of the show, Michael enters the fray riding a bike. I had visions of Tom falling off the bloody thing or worse, cycling straight into the orchestra pit. But everything went well. His bike handling was superb, as good as his tap dancing, and the fact that he performed in the West End could never be taken away from him. I am still unaware of it at this stage, but this story, *Eclipsed*, is now well and truly under way.

His first night playing Billy was another level of intensity all over again. Perhaps a hundred friends and family had booked tickets. Tom's training had been intensive and long and to account for his education, it was necessary for him to move into the Billy house, coming home just at weekends. On Monday 8th Sept 2008, I took him on the train to the theatre in Victoria. We were early of course because if you recall, I don't do late. Today, I wanted to be early to give the whole day a sense of ease and no big deal. I thought it would be a good idea to have a meal on the concourse of Victoria Station to make sure he had plenty of energy. I chose Yo Sushi because Tom likes it, but also because it was from this very balcony that I had spotted Nikki and Tom on my birthday when we first went to see the show. Tom didn't eat much, which worried me a little, but I didn't mention it. I dropped him at stage door at 2.00 p.m. for his final rehearsals and run-through and I went off to various meetings in Soho about various projects all at different stages of not being made.

Billy is a strange role because no amount of training can adequately prepare any child for the role. It can just get the child to a level of technical ability and stamina to complete their first show, but then the real learning of the role takes on stage during their run and in front of thousands of people. Some learning curve then, and not dissimilar to one facing a prospective comedian. No matter how much the fledgling comic practises in front of the mirror or in the park or in the car on the way to the gig, nothing can replace stage time, with the lights in your eyes, the expectation in the air and that dreaded silence in your ears.

So, when a child plays Billy for the first time, it is reasonable to say that he is about to give his worst performance of his run and conversely, that his last show will be his best. This was certainly the case with Tom for other reasons besides, which we were yet to discover. Not that we noticed this at the time though, as excited as we were. Nick Evans took to the stage before the show to announce that tonight a boy was making his debut as Billy and he even thanked his parents by name for lending out our son for so long. I wondered why the company felt the need to make this announcement and I suspect it is to provide something of a security blanket for the young actor, to create a feeling of kindness and understanding amongst the audience in case the poor lad falls flat on his arse.

Tom's first show was certainly a lot less involved than the show he gave at the fifth birthday performance with Sir Elton in residence. Each boy cast as Billy performs a different show to account for their strengths and to avoid some of their frailties. If a kid is a very strong acrobat like Fox, then it makes sense to include a lot of acrobatics and as a boy develops in the role, so his show will become more complicated and demanding.

A pivotal part of the show is when Billy, dancing at a miner's refuge, demonstrates his special talent for ballet and his teacher and fellow pupils all notice his ability for the first time (not to mention the audience in the theatre who watch the boy complete the ugly duckling to swan routine with a dance called 'dream ballet' in the second act, suitably accompanied by Tchaikovsky's 'Swan Lake'). Billy's talent reveals itself when the whole class is asked to assume the classic ballet position by their teacher, Mrs Wilkinson. Think of the fairy on the top of a music box and you get the idea: standing on one leg with one arm stretched out aloft. To really understand this anecdote, you might want to try and assume this position yourself now. It's practically impossible, especially how Billy is expected to finally take up his pose. Spinning around on one leg clumsily, Billy finally finds his balance and starts to get himself into the classic position, but this has all taken time, perhaps a minute or so, and all on one foot. So, when Billy finally catches his teacher's eye, the lactic acid is practically pouring down his leg. The scene ends with the teacher stepping back in wonder to take in the boy's poise and beauty. It is beautiful and something to behold. In life, there are times when we need to put our foot down, but this was not one of those moments. So, when Tom's foot hit the stage, everyone in the theatre, the company and Tom himself felt a little disappointed. Damien Jackson was Tom's main ballet teacher and he still ribs Tom to this day for that moment, and fair enough. In text speak, WTF. Billy did put his foot down!

The show continued and at the end, the audience screamed their approval. Like all musicals, a finale is performed. It's a tradition that really defines the musical. A play just gets a curtain call, but a musical gets to perform a medley of all the best bits that have gone before. The actors look like they enjoy themselves, which the audience pick up on and the fervour spreads. The cast might be pretending of course but no matter, the effect is the same and the audience stand and clap their approval. And then it was suddenly all over. Bloody hell! Years of training and auditions and my son is Billy Elliot.

After the show, there was an impromptu reception to congratulate Tom. Damien ribbed and patted him on the back in equal measure. Georgina, another of the ballet coaches, told me how pleased she was with the way he pointed his feet. I hadn't noticed but I made a note to look out for this in future. Nick Evans, the resident director, made a speech and despite all the attention on Tom, he looked shattered and we decided to take him home. He was scheduled to perform three shows that week, which is always the schedule for a new Billy, but he would be unable to complete any of them. That night, he didn't sleep very well, which we put down to excitement until the morning came and we realised that he wasn't well and the doctor diagnosed tonsillitis. He hadn't been well for a couple of days, but he had kept it to himself because he didn't want to let anyone down. But now it was to bed for rest and no more shows. But no matter, he was now a Billy – but just one on sick leave!

Lots of people were responsible for this achievement, chief amongst them, Tom himself and his mum. But let's not forget Des O'Connor, Janet Jackson and Stephen Daldry of course. A strange set of fluky occurrences had conspired for this to come about and Tom's life would never be the same or very normal again.

Tears of a Clown

We have already established that I am no genius and incidentally, as I write, Tom has just received his GCSE results, exams that have been a great source of stress in the Holland household, particularly for Tom and his mum. Having missed so much school on *Billy* and *The Impossible*, Nikki was very worried how Tom might fare; her reasoning being that a career in show business is too precarious to be ever taken for granted. Yep, I hear that loud and clear, but still I was less worried about Tom's exams, although I still wanted and expected him to do his best. Indeed, this is the only thing that I demand from my children. To use a football cliché, don't 'leave nothing out on the park'! And as things turned out, you will not be surprised to read that Tom completely outgunned what I managed to achieve some three decades earlier. But this was bound to happen and I realise this now because it fits with this story, which is pre-ordained?

But I am no comedy genius either, which is the moniker that some comedians it seems crave the very most. I don't get this. Doing comedy, myself, I am much happier getting laughs rather than nods but maybe this has been another of my mistakes.

I also think that the term genius is used far too liberally and should really be confined to the sciences and engineering. I say this because science is objective and comedy is not. It is difficult to argue that heart transplants don't involve genius or the engineers who can conceive and execute cross rail in the world city of London? But now we have genius footballers, cooks, rappers, actors, directors and the biggest culprit of all, the genius comedian. I do not really understand the correlation between being clever and being funny. I would like my surgeon to be clever but I just want my comedian to be funny.

It is generally accepted that genius often flirts with madness. The two are closely linked and joined by a grey area. And it might follow then that the artist aspiring to be a genius might improve his chances by hinting at a dark side and even a bit of madness. This is made even more likely because so many of our most revered comedians certainly suffered with mental illness. There are different requirements for different jobs; to become a pilot, it is probably best not to mention depressive tendencies, but in comedy, it could make all the difference. Tears of a clown, like so many clichés, has a strong ring of truth to it.

And because of this unlikely upside, I am always mindful of comedians and their very public declarations of their mental frailties. Or perhaps being a comedian merely exacerbates the mental frailties in us all. To start with, it is a very public job. The comic's success is there for all to see and similarly their failures also. Their work is for public consumption or not. Their work is discussed and reviewed or even worse, ignored. And in our internet age, a reviewer can be anyone, a bloke in his stained pyjamas with a grudge. A comic is only as good as his last gig, his last DVD or last Arena tour. It is relentless and exacting: self-employment in its purest form. For its shear brutality, it bears repeating; no gigs, no income. No laughs, no gigs. And this all creates pressure and often we succumb. But isn't pressure relative? Doesn't pressure affect us all, whatever we do? Life comes with pressures and my real point is that life is meant to come in waves, with highs and lows. It must because if our life does not have any lows then how can we recognise and appreciate the highs? So, low points in anyone's life are normal and yet too often they are considered abnormal and something that needs to be explained, solved or medicated.

I once worked with a young comedy writer called Debbie Barham. We worked together in a writing team for a Clive Anderson television series. Debbie was not much of a team player. She was the only woman in the team. She was a much better writer than any of us and didn't need to collaborate with anyone artistically, but she clearly found company difficult as well. It was apparent that Debbie was unwell, probably depressed and certainly underweight, but none of us felt comfortable discussing this with her. It was just too personal. Plus, our jokes were being roundly rejected by Clive and hers were being used, so Debbie's problems paled by comparison! Some years later, I recognised her face on the front page of *The Guardian* arts section. No doubt, her writing continued to flourish and she had penned a masterpiece novel? I read with utter sadness that Debbie had died of anorexia. No one could argue that mental illnesses are not real but they are undermined and trivialized by people who feign such maladies for whatever their reason. By which I refer to well-timed and very public breakdowns, which can be so good for business and – dare I say it? – even a career move. They are akin to the sob story that accompanies so many of the contestants entering the arena of reality television. As well as garnering sympathy, a breakdown can explain away certain behaviours and crucially, they can generate publicity, which is why their revelation so often comes after a career has peaked and the spotlight is elsewhere.

Lord John Prescott's frank and rather extraordinary admission that he had suffered bulimia for years came after his career in government and just ahead of his request that we all buy his book. This was a revelation beyond satire, like manna from heaven, provided by Lord Prescott himself because, presumably, he couldn't keep it down any longer.

And why am I mentioning all of this and purporting my half-cocked theorems about mental health and fame? Well, to introduce my own mental health issues of course in the hope that some publicity might follow. So here we go – I too have had a mental breakdown.

Actually, I haven't. Not really. I do have some mental frailties, some of which have probably become apparent to the more attuned reader. Remember the kippers? And some of these frailties and quirks make my chosen profession even more difficult than it already is. Certainly, I have had bouts of melancholy but I suspect all within the range of being normal. But haven't we all? But what use is a book about a comedian with a film star son if the author cannot explain the painful episodes of his career that have accompanied the laughs?

So, onto my mental breakdown then; it happened when my twins were very young and precipitated my leaving the comedy circuit altogether for ten years or so.

Our twins, Sam and Harry, were born on Valentine's Day, 1999, at a time when I was doing up to ten circuit gigs a week, often four on a Saturday night alone and so by the end of the year 2000, just ahead of my appearance on *The Royal Variety Show*, I was stressed and exhausted. I was having panic attacks and sometime struggling to get on stage. On one occasion, I almost ran from a venue as the compere was about to introduce me. I recall doing a one-man show around this time at the Komedia in Brighton. Brighton is a funky town and has always been a great place to play. I had headlined a famous and much-loved comedy club in Brighton for years and long since progressed onto one-man shows in the town. This show was sold out, but on this night, I felt highly anxious and couldn't settle down on stage. What a comedian says is important but how he says it is what really matters. Utter conviction and belief is the very least that a comedian needs to be successful on stage. Tonight, my tongue felt fat and nothing was particularly flowing. From the back of the room, I saw a man emerge from the darkness and he slowly proceeded to walk down the centre aisle towards the stage. Call it instinct, but I knew that this was not good news and it wasn't a call of nature either. It was just something about the man. He had a swagger and he was too deliberate. As he got to the front of the room he announced, loudly enough for the whole room to hear, 'It said comedian on the poster,' and with this he left. And I allowed this to happen. Despite having a microphone, I allowed him sufficient quiet to deliver his blow and even worse, I didn't respond adequately and neither could I laugh it off. Rather lamely, I was crushed and limped to the end of my set. In my dressing room afterwards, I sat in silence and eventually drove home in tears. I collapsed into bed and when I woke up the next morning, I couldn't move. I mean I literally couldn't move the left-hand side of my body.

I thought that I was having a stroke and Nikki worried that I might be dying. My face felt numb and I was slurring my words. There are plenty of examples in show business, where premature death can be the ultimate career move – Marc Bolan, Bill Hicks, Curt Cobain, James Dean, John Lennon, River Phoenix, Heath Ledger – but with my achievements to date, I knew that my untimely death would have no economic upside for my family and so I had plenty to live for.

The doctor was called and did some on-site tests. He prodded and probed and could assure me that it was not a stroke and nothing else sinister. He diagnosed severe nervous exhaustion, which was something of a disappointment. I'm just tired? Is that it? He explained that I needed a prolonged period of complete rest and I would be fine in three weeks, maybe a month. I looked at the man a little oddly. Rest? Was this doctor blind? He was suggesting that I have complete rest in a house with three very young and very male children, one of whom was continuing to dance to Janet Jackson and was still intriguing his mum.

But rest I did and it was this rest that I would come to regret because shortly afterwards I practically gave up performing in public, or at least on the comedy circuit. I was allowed this luxury because my book deal for two novels had arrived with Swiss timing. So, I was going to become a novelist instead. And continue with screenplays of course. And perhaps write a column or two in the nationals and give the odd lecture at literary festivals and drink mint tea.

These lofty plans are still on-going as you will discover.

The Sweat Smell of Success

I have talked much about serendipity in this book and perhaps not enough about talent and sheer hard work - so let's stay with me then? No, don't worry, I am kidding. I am reluctant to write here that Tom is extravagantly talented as an actor. I like the idea that readers of this book can make up their own minds about the merits of Tom and the author of this book. Readers can watch his films or my stand-up or read my novels and make their own minds up. Plus, other people tell Tom on a very regular basis how marvellous he is and so he doesn't need to hear it from me as well. The gushing is particularly high in America, which is partly the reason why Nikki or I insist on accompanying him across the pond. Whilst I want all my sons to maintain their spirit and their confidence, I am equally keen that they keep a level of normality and perspective in their lives also, whatever they end up doing. The big airline seats that Tom now qualifies for is a bonus as well and makes the trips even more special.

I should also add that I don't really believe in the extravagant talents of actors per se about which I explain further a little later in this book. This said, I am certainly never very easy talking about the 'talents' of my son but I am comfortable discussing just how bloody hard he has worked to achieve his success to date. In life, I think that there is far too much emphasis on final results and not enough value placed on endeavour, whatever the outcome. My film career is a good example of this. In terms of output, income and films made, it could only be viewed as a disaster and a complete waste of time. But I don't see it like this at all. To begin with, I enjoy writing and enjoyed writing every unproduced script or unpublished novel. But this is not their full value either because these individual projects have provided me with an invaluable commodity, which is quite simply, hope.

In my view, hope is always seriously undervalued and underestimated. It comes with endeavour and it comes a close fourth in the make-up of a complete human being, behind oxygen, water and love. Many clichés distil this very well.

Better to have tried and failed than never to have tried at all.

And better to have failed because we would have 'hoped' that whatever it was we were doing was going to be a success. And it is this hope that is key to everything that we ever achieve in life.

Our 'just desserts' is what we all hope for in life, to get what we feel we deserve, and Tom's success to date is certainly commensurate with his extraordinary commitment and hard work. Over the years, I have fully expected all my projects to get made, produced, published and commissioned. Enjoy writing as I do, but I didn't write any of them for the fun of writing alone. And the fact that I have almost never had the result that I have been hoping for, each project has served a purpose and critical function nonetheless.

This is a picture of me outside the Victoria Palace with Stephen Daldry for Tom's last ever performance as Billy.

A very much in-demand tall film maker – what's to like?

I don't recall what I was saying at the time in this photograph, but from his reaction, it might have been something like 'I write films you know' and who knows, one day...

And to illustrate Tom's commitment I share here a brief anecdote. As Tom's debut as Billy neared, we took his brothers away to France for a half-term break. Tom stayed with his Granny Tess (my mum) whilst his training continued. On our return, having not seen him for a week, we all charged into Marylebone to the Sylvia Young Stage School where Tom was having a lesson with Damian Jackson, one of the head choreographers of the show.

When we arrived, Tom and Damian were busy running 'Electricity' together, the signature tune and dance of the musical. It's the moment in the show where Billy auditions for the 'ultra-posh Southerners' at the Royal Ballet School and completely wows them with his impromptu dance routine. As such, this dance needs to be spectacular and would eventually climax with Tom running up and doing a backflip off a wall (a move that always worried me, but always had the audience whooping their approval). At this stage though, Tom was a long way off from performing such acrobatics.

We shouldn't really have entered the studio but so excited were we to see Tom, we pushed our heads through anyway and so intense was the lesson that neither of them seemed to even notice us. As discreetly as five people can be, we all sat down and gawped as Damian ran Tom through the dance, repeatedly. Elton John's accompanying music blared out loudly and yet Damian could still be heard clapping and shouting encouragement and marking out Tom's mistakes and missed marks. Tom was wet through with perspiration and barely looked over in our direction, concentrating only on his teacher and forcing himself to run it one more time. As spectacular as is it was, it was not an easy watch and made me feel a little uncomfortable after our relaxing break away. And then at just after 5.00 p.m., the lesson was over. Tom and Damian slapped hands; Tom wiped himself down with a towel and finally ran over and embraced us all. I can remember thinking at the time that I don't think I had ever exerted myself in such a way.

I got to know Damian well over the years. One conversation that we had particularly resonated and has always stayed with me. Damian had been a professional ballet dancer and so he is in a good position to judge. He explained that an adult probably could not perform the role of Billy because they would not be fit enough and he went on to say that a kid playing Billy needs to be as fit as a person can possibly be.

One thing that I will never thank the producers of *Billy Elliot* for is a section of the show called 'Angry Dance'. It closes the first act and is basically a representation of a child's anger at the world and his own set of circumstances. Billy is required to tap dance and fling himself across the stage and against riot-clad, baton-wielding police officers, accompanied by a deafening wall of rock guitar. It's a dance I always hated watching because I knew what pain it was causing my son. When the musical first opened, as the spell-bound audience would retire to the bar to catch their breath, the boy playing Billy would too often be just off stage, vomiting. One boy even vomited on stage during the dance, such were his exertions. This was a situation that clearly could not continue and it gave the producers a stark choice; either they could tone down 'Angry Dance' or they could opt to increase the strength and the stamina of the boys playing Billy. They chose the latter and therefore Damian could make the statement that he did and with some confidence. Through his training, Tom became as fit as any kid in the country. The kid who swims or runs nationally might be as fit but certainly no fitter than a Billy Elliot. Tom was super-duper fit then, which was another thing to widen the gap between father and son.

And Tom was a particularly angry Billy and as such, he always dreaded the upcoming 'Angry Dance'. Because no matter how strong and fit he was, it always hurt like hell. I sat there one night in the stalls and timed the wretched thing. It was only two and a half minutes, but by the end of it I knew that his little body was screaming in pain. He always finished the first act exhausted. But this was not the case with all the boys playing Billy. This was acting after all and a kid could choose to feign his anger if he wanted to – so less 'Angry Dance' and more 'Upset Dance' – but Tom never did this. He went for furious every time and I think this told in his performance and is perhaps why things have so opened for him since leaving the show. He certainly became the very best Billy Elliot that he could have been. And this is really Tom's talent as I see it: his personality and his application.

You will recall his first audition and how Stephen Daldry attended. Once Tom had started playing Billy, various people admitted to us that Tom had confounded all the odds in getting cast. With no ballet and gymnastics at all, his learning curve was practically a cliff and the professionals charged with training Tom in lots of different disciplines didn't give him much chance, and I agreed with them. But what his teachers and I hadn't counted on was his determination. His bloody mindedness to be the best he can be. And this is as valuable as any talent.

The profession of acting takes itself very seriously indeed. Successful actors are lionised and sometimes practically deified. But acting is always fatally undermined by the many examples of debut actors giving award-winning performances. Mike Leigh is a director who makes great capital from casting completely untrained novices in his films and who often perform with remarkable aplomb. Imagine such an approach to other professions: medicine, law, dentistry or architecture? Barkhad Abdi was a taxi driver in Detroit when Paul Greengrass cast him in his film, *Captain Phillips* with Tom Hanks. A Somali immigrant, making a crust driving a cab in one of America's toughest cities, presumably Barkhad was intent on keeping himself fed and warm and not attending drama lessons? And yet he bagged himself an Academy Award for his efforts.

I spoke to an American talent agent once and he explained that talent is the only thing that really counts; that talent will always out and that film 'stars' are simply more talented than their contemporaries waiting tables. Really? I simply don't believe this. Of course, I can see that Robert De Niro is a fine exponent of this craft. For his versatility alone, he sets himself apart. As funny as he is in *Meet the Parents* and as menacing as anyone on screen in *Raging Bull, Taxi Driver, The Deer Hunter, Cape Fear...*

And sure, Tom is talented. I have just written a second series of a Radio 4 sit-com and sitting with some hopeful actors, it is glaringly apparent that some people can act and that others can't. I believe that this is largely innate and why drama schools are little more than an employment racquet. Tom certainly has an ability to appear natural on both screen and stage. But is he just more talented than a lot of kids who just won't ever get their chance to shine? I suspect not and furthermore, I don't think that Tom is any more talented than his three younger brothers. (All enquiries to me via social mee-ja).

Tom's success is indeed sweet but it smells of sweat because he has worked so incredibly hard to achieve what he has. His hard work rather than his talent is something I am a lot more comfortable discussing. It is something about him that I also greatly admire. I believe that endeavour is never wasted. It always counts and if it doesn't bear fruit immediately, then it will at some later point and in an area, you might least expect. As things transpired, the efforts of writing The Faldovian Club were a complete waste of time? But for inspiring Only in America which is now the spine of this book...

The efforts Tom invested in getting cast as Billy and then playing the part might be lost now because his performance can't be viewed or represented here in this book. Only the people who saw him in the show can really attest to what I am attempting to explain. But The Impossible can be viewed and why I am pleased that Tom brought the same work ethic to the making of this film. And a good thing too because the hours were gruelling for him to complete and for us to watch.

And it is this that I think marks Tom out and why I am never very at ease when people tell me how 'incredibly talented' he is. Opportunities appear for us all. The skill is to recognise them and to apply every fibre available to exploit them. I like the phrase 'smashed it'. I first heard it used by a friend of mine called Terry Alderton. Terry is more a clown than a stand-up comic but this is not to take anything from him. Not many comics in Britain, famous comedians included, would relish the prospect of following our Terry on to a stage. An amalgam of voices, alter-egos and brilliant physicality, Terry rips gigs apart. Terry and I were backstage at a gig discussing various comics we used to work with who now play arenas: some very deserving, others less so and few of them as talented as Terry. One comic was in the middle of a sold-out arena tour. We speculated on the money he was raking in.

'I tell you what, Dom,' Terry said, 'he's completely smashing it...'

And this is what Tom does. He smashes it, and good for him.

Batman and Robin

Tell anyone in show business that you are writing a screenplay and watch their eyes glaze over. Yeah, good luck with that. Why don't you try for something that is more likely to come off? Like becoming a heart surgeon? Or winning Wimbledon? This is because writing a hit film is a little bit like boarding a non-stopping train as it flashes through a backwater of a station. It can be done but most people will get creamed trying. And those few writers who do manage to clamber aboard will not do so unscathed. Becoming a film writer is a painful experience and injuries are inevitable.

Pitted against the fledgling writer is the fact that there are very few individuals who can genuinely affect the chances of a movie getting made. Getting to these people is virtually impossible. It happens by chance in my story *Only in America*, but such people are heavily guarded and protected. But there are plenty of people in film who pretend that they can get movies made. These types are in abundance and unfortunately, getting to them is a piece of piss.

Over the years, I have attracted my fair share of time-wasters, two of whom bear mentioning now, if not to entertain then to serve as a warning. To save them any embarrassment I will call them Batman and Robin. I was introduced to them by a friend of mine, a celebrated stunt coordinator and second-unit director whose credits include, appropriately enough, *The Dark Knight*.

According to my friend, Batman and Robin had spent 'years' designing a revolutionary film-financing model based entirely on product placement. It had taken meticulous honing to perfect not to mention secrecy and delicate and protracted negotiations with some of the world's biggest banks and companies. For once in my life, my timing was excellent because they were now ready to launch this revolutionary platform and first in their barrel was a movie called *Only in America*: a script by a comedian who was now starting to panic.

Their system was relatively simple. A branded product would be placed prominently in the film and in return pay 20% of the film's budget, an investment which would trigger the remaining funds required to finance the film from the Bank of America. They explained that it was going to revolutionize film-making and change the studio system forever.

Batman was the first to read my script and hastily arranged a meeting with me at Pinewood Studios. Our mutual friend called and explained that Batman needed to meet me quickly because certain brands were manoeuvring who were perfect for my script. I was delighted and completely available. On the morning of the meeting, driving my twins to school, my mobile rang. It was early to receive a call and it was most likely Nikki to say that there was a PE kit still in the hall. But it wasn't Nikki; it was Robin. He had read the script also and was so excited by it that he just had to call. Bloody hell, maybe this was it.

The meeting with Batman didn't go well. It went spectacularly well. Batman was optioning the script and within six months he would have raised £4m and we would be in production. Now, Dominic, who would you like to direct this film?

Erm...

This remains the third most ridiculous question I have ever been asked in show-business, behind, do you know Elton? And do you know Van?

In film, it might be the actors who get the public's adoration, but in Hollywood it is the director who is king. In the movie world, the director is known as the film-maker, which is right enough. The director not only makes the film but often, it is the director who gets the film made as well. As such, attaching a bankable director is the first and highest hurdle that the screenwriter faces. A script remains just a hundred pages of ink, pulp and effort until a director attaches, whereupon it becomes a film project. Star actors can be approached before a director, but their agents will want to know who is directing and if this question cannot be answered, then, please, stop wasting our time.

So, attracting any director is difficult and attracting a director with traction is the stage where most writers bounce off that speeding train. Let's say that a film project takes two years from director's attachment to cinema distribution, assuming it makes it this far of course. Many films get shot but remain unedited and many edited films will not be sold and will never see the light of the silver-screen. Straight to DVD is the cliché to denote failure, but these are really the success stories because a great number of films fare so much worse than this.

Decent directors are not necessarily better film-makers than others, they just have some currency, which means that they are inundated with scripts and they need to choose carefully. A film will consume years of their career and could be the death knell if they choose badly. I know this now, but I didn't when I first met with Batman. Having explained his new system, he told me that I could basically choose whichever director I wanted. You want Terrence Malick? You can have Terrence Malick. As it happened, I didn't but I was quite interested in Mike Newell who had scored such a hit with *Four Weddings* - a movie in the vein of *Only in America*. Fine, we'll get Mike Newell, not a problem. I think I even wrote this down in my diary – Director, Mike Newell – just in case I forgot. And how about Clooney for the part of Mitch because the same theory applies to talent: they do as we say. With this new model, we call the shots. Really? We kicked a few names back and forth and settled on Brad Pitt starring with Mike Newell directing. Another coffee? Fuck it, why not?

The whole thing was preposterous and I am somewhat embarrassed now when I think that I believed all this guff. I was either hopelessly naïve or a little desperate, which is of little comfort now.

A little giddy, I left the meeting and called Nikki once I got back to my car. An Aston Martin had been parked adjacent to my Fiat Multipla, which I admired and thought was only a matter of time. I wasn't as excited as I had been in the past, like the time I had run from Ginger Productions to the London Studios. I felt numb and a little bemused more than excited. That after all these years of waiting and all along there was such an easy way to get a film made? And all it takes is a neatly placed bar of soap.

A series of phone calls back and forth with Batman and Robin and the good news continued, and even Nikki started to believe. The whole business model hinged on Publicis, one of the world's biggest advertising agencies. I had never heard of them, but so what? It wasn't very long ago that I hadn't heard of Frank Capra, and Terrence Malick will not be impressed to hear that I needed to Google him also. Batman and Robin had been true to their word and brands were queuing up to buy into my protracted film project, *Only in America*.

Then I met Robin for the first time: a quietly spoken man from the North East who liked to name-drop brands rather than people. It was an odd listen but as desperate as I was, I was listening and was suitably taken in. His background was advertising and he fired up his laptop, keen to show me any number of film clips demonstrating how we were going to conquer Hollywood. I recall a scene from *Get Shorty*, a film I hadn't enjoyed at all but I didn't mention this. It involved a Toyota Prius and John Travolta. Robin spoke so softly, I could only catch a little of what he was saying, but it was a big number. Millions of dollars were involved and the script was rewritten to effectively advertise the new wonder hybrid. It appears Robin had brokered this deal himself, which might explain why he spoke so quietly because I would soon discover that he certainly had not.

My two caped crusaders set Renault in their sites for *Only in America* and they had already met with Publicis about it on numerous occasions. There was strong interest also from Ford but Renault was currently on pole. The Intercontinental Hotel Group were also keen as were various international cosmetics giants. The more the merrier as far as I was concerned. Perhaps I could get Nikki some face cream.

As well as my instincts, I did have ample warnings that all was not normal. Richard Holmes is a real-life film producer who has made some real-life films. He had flirted with *Only in America* for a few years and put me in touch with Sony in LA. I now had an option agreement from Batman and being between agents, I thought I would run the contract and this financing vehicle by Richard. He listened for a moment or two before phasing out. Product placement was nothing new in film – Aston Martin and Martinis being notable examples in Bond – but this was something new altogether and Richard was unequivocal. It was all complete and utter bollocks. His advice was that I should run a mile but desperate as I had become, I stayed put. Richard was just jealous, obviously.

Further meets and phone calls ensued. By now, the board of Renault, including the chairman, had read my script and all had signed off on it. Then came a crunch meeting with me and Batman and Robin. They put to me a question that no writer ever wants to face. Very basically, was my artistic integrity up for sale? Renault were able to commit but naturally, they had some demands. Namely, they wanted their Renault Clio to appear throughout the film. 'Embedded' was the word they used. They wanted my lead, Ann Hathaway (who else?), to drive a Clio in return for two million quid. For other film-writers, this might be a step too far but for me, not a problem. I would have changed my lead character's name from Milly to Nicole if it had helped and written in Papa as well. Selling out? Me? Yeah, and? C'est la fucking vie, pal.

As protracted and slow as the film business is, I have never been one to procrastinate and so the new script was ready within days and the suits in Paris were ecstatic. LG were also now on board for a further £1m. Welcome LG. But I hadn't yet signed anything and I decided that I really should employ the services of a lawyer. Not knowing anyone, I turned to Google and plugged in 'entertainment lawyers'. I selected a firm and placed the call and now as a buyer in the film world and not a seller, my call was returned instantly. The lawyer explained that before any money was charged, he needed to look at the contract as it stood. I mailed it to him and waited, hoping for his immediate approval. What I really wanted to hear was, 'Blimey, sign it!'

I am not a complete idiot. I do recall asking Batman if I could attend any of the numerous meetings that were taking place with Publicis. But alas, I was not allowed. To start with, they all took place in Paris, which for some reason I didn't bother to question. I had a passport, I was handy for the Eurostar and I quite fancied the idea of meeting some Parisian Grand Fromages who wanted to make my film. But this never happened.

My lawyer now got back to me and was happy to take me on as a client. A thousand pounds was needed as a retainer, which I paid readily because for a £5m movie, it was a small price to pay. I met him just once in his office. It was just along from the BBC in Portland Place. He explained that their business model was highly irregular and in his opinion, probably would not work. Right, thanks for that. The meeting lasted about twenty minutes and it remains to this day, the most expensive cup of tea I have ever bought in my life.

Yet, despite all the evidence against, I still wanted to believe in Batman but then he suddenly went quiet. He went dark as it were, which would not have been a bad thing if he had been the real Batman. The phone calls stopped and the silence began, which is much more like the film world I had become familiar with.

Three weeks elapsed with no word and then finally, Batman called. It was late one evening. I was in a bedroom at The Grosvenor House Hotel, about to entertain a thousand guests after their black-tie dinner in The Great Room and so I could use some good news with which to hit the stage. Batman, however, could not oblige.

He explained that Robin was a crook and was not to be trusted, but that he was dumping him from the business and proceeding on without him. No sooner had I ended the call, Robin rang and explained that Batman was a fantasist and a liar, and now I was thoroughly confused and dejected. How could these two men fall out like this? They had spent ten years putting this model together. They had both put their houses on the line or at least they claimed they had. Their labour was about to bear fruit, making up to ten movies a year. And now they have fallen out? How can this happen? They are Batman and Robin. They can't fall out.

My head in a spin, I got in the lift and hit ground on my way to The Great Room, the most famous banqueting suite in Britain. The noise hits me before I even see the room from the balcony overlooking the diner's coiffing their drinks without a care in the world. A thousand conversations make a lot of noise. Add in cutlery, glasses, background music and serving staff, the cacophony is as foreboding as the sight awaiting me. And all this noise will need to be silenced by just one man and his jokes, and then replaced with equally loud laughter? What a ridiculous job I have and little wonder I want to get my films made. I try to feel positive as I go on stage. As nervous as I get, I like to have a sense that all will be well for the next half hour, but this is not a feeling that I can easily cheat.

The gig went well enough – brilliantly, given the circumstances – which meant I could happily invoice for laughter rendered. Waiting for me at home was an email from Robin that he had promised me. It was a letter from the worldwide head of Publicis or more accurately, a disclaimer, stating that his group were not working with Batman. Obviously, the letter used the man's real name. It went on to say that Batman had been misrepresenting the Publicis Group to their clients (presumably Renault) and that no parties involved should assume any interest on the part of Publicis or on the part of any of their clients. Just as Richard had said, it was bollocks all along: two fantasists operating in never-land and I had briefly accompanied them.

The whole process had taken probably a year and cost a lot of false hope, not to mention the grand to the lawyer, and yet there was another kick to come in the years ahead from this whole episode.

At the time, there was another funding avenue for *Only in America*, which involved using a brand-new film studio in Alicante, Spain that was struggling to attract movies. Because *Only in America* was rooted in the film world, there was talk of recreating the LA scenes in Alicante and the facility in Spain part-funding my film. Apparently, the head of the Spanish studio had read the script and this was a distinct possibility. Could I go to Spain to discuss? Sure, when?

I never went of course, although in years to come I would spend six weeks in these very studios watching the making of the wave sequence for the movie *The Impossible*. It wasn't until I was on set that I made this connection and when I did, I laughed. It was another link between father and son and I would enjoy including it in a book I had already started to write.

Don't Book it Danno

I had tried to get Tom out of *Billy Elliot the Musical* a couple of times already. We had delighted in watching him strut his stuff of course. All our close friends had been to see our 'dancing boy' and we had dined out on *Billy* for a few years already. Our twins, Sam and Harry, were in their final year at the same primary school Tom had attended and where he had trained in the gym for the role. I am frequently asked about sibling rivalry in our household and how Tom's brothers have coped with their illustrious older brother. Firstly, Tom is not more illustrious than his brothers, not at home at any rate, but it is probably a little irksome for them when as a family, we encounter people for the first time and the first enquiry is often, 'And which one is Tom?' But I can honestly say that my boys are much prouder of their brother than jealous and this was amply demonstrated during a school trip for their entire year group to see the show.

Sam and Harry revelled in their friends seeing Tom on stage and they were the first to cheer and leap to their feet at any given opportunity. During the finale, Tom gave their whole group a little ovation of his own with a thumbs-up and a wave.

However, it should be said that Paddy was much less impressed by Tom in the show. Paddy was only four at the time, which is far too young to enjoy such a show. The swearing aside, Paddy couldn't understand the story but no matter because seeing Tom in such an unusual setting would be intriguing enough. One moment that stood out from so many 'Billy' moments occurred during the matinee show on New Year's Eve. It arrived just after the interval, during a sequence called 'Dream Ballet'.

In this section, the young Billy dances with an apparition of himself as an adult to Tchaikovsky's Swan Lake, during which Billy is hitched to a wire and flies about the stage and auditorium. Along with running up the wall, this is the 'wow' moment of the show when the audience usually breaks out into applause. Not Paddy though. He now had a tub of ice-cream and this held his attention more than anything Tom could do above his head.

Sitting on his mum's lap, even though he had an expensive seat of his own that we had purchased, Nikki was excited about his reaction to this flying sequence.

'What do you think Paddy?' she asked, to which Paddy replied, 'Mmm, lovely.' He was referring to his ice-cream and couldn't give a flying toss about his flying brother. A perfect reaction in some ways because keeping Tom's feet on the ground is what Nikki and I are determined to do and in this we are abetted by his brothers.

But now we were ready for Tom to leave the show and finally hang up his leotard for good. He was approaching two years in the role and a lot of the novelty had worn off. I don't mean the show itself, but everything else that comes with it: living away from home, the late nights, being away from school and just missing his mates and a more normal environment. Plus, we all wanted him home.

We hadn't all been away on holiday together for a long time and as exciting as *Billy* had been, we wanted to get a family holiday in before it was too late. Such holidays rank high in most people's memories of childhood and because of the show, we had some ground to make up. And I had big plans to correct this imbalance.

Tom's last performance was scheduled for late May 2010 and ever hopeful that we would have a good English summer, we plumped instead for this big family getaway over the forthcoming Christmas. We have rarely holidayed over Christmas and the whole idea really appealed. Leaving cold England for sunnier climes? This is what rich and successful people do and I thought it was time that the relatively rich and very successful Holland family got with the times. The only criterion for our destination was that it needed to be somewhere hot. No point in leaving England for somewhere cold. With typical bluster and no research at all, I quipped that I would like to be brought down to breakfast each morning on an elephant. And cost wasn't a factor I told Nikki. What price memories, eh? This was not going to be a regular Christmas jaunt for us, in the way it is for the genuinely rich, the people who jet off every December to somewhere far flung. This was going to be a Holland one-off, so I could suffer the cost just this once, no matter how big the hit. I left it up to Nikki and told her that the world was our oyster. Wherever you fancy. Stick a pin in the globe. I'll charter a boat if needs be. Just nowhere near Somalia, obviously.

Not for a moment did it occur to me that this was 2010 and we were amidst the worst economic maelstrom since the 1930s. I should have noticed, especially since my income had more than halved since 2007 and a creeping panic about my future income had already taken root and was developing very nicely, thank you. My income has always been ad-hoc and somewhat precarious. No basic pay and no sick pay, I only earn when I stand up on stage, and looking at thin months ahead had never worried me in the past. Because when these months finally arrived, something had always come in – a little bit of telly or some corporate events – but by 2010, this was all becoming a little bit more strained. My television appearances were now exclusively day-time and such appearances do not feed into corporate bookings on which I have relied for so long. But I suppose I could always write another hit film?

So, economic circumstances forced me to make a return to the comedy circuit, but it had been a while and now there were promoters who had never heard of me? Yikes! Again, my timing is poor because the halcyon days of circuit comedy are now over. Club comedy is in contraction. Clubs are paying the same as they did twenty years ago; there are fewer gigs and more comics. Not a great time then to book the holiday of a lifetime.

Too late, however, because Nikki is surfing the net and I am still in complete denial. I have always been a glass-half-full man. It'll be fine. By the time, I am straddling Dumbo on my way down to breakfast, either the economy would have righted itself or more likely that one of my film projects would have been green lit.

South Africa quickly nudged ahead of Kenya (safer?) which was replaced by Malaysia, which then lost out to the Maldives, where we had honeymooned. A nice touch to bring our four boys to the island where it all began, but this eventually counted against as Thailand screamed into view and finally emerged as the winner.

Thailand is an evocative place that occupies a special place in many people's hearts. It is just one of those places, even for people who have never visited. Whether it's the fragrant food and beautiful people or the stunning beaches made famous by that novel and the film starring Leonardo DiCaprio. What's not to like? And then there is Bangkok of course, one of the world's most vibrant cities, famous for so many things that they hardly need mentioning. So it was settled then; we were Thailand-bound for Christmas, for a holiday that our boys would never forget.

Then Nikki hit me with the price and my vision blurred. I can't remember what it was exactly. But it was high and way more than I could ever afford even during the good times that were now in the past? Realism quickly kicked in and Center Parcs screamed into view and even then, with only one of the basic bungalows. Sorry boys, there would be no elephants this Christmas aside from the tattooed variety clad in pastel velour.

It was typical of me that I hadn't waited for a provisional budget for the Thai Christmas excursion before telling my kids that Dad was taking them to a tropical island and assuring young Paddy that Santa was coming too. I even got the bloody globe out to show them. Understandably, they were all very excited and they all agreed that the long flight was going to be best part of the adventure, and so I worried how a trip down the M4 to Longleat Forest was going to fare in comparison, especially the stretch passing Heathrow with as many planes in the sky as cars on the road.

And so, it was good news indeed that Tom managed to get himself cast as Lucas in the film *The Impossible*, which happened to be filming over Christmas in Thailand. Bloody hell Tom, good work mate. Really good work.

The boys in Thailand at the location where *The Beach* was filmed

And naturally, with Tom comes his brothers and let's not forget his mum and his dad. So, the Holland family did get its mega holiday after all. Only it was a holiday with a difference. It wasn't for the usual two weeks but for four months. Plus, it would be preceded by a six-week stint in Spain during the summer. And there was little worry that we would ever forget this experience either. Not because we would take the odd photograph as memories but because a feature film was being made and would be ample reminder.

And furthermore, this extraordinary holiday was set to be free as well. The holiday that I could never have afforded was being gifted to me. So, I say again, well done, Tom! Good work.

Three More in the Barrel

Of the many reasons to write this book, one of the most pressing is to refute the inevitable accusation that we are pushy parents desperate to get our kids into show business. As I said in the prologue, it is normal and correct for parents to be ambitious for their children. After all, it is the human race and not the human fun run. Charles Darwin ranks as one of the greatest all-time Britons for explaining that only the fittest will survive and yet there seems to be a difference between a pushy parent and an ambitious parent. The ambitious parent is irksome and often unattractive but the pushy parent is always beyond the pale.

So, let me be clear; I am a pushy parent but only in the field of golf and even then, my ambitions are moderate. None of my boys are going to play in the Ryder Cup, but I hope they all become decent players and much better than I ever managed myself.

The mantra of the ambitious parent is 'Education, Education, Education', an arena where the bar is being continually raised and parents will stop at nothing. Faith schools keep the churches busy on a Sunday and their numbers swell with atheist parents having a sudden vocation and dropping to their knees to pray, presumably for a place at their local school.

And in every grammar school catchment area, a cottage industry of tutors exists, raking in much booty in cash; which is not something we have ever been a part of, happy for our children to take their chances at their local comprehensives. This is a practical decision rather than a political one. We just can't afford the fees.

So, ambitious parents want their children to become doctors and pushy parents want their kids to become famous, so, naturally, they congregate in the tawdry and clawing world of show business. Anyone who has seen that clever film *Little Miss Sunshine* or any episode of *The X Factor* will see that it is so often the dreams of the parents on display and on stage.

One of my all-time favourite jokes goes like this:

A man at a job centre is told that the only vacancy is for a 'buttocks down hair stylist' and is he interested? Confused, he asks for a job description and is told that lingerie models have a fine layer of hair covering their buttocks and that before a fashion shoot, this layer of hair needs to be smoothed down and it is best done by hand. The job pays £40-50k per annum. The man is immediately interested and is told to go to Cardiff for the interview. 'Why? Is that where the fashion shoot is?' he asks. 'No, the interview is in London, but Cardiff is where the end of the queue is.'

Show business is a lot like this. It's impossible to quantify, but it must be the most oversubscribed businesses of all. By which I mean, for every job there are thousands of applicants, many of whom are just as capable as the successful candidate, but the stars just didn't align for them. In other words, there are legions of talented people who are never going to make it.

Given such statistics, the story of *Eclipsed* is an unlikely one. It is particularly extraordinary as it is not just Tom who is overtaking his dad. My other boys are flirting with the idea as well. Just to recap, we have four boys: Tom, twins, Sam and Harry, and then finally Patrick.

In May 2010, Tom has finished playing Billy and is looking forward to a summer of doing not very much. You already know by now how this plan worked out. Now, I got a phone call from the drama teacher at Tom's old school, where Sam and Harry were in their final year. She was calling for my advice on a showbiz matter and as needy as I am, I was naturally all ears. She had been contacted by a film company who were producing the movie *Horrid Henry* and they wanted to see the entire year 6 of the school to find their Henry and Peter. The teacher was worried about the legitimacy of the project and allowing anyone access to the boys, so I made some calls. Everything checked out and the mass audition took place; nothing more than each boy doing a quick identification to camera and answering a couple of questions, Sam and Harry Holland included.

I didn't even know that this had taken place, so when both my boys were recalled to see the producers again I was a little bit surprised. The man on the phone was at pains to explain that both of my boys had made big impressions on the producers and I wondered if they knew who their dad was.

By the time the twins' second audition came around, at the Welsh Centre in London, Tom had already been cast in *The Impossible* and we were making plans for a six-week filming stint in Spain. But with Thailand to follow in the autumn, it would clash with *Horrid Henry*'s filming and so the boys being involved would be a logistical nightmare. I was relieved that their second audition was absolutely rammed with hopefuls. Shortlist, my backside! Linda Lusardi was there with her young son. I had met Linda's husband before and so we got chatting in the way that 'celebs' do. I rather enjoyed the attention from on-looking dads wondering just who the hell I was.

By now though, Nikki was panicking that either of the twins might get cast, which would mean that they couldn't go to Thailand and the family would be split up. Such feelings came with some guilt because what an opportunity for either of them and maybe even both. I assured Nikki that they wouldn't be cast, but this wasn't much comfort given my predictions about Tom's chances of playing Billy. At least Paddy, our youngest, was not being pestered with offers to be in a film. Not yet, as we were about to discover.

With no decision made on *Horrid Henry*, the whole family headed off to Spain for six weeks to shoot the tsunami sequence for *The Impossible*. At our apartments on the second day, we met the director, J.A. Bayona, and his team. As J.A. shook the hands with my boys individually, I could sense something afoot.

Finding the boy to play Lucas had taken well over a year and the producers were about to give up on the UK and extend the search to America until they found Tom. And once Tom was cast, they had to find boys to play his younger brothers, which again was not easy and had yet to be resolved. And then J.A. meets Tom's real-life younger brothers who looked like brothers and crucially, were also available. Furthermore, they were on the location as well accompanying their big brother.

Tom and his brothers in Spain with JA Bayona

The boy who had been cast to play Lucas's youngest brother, Simon, is also on set but for rehearsals only with the director, JA Bayona. He is five years old, the same age as my Paddy. It is hot and dusty on set and the young actor, like most kids of his age, has a problem concentrating and would rather be playing with other children than interacting with a film director. For whatever reason, JA is not convinced that the boy is going to be able to do what he needs and this is a major problem: a problem with a possible readymade solution in Paddy Holland? Sandra Hermida, the line producer puts this solution to me and immediately I panic. The boy's mother is on set and has no idea about this developing situation and I feel anxious for her and her family.

Naturally, Tom is keen for Patrick to do it and we don't even think to ask him, not yet anyway, and then we get a phone call from London. Sam and Harry have been shortlisted for *Horrid Henry*. According to the casting agent, they are looking at Harry playing Henry and Sam playing Peter. I put the phone down, numb. What the hell is happening to my life?

At this rate, we might have four kids in films at the same time. We are never going to be able to explain this away. None of these were roles that we had sought, but no one will ever believe this. We are going to look weird freaky pushy parents hell-bent on making our kids famous. Nikki is now completely freaking out. The whole thing feels like one big practical joke or worse, a conspiracy against me and my own efforts in the same bloody business. The upside is that this story I have in mind to call *Eclipsed* is going to be a belter and I fire up Tom's laptop and make a general start. Maybe I will start it as a blog? Naturally, Tom has an Apple and not a PC and I struggle with the process at first. I sketch out some chapters and decide that I will certainly need a chapter based on Tom's brothers. I make a note of a potential title, 'Three More in the Barrel'.

Nikki is still beside herself. What if they all get cast? We can't very well agree to Tom playing a part and not letting our twins do the same? If it comes to it, the plan is that I will stay in London with the twins and Nikki will go to Thailand with Tom and Patrick. This is not ideal. The prospect of being apart from the twins fills Nikki with dread and I'm not overwhelmed at getting Twickenham Studios instead of Thailand either.

For now, though, we sit Patrick down at the studio in Spain and put the idea to him of being in the film with Tom. He is going to be in Thailand anyway, so it does make good sense. Patrick takes a moment to think about it and then gives a firm and very flat no. This is a little surprising and we need to be sure and so we ask him again. Once again, it's a no. Fair enough, but this time we ask why. He explains very straightforwardly that it will be too embarrassing. Tom now gets involved because he thinks Patrick is perfect. He is being asked to play Tom's younger brother, a role he was literally born for. Paddy is persuaded by Tom to take the role but still he has a special proviso on which he will base his final decision. And it is non-negotiable. He wants to know if there is going to be any karate in the film, which is his current obsession. Then he gets a little more specific and asks if Jackie Chan is going to be in the film. I know that Chan is not involved and I check the script again and there is no karate. We explain this to Paddy and he listens intently and gives us his final answer... No. No Karate, no Paddy. Nikki is relieved. One down, two to go.

As it turned out, the boy cast to play Simon in the film was Oaklee Pendergast. Oaklee is a force of nature who really must be experienced to be believed. And he happens to be a dead ringer for Paddy and they were often confused for one another.

Paddy's decision to pass on a potential career in Hollywood was a little at odds with his obsession with films characters at the time. Paddy had always been an avid dresser up. He had gone through the usual suspects; Spider-Man, Batman and Hulk. His longest faze was Indiana Jones, getting through at least two outfits and possibly three. And when we arrived in Thailand, it so happened that he was mid-way through his Luke Skywalker obsession. Not ideal given that Luke's outfit is nylon and Thailand is boiling hot but a good thing given that Obi-Wan Kenobi (Ewan) was pretending to be Tom's dad. Paddy celebrated a birthday in Thailand and had a shared party at a beach bar called Memories Bar with Naomi Watt's youngest son. Naturally, Ewan was invited and Paddy went as Luke. A memorable birthday party then? On a beautiful beach in Thailand with the real Luke Skywalker's mentor in attendance.

Memories Bar is aptly named and would become so important to the production of The Impossible, it really should have got a single card credit on the movie.

Back in London after Spain, Sam and Harry are seen for *Horrid Henry*, only now things have changed again and the odds have considerably lengthened, which is good news. Sam is now being considered for Perfect Peter and Harry for Aerobic Al. But as it turns out, only Sam is seen again and neither of our boys are in fact cast. They are both disappointed but Thailand is some consolation. Nikki and I are relieved.

To add to this rather bonkers state of family life, over this same summer, I was back in London to do some gigs, including a week on the TV show, *The Wright Stuff*. After I appeared on the show one morning, I received a phone call almost immediately afterwards. A casting director had watched the show and seeing the caption 'comedian' on the screen and seeing my face, she thought that Dominic Holland might be worth a punt and that he should at least be seen.

She was casting *The Hobbit* and wanted me to read for the lead. Blimey! Were this to come off, this would technically be known as a career break and would immediately put a halt to my plans to write a story called *eclipsed*. And so what? Get in the shade again son and bring on the Hobbit. I was interested and obviously, I was available. Looking back now, it was almost four kids in movies then and a hobbit as the old man. Nikki would have had a breakdown.

You will know already that Martin Freeman was cast. As it turned out, the actor from *The Office* and *Nativity* got a little lucky because I never even got to read for the part. Like that famous film *Raging Bull*, I could have been a contender.

But now *Eclipsed* was back on and here we are. And as it transpired, my twins were included as extras in The Impossible.

Sam and Harry as extras in *The Impossible*

Only Sam would make the edit, a source of great amusement even to this day in the Holland household.

Profit Warning

Hearing about Princess Diana's crash was one such occasion, and eerily I was in the Piccadilly underpass at the time, on my way home from the Comedy Store, having done the late show. 9/11 was another. For this world event, I was idly at home, my father-in law fitting a new porch to our house when my neighbour, Chris, popped round and suggested we put the television on. 'Why? Am I on?' I might have joked? The 2004 Asian tsunami was another event when I can recall when and where I was when I first heard the news.

Now, I don't think I had ever heard the word tsunami before and I stood in my kitchen spellbound, listening to the radio and the unfolding tragedy. The numbers were staggering, which I visualised by imagining multiples of full Wembley Stadiums. It felt even more poignant for the fact it was Boxing Day, a day to be with family and to reflect. No doubt pictures recorded live were available also and I was rather pleased with myself that I didn't turn to the television. As much as I was intrigued by a thirty-metre wave, I didn't wish to see people who had drowned or the traumatised survivors either.

All day the shadows lengthened over Christmas when numbers of even two hundred thousand people were mooted. It was possibly the greatest natural disaster in living memory. Of course, there are natural disasters every year, taking lives with glib abandon and we watch and we gesture and sometimes we respond to the appeals and sometimes we don't. But this event was different, because of the sheer numbers involved, but also because Westerners were killed and in great numbers. Tourist destinations as they were, the Western world felt connected and grieved collectively. The 2010 Pakistan floods affected seventeen million people, but the appeals struggled to make headway because the West didn't feel engaged. Another tragedy then and a subject for another book and by an author more worldly-wise than me.

The Asian tsunami enveloped Scandinavia, Britain, France, America and indeed the whole world. News crews darted about the place mawkishly recording whatever they could and individual stories began to emerge. Rumours that Sir Richard Attenborough's family had been decimated and endless pictures of survivors on location scouring notice boards in the hope to find their loved ones made heart-rending viewing.

The tsunami became a world event and I couldn't have known then what an impact it would come to have on my family: the opportunity it would create, the experiences we would have and the friends we would make – an awkward reality emerging from such a tragic event, which I am always mindful of as I write this story.

The first time that the tsunami physically touched me was during a phone call from my friend, John Inverdale, the BBC sports journalist already mentioned in this book. John was involved with a charity golf day and dinner at The Royal Wimbledon Golf Club close to where I live. By now, the story of Sir Richard Attenborough had been confirmed, that three generations of his family had been killed in the tragedy, and the golf day was being organised by his son-in-law, a man called Jeffrey Holland. John Inverdale asked if I would talk for twenty minutes after the dinner. Although I am much more of a stand-up comedian rather than the raconteur who is better suited to such gigs, I didn't see that I could refuse. Add to this a rarefied venue and the occasion and I inked the date in my diary with some foreboding.

The day began on the putting green with an array of sports stars, a collection of celebrities of sort, friends, family and the most important people of all, the individuals paying top dollar to play. A welcome was followed by a two-minute silence and then the golf got started. Colin Montgomerie hadn't yet arrived having finished second in the British Open the day before, so everyone understood and hoped he would make it along later.

I didn't enjoy my round very much, thinking on every shot about the evening ahead, and with Bruce Forsyth and Jimmy Tarbuck in the field, I wondered why it was me speaking and not them.

Most of the sports 'stars' left before the meal as is sadly their way, but the evening was significantly augmented by the presence of Sir Richard Attenborough himself along with his family. I sat with the club pro during dinner and he remarked without knowing who I was that he pitied the poor sod who was having to speak after the meal.

There was no stage or lights and I felt very exposed and frankly, out of my depth as Jimmy Tarbuck suddenly took to the floor and did something rather extraordinary. I had never seen or met Jimmy before but of course I knew that he was a cheeky Scouse comic with a great line in the pub gag. On this evening, Jimmy was conducting the auction and before he began, he did a quick ten-minute routine, but not from his own repertoire. Instead, he used anecdotes and quips of our now-deceased and best-loved comedians. He told the one about Eric Morecombe, when Eric was asked by a one-armed doorman if he could attend the recording of *The Morecombe and Wise Show*, to which Eric replied, 'No, because you can't clap.' A brilliant joke by the late Eric Morecombe, told now by the famous Jimmy Tarbuck. Everyone laughed apart from me. I sat there stony faced. More followed from the canon of Tommy Cooper, what Tommy said or did, and my mood darkened even further. Not only was I following Tarbuck, one of the UK's best-known comedians, I was following him doing the greatest lines of the very greatest British comedians ever. If Chaplin had spoken, no doubt Jimmy would have done him as well.

Before the auction, Jimmy brought the mood down and reminded us about the tragic events that had brought us together and that we should all give generously. Dessert followed and then I was due straight up after coffee, but before then Sir Richard indicated that he would like to say a few words. The room fell silent as this great man from such an illustrious family stood with the support of those on either side of him. I am not a skilled enough writer to adequately describe the pain that was etched on his face or the atmosphere in the room. He wept openly as he remembered those who had passed and finally, unable to continue, he needed to be helped back in to his seat. People were crying openly, but by some distance I was the saddest person in the room.

Anyone who has ever seen me perform will know that my boys and being a dad is a large part of my act and now suddenly, none of this material would be appropriate. It all had to be jettisoned and I frantically tried to think of material that might chime. I started to panic. What would I open with? Should I reference Sir Richard and then proceed to try and be funny and at least as funny as Eric Morecombe, Arthur Askey, Max Wall and Tommy Cooper, courtesy of our Jim. In that moment, I decided that I just couldn't perform. There was nothing I could say for the occasion and I just could not go on. I quickly rushed off to find Jeffrey Holland, the organiser, and hoped that he would understand. He was on his way to see me because he too had concluded the same thing. Now was not the time for levity. He told me to relax and enjoy the evening and I could have cuddled him with relief.

It was a crying shame then that no one thought to explain this to his son who after coffee took to the floor to respond on behalf of his grandfather. He thanked everyone for coming, probably gave an indication of the amounts of money raised and then proceeded to introduce the very funny Mr Dominic Holland.

I sat there aghast with all eyes on me. I had a stark choice and both were humiliating. Do I take to the floor and struggle or do I refuse to go, something I had never done before or since? I chose to stay in my seat. At least this way, it was only me being embarrassed and not the whole room as happens when a comedian struggles. And that's how the evening ended. I wanted to leave straight away but I was determined to stay. I needed to stay to front it out, even though I felt hollow inside.

Charity is all around us. The acts of carrying a fellow passenger's bag up a flight of stairs or giving up a seat to someone more in need are small examples. But in the main, charity is confined to what or how much we give to others, either in a collection box when the need takes us or more formally through our bank accounts. And then there are those of us who more fully embrace their charitable deeds and I would like to draw attention to one individual I met on location in Thailand. His name is Thomas Sonnerson, a very successful Swedish businessman who I greatly admire and have stayed in contact with.

The film *The Impossible* is the story of The Belon family, a Spanish family of five: Maria, Henrique and their three boys, Lucas, Thomas and Simon. They were holidaying in Thailand in 2004 and stayed at the Orchid Beach Resort in Khao Lak, Thailand. And being scrupulous about details and wanting the film to be as authentic as possible, it was decided to use the Orchid Beach Resort both as the film set and the hotel to accommodate most of the cast and crew for the four months of shooting.

Liev Schreiber, the partner of Naomi Watts, promptly found a surf beach close by with a simple bar/restaurant called Memories Bar, and it immediately became the meeting point for the entire crew every weekend.

Memories Bar

From J.A., the director, down to and including Naomi and Ewan, everyone convened at Memories every Saturday lunchtime and some didn't leave until Sunday night.

'Memories Bar' was owned by a beautiful man called Ching, who I cheekily renamed Ker Ching to account for all the extra business he was suddenly enjoying.

He became a father for the first time during filming, something which was celebrated by all and was particularly poignant given his history and how he came to name his bar Memories.

The beach where his bar is located is remote and separated from the road by dense jungle. It is not accessible by foot and not even very easily by car. The dirt track from the road to the beach is at least 3km and really requires a four-wheel drive vehicle and ideally a tank. The first time I made the trip, as the track narrowed, I almost turned back, thinking that I must have made a mistake.

Elephants on the road. Only in Thailand?

Having already passed an elephant farm and continuing through thick jungle, eventually the track leads into a clearing and the most beautiful beach that our planet earth has to offer.

Ching was riding his motorbike on this track heading to the market on December 26th, 2004 when suddenly he heard an unearthly noise behind him and his whole world changed irrevocably. The sea that is so impossibly beautiful and the source of their livelihood had suddenly become their nemesis. It had risen and forced its way miles in land, obliterating everything in its path. Many hours later, after the waters had receded, Ching finally managed to return to his bar and discovered that many of his family had been killed. Young children who were orphaned that morning still live there today as a kind of extended family and are now fast growing into young men. Their whole story was humbling, especially as we all sat and played on this beautiful beach without a care in the world, just as people had done in 2004. Ching showed me a laminated newspaper story covering his personal loss and it reminded me of my evening in a golf club some years earlier.

Thomas Sonnerson and his family regularly visited Thailand, but at the time of the tsunami their good fortune was to be at home in Sweden watching the news like the rest of the world. Thomas knew Ching well and establishing that his bar was in the middle of the disaster area, he frantically tried to contact his friend but to no avail. He left messages with as many people as he could and hearing nothing back, he assumed the worst. Two months later though, Ching finally contacted him. He was alive and immediately, Thomas jumped on a plane.

And the result of the two men's happy reunion and their endeavours is now plain for all to see. The bar has been rebuilt with bungalow accommodation to rent, plumbed toilets and showers and a kitchen which would witness one of the greatest moments in the Thai arm of *The Impossible*, and warrants a later chapter all on its own.

Thomas visits regularly and has further plans beyond. I don't know how much he has contributed, but I am sure it is considerable and what they have managed to achieve together is magnificent. Memories Bar is so called for obvious reasons, but there is nothing mawkish or sombre about the place. The place is brimming with life and endeavour and we all felt very privileged to spend time there with Ching and his thriving extended family.

Later into filming, there were many scenes that required huge numbers of extras, as many as five thousand in total, and it was necessary to recruit children of all nationalities to represent the children who had been separated from their parents. And because of the tsunami, there is a plentiful supply of genuine orphanages in the area. During one scene, Tom was surrounded by young children, not actors but real orphans, and he had no trouble emoting I'm sure. A little girl took a shine to my wife and sat on her knee at every available opportunity.

One day towards the end of our stay in Thailand, we were keen to visit an orphanage and hoped that we might see some of the children we had met on set, but it was not to be. The tsunami devastated so many families that the orphanages are too numerous, all staffed by people of extraordinary fortitude and kindness.

We had an address and were heading to one orphanage, but without a sat-nav our hopes of finding it were fading fast. I suggested that Nikki should call to get some directions but the lady on the phone had very little English and wasn't able to help. Our Thai was of no use whatsoever. We carried on a little further and tried calling again and this time Nikki started to describe our car, which I thought was a little odd as non-descript as it was. Nikki got off the phone and explained that the lady was standing on the road looking out for our car. Blimey! Good luck, I thought. We didn't know how far away we were and how long the poor lady might have to wait. As things transpired, it wasn't long before we saw a tiny lady waving her arms frantically at us and beckoning for us to turn; a good thing too, because we would have driven straight past. She would have stood there all day if needs be, because visits such as ours had become their lifeblood.

Whether the children had been primed, I don't know and I don't care, but they all came out to greet us and give us a glass of cool water each. The lady and her husband, in typically Thai fashion, smiled broadly and proudly and showed us their orphanage: home to probably thirty children, scrupulously clean with a chicken coop, some plantings, a classroom and basic living accommodation. It was a life lesson for my boys in humility and for Nikki and I as well.

These kids had nothing by comparison to what we lavish on ourselves and yet they radiated happiness and we all felt humbled.

I gave the man some money and we promised to return with stuff that we had accumulated during our stay that we could leave with them. This orphanage had been founded and entirely funded by a Swiss doctor who, like Thomas, had holidayed in the area and felt compelled to act. The Swiss get a bad press. War record, gold, wealth, watches and boring are all insults casually banded around, but what a remarkable man this doctor was. He bought some land, had the structures built and completely funded operations for five years before asking them to stand on their own: an incredible legacy to leave from his well-paid endeavours, caring for people in Europe.

The film is called *The Impossible* for obvious reasons, that a family of five should have survived such a freak of nature when all around them people perished. Maria was so badly injured that she really should have died and when I first read the script (way before Tom was cast), I was convinced that she would die and her son would need to bury her. So, the ending surprised me and even disappointed because they had gone for a Hollywood ending, no matter how unrealistic. I was stunned when it was explained that it was a true story.

Meeting and becoming friends with the Belon family was one of the great experiences of seeing *The Impossible* being made. They are a lovely family and Maria is a formidable lady. She is a doctor herself, which might have helped her to survive, but what she did indisputably draw upon was her love for her family. Lucas too is a remarkable individual, the character that Tom plays in the film. Thinking his dad and brothers are dead and seeing his mum so gravely injured, he was a ten-year-old boy who suddenly needed to grow up. Being present and strong for his mum no doubt helped Maria to survive and the way that he helped others too in the hospital it is fitting now that Lucas is training to be a doctor himself and here in London.

The Trump Hotel, Toronto – with the real Maria and Lucas

This picture was taken in Toronto after the world premiere - the real Maria and Lucas with Nikki and Tom.

The very last scene of the film is the family being flown out from Thailand to Singapore on a medical plane that has been organised by Henrique's insurance policy. Maria was sedated but conscious and still gravely ill, having already been operated on three times in Thailand. This final scene was shot in Madrid, an emotional occasion for Tom and J.A.Bayona, who by now had become as close as father and son.

It is a happy scene of course but also a sad one for the Belon family. They were injured and broken but still whole and together. Below them was carnage, people who were not as fortunate, and this burdened them with a sense of guilt. During the publicity for the film, J.A. made an interesting point that particularly resonated with me.

'The Belon family was lucky. They did nothing to survive. To state that they did is to disrespect the people who did not survive; that the people who died could have done something to avoid their fate. The tsunami was indiscriminate. The Belon family did nothing to affect this outcome.'

A quarter of million people died that day and many millions more directly affected. Lives lost and lives changed forever, including the lives of the Holland family I might add. I wouldn't be writing this book without that fateful day and I am mindful now and sensitive to this reality.

Anything worth Achieving is Difficult

There is a lot of wisdom in this expression and it certainly chimes with me. It is why hard work underpins almost all high achievers. That said, the playing field of life is certainly not a level one and this means that some people need to work harder than others, depending on their personal circumstances. Some people just have it easier than others but there is no real gain in complaining about this. It's life. Beautiful people always strike me as being particularly lucky bastards.

The ugly person turning up for an interview has a steeper hill to climb than the attractive candidate. There are plenty of plain-looking broadcasters in radio; not so many on television, though.

Intelligence too is highly prized, but unfortunately academic intelligence more so than the emotional variety. And let's not forget lineage either and not just those with famous forebears. These days, just having two parents puts a child at a huge advantage.

But much more valuable than these advantages of birth is an attribute less immediately apparent and more difficult to gauge. I refer to confidence, which is literally invaluable to those who have it and to the 'professionals' who peddle it. Billions of dollars are spent by people desperate to acquire confidence. It seems almost all the non-fiction books are self-help books, which mostly appear to be the same book with just different jackets and titles. Self-help gurus are rooted in confidence and the power of thought. Paul McKenna is a well-known exponent. But if he can think himself happier, richer and more confident, then surely, he would be able to think himself a full head of hair. Do that, Paul, and I'm in.

I am just dubious that confidence can be distilled into a book and acquired so neatly. To an extent, beauty can be bought with surgery and grooming and so can intelligence with practice and cramming. And to a point so can confidence by attending the right sorts of school and mixing in certain circles. All kids might get 'A' these days but don't be fooled. Grades are a factor for a short time only, but confidence endures and keeps on giving. Or does it?

I say this because in the area of confidence, I am hopeful and fretful in equal measure for my boys. On the looks front, things are looking good for them. None of them have my scrunched-up face and for now at least, they are all seem abundantly confident, a quality that neither of their parents would lay claim to gifting them. And therefore I worry because I can recall being amazingly confident as a kid, much more so than I am now, which makes me wonder; is confidence like cartilage, something that works perfectly in youth and cushions any blow but diminishes with age? Does confidence wear out? And if so, how can I preserve it in my boys?

I have no doubt that it is my fragile confidence that has led me to village halls and not a lack of talent or 'funny', and I am interested to see if I can trace where my insecurity springs from. It will be a useful exercise if it can inform my job as a dad.

At primary school I was very much an alpha male. I was one of the fastest kids, one of the best football players, the funniest, obviously! The cutest. The girls loved me and I loved them. First there was Loretta and then Michelle, who was very tall and very fast but rather tellingly she slowed down enough when she needed to. Caroline, Debbie, twins called Louise and Janice, Rebecca. These are all indelible names in my head and despite being relationships as fleeting as they were innocent, they are all knots in my handkerchief. I was a catch and life was a doddle. And as young as we were, although I was always small, the disparity with other classmates was at its least and this might be the key.

Because when I went to secondary school, almost immediately my alpha male status was ripped away from me. The most formative race of all had begun; the race through adolescence and into manhood and I was going to finish flat last. All through my childhood I was late with advent moments: losing my teeth, voice breaking, shaving, even one of my testicles refused to drop down and needed surgery. I just grew up very slowly, something compounded by being young in my year. So much in life hinges on how we perform in school and not just in exams either. I didn't know I was small at primary school but in secondary school it was glaringly apparent and yet I was constantly reminded of it as well. Even now it is a joke that people are happy to level and I am 'big' enough to laugh along as well. I caught up in the end development-wise, obviously. I did become a fully grown and mature adult but by the time this happened, I think I had developed my lingering sense of doubt.

Throughout my teenage years, an area of life that worried me greatly was whether I would be able to snag myself a mate. Nature programmes on TV appalled me. I would pay attention to the stags rutting, the whales thrashing and the hippos and walruses smashing heads together to attract a female. Even worse, too often, these disputes were settled with the winning male siring the entire herd, a fact that kept me awake at night every bit as much as Spielberg's *Jaws* had done. I looked at my parents and figured that my dad had done well. He had a wife (mate) and four children and he was small. But he was handsome on his wedding day in a dark and swarthy kind of way and he didn't look like a kid who was called ugly at school as I was throughout my childhood.

I was terrorized by the phrase 'tall, dark and handsome'. At fifteen, it seemed that I was only going to qualify in one of these areas and of the three, being dark was the least desirable. Peter Sutcliffe was dark I seemed to notice.

So, when I got my first proper girlfriend I was taking no chances and promptly married her, and in this area, I am constantly reminded that I am punching way above my weight, so well done me. And it's a good union. Our gene mix has a synergy to it. Each of my boys is a greater whole than their parents' constituent parts.

On the girlfriend front, Tom is certainly not having an adolescence like mine and I expect that he worries a lot less than I did.

I should add that my lack of confidence is rather exposed by joining a profession that is so public and where having big balls is pretty much essential. Possibly in a more normal career and life, my confidence reserves might even be considered full. But comedy has exposed an Achilles' heel of mine. I don't expect any of my boys to become stand-up comics but no matter, I still want them to be confident and more robust than their old man, and if Tom is anything to go by, then I might even be on course to getting my first ever grade A in my life.

Author Footnote

A quick word on confidence and my lack of it because whilst it has certainly contributed to my fallow years, it does not entirely account for my extended career plateau.

Because by the time I got my head and act together again (literally) and could headline gigs again, up against me for TV slots is diversity.

I get diversity and I understand its good intentions. To reflect the nation and to encourage further proponents from whichever minority it is?

One night in the previous century at the Meccano Comedy Club in Islington (sadly, no longer a fixture on the dwindling comedy circuit), I was present for Eddie Izzard's very first gig in a dress. Eddie has always been way ahead of his time. Nowadays, the acronym LBGT is as well-known as any and everyone knows what that the T stands for. Coming out as he did in the early 90's, Eddie was fully twenty years ahead of this particular curve and I smile ruefully when I recall how he explained his attire to his audience at the time.

In his act, he would say something like the following and you may wish to read it with his voice and inimitable mannerisms.

I am a comedian – a stand-up comedian - and in comedy these days it is important to be different. But look at me. I am white. I am middle class. I am straight... And so, I thank God that I am a transvestite...

In fact, Eddie was plenty different enough from his fellow comics without donning a dress. As well as being unique; at the height of his powers, he also happened to be funnier than everyone else. And touring with Eddie as his support act and watching him say this each night on stage, I confess that it didn't really resonate with me at the time. I didn't really understand his point about needing to be different and needing to stand out. But I certainly do now.

In many areas of the arts, I can see that diversity can be applied without any impact on the output. Newsreaders are a good example. If the person can read out loud in a clear voice, then who cares whether the person is white, black, brown, disabled, male, female, gay, straight, bi, trans...

But comedy is tangible and it can be glaringly apparent when a person is booked for meeting criterion other than how funny they are.

Always better to show rather than tell, so I share here a salutary tale now which explains why in the last few years I have needed to pursue other sources of income in addition to my comedy.

BBC Radio 4 booked me for a show being hosted by the comedian, Jo Caulfield. It was being recorded in Edinburgh and I was asked to tell two funny stories to a live studio audience. The stories needed to be true and each run to six minutes. So not stand up per se, but funny true life stories delivered by funny people. I submitted transcripts of both stories for approval. I was booked and I was delighted. The producers sent me a train ticket and suggested that I record both stories and they could decide afterwards which one they would use.

The recording went well and because it had been so long since I had appeared on BBC R4, I was thrilled to be included again. However, a month later I got a phone call from my agent. He sounded sheepish explaining that I hadn't made the edit and would not be appearing on the show after all.

Comics instinctively know when a show has gone well and whilst I hadn't 'smashed' the gig to use a previous expression, the recording had gone well and certainly well enough. I recalled that the producer after the show had been delighted.

But no matter because it was explained that BBC senior management had become involved and they were demanding more female and regional male voices on this show. There is nothing I can do about either of these requirements and so I hit the floor in more ways than one.

My lack of confidence is something I can contend with and keep in check. Watching me perform, I don't think anyone would ever suspect the struggle I sometimes have to get on stage. I can continue to write the best comedy I can, but I can do nothing about being in Eddie's words; a middle class, pale male, straight comic of a certain age – characteristics which conspire against me now. The same barrier that Michael McIntyre so easily vaulted but Michael is a rare thing; a once in a generation comic who could not very easily be ignored but there are many excellent comedians who readers of this book will never hear of because they don't meet certain criteria and this is a shame and a waste of their talent and hard work.

This same criterion could not be forced upon other professions. Racism is an issue within football and particularly so on the continent. But only amongst certain moronic fans and not the clubs? Watch any Premiership match and it is noteworthy how many black players there are. An awkward description perhaps, but non-white players are often the majority. And why is this? Because they are the best players of course who are preferred by the manager in his quest to keep his job. It is sometimes lamented the lack of Indian football players in the top flight and whether racism is to blame? I suggest that it is not and that it is simply because there are no Indian players good enough to play top flight football. And if racism is at fault then how is it that there are any number of top flight cricketers of Indian ancestry, many of whom are the best in their positions and why they play for England?

Furthermore, I accept that until say a decade ago, comedy has been the preserve of white men and very often, privileged types from public schools and Oxbridge. But none of these men, or very few, made it in comedy just because they were white and posh. They made it because they happened to be the funniest people of their generation? Just like Victoria Wood made it and became a national treasure. Victoria Wood was brilliantly funny. As funny as any of her male counterparts. A great loss to comedy, I worked with her only once but imagine explaining to Victoria Wood in her heyday that she had been booked because of a new diversity quota? She would have been livid and rightly so. Similarly, Kathleen Madigan who I shared a bill with at the Kilkenny Cat Laughs Comedy Festival and who remains one of the best comedians that I have ever worked with.

Richard Pryor enjoyed an extraordinary life and an incredible career. Richard was not booked because he was black. His colour had nothing to do with his success and everything to do with his talent for making people laugh. Same story for Chris Rock and Eddie Murphy and Kevin Hart. Again, good luck explaining to Chris Rock that he has benefited from affirmative action which he lampoons so effectively in his comedy. He appears on TV and fills arenas because he is bloody funny and people in their droves want to see him work.

Not that performers have to accept such arbitrary laws and here technology can be harnessed and has a role to play. YouTube is the place where creative minds can showcase their output which is otherwise surplus to requirements. As I write, I have just seen an initiative on Facebook by my old mate, professional comedian and circuit stalwart, John Moloney.

John Moloney is a comedian who can rock a room and has done so the world over and for many years. But like many other very able pro comics, John has never managed to appear on *Live at the Apollo*. Ditto, Sean Meo, Mike Gunn, Paul Thorne, Andy Askins, Addy Van De Borgh, Jimmy McGhee, Bob Mills, Mick Ferry, Ben Norris, Otis Cannelloni, Jeff Innocent, Roger Monkhouse, Paul Tonkinson, Tim Clarke, Pierre Hollins... and many others besides.

So, John Moloney in his mischievous way has an idea to create his own TV show to be funded by the contributing comedians themselves. He has it in mind to make the show available to comedians over the age of 50, rather like the senior's tour that they have in golf. I will encourage John to broaden his stable to include any comic of any age (at the time of writing, I am 49). But it is his working title of his show that appeals so much – *DEAD at the APOLLO*. He is being flippant here and will not use this title but I hope he gets this venture away as I imagine would so many TV viewers who used to enjoy *Live at the Apollo* back in the day when it was funny.

Like Father but Not Like Son

Eddie Izzard is a good subject for any case study on confidence. He's one of the world's most successful comedians and happens to be one of the most self-assured people I have ever met. But what feeds what? Eddie's success feeds his belief or his belief feeds his success? And let's not forget his large slice of talent and his unique style and originality.

On tour together, three things occurred which are relevant and worth recounting. It was the autumn of 1993 and my stock was high. My debut Edinburgh had been marvellous darling and touring the UK with the country's hottest comedian was the climactic end to a perfect year.

One of Eddie's great skills as a comedian is to give the impression that he is making everything up as he goes along. It gives the impression that each show is unique, a performance that is not generic, but one that is being crafted for this audience and for them alone. This flatters the audience as much as it impresses them and they laugh even harder. It's a technique used by many comedians, but Eddie was particularly pioneering and he has been much copied since. To be fair, his routines do evolve on stage. His shows are genuinely 'work in progress' but nevertheless, even when a routine becomes set, his style remains that of the free-wheeler, conjuring and spinning comedy gold from apparently nowhere. To support this style, deliberate mistakes are a well-used technique of comedy. They provide an opportunity for some beautifully witty and deliberate ad-libs, which the audience love and most usually applaud. And nothing wrong with it either. If the punters are laughing then keep going. However, such ploys only work if the audience is caught unaware. In Frank Skinner's second book, he talks about an 'ad-lib' that he did each night and was enjoying enormously until it was ruined one night when a group of fans came to see him on consecutive nights. This is precisely what happened to Eddie on 'our' tour one evening. As popular as he is, some fans book to see him on various nights throughout his tour. In the North West, we played the Blackpool Opera House and a group of fifty had seen him the previous night in Manchester. I only discovered this when I was on stage and I was mortified. I was panic stricken that these fifty people wouldn't laugh at my material again or even worse that they might shout out my punch-lines. So, on stage I edited and changed my entire set as best I could. Never mind the other thousand people who hadn't seen me the night before in Manchester. So, I did a less strong set and effectively played to the fifty people who had come along again. During the interval, I explained all of this to Eddie thinking that I was doing him a great favour. In his second half, he had a beautiful piece of material that hinged on his 'deliberate' mistake and I reasoned that he would moderate it accordingly. But he changed nothing. 'If they come again, it's their issue not mine.' And I compared my flat performance to Eddies triumph. Eddie had the other people in mind: dare I say it, the bigger picture. The much bigger picture.

Something else noteworthy is that at every show we did together, during the interval, several his audience would always leave. Eddie was at the height of his powers and yet for some punters, his surreal ramblings left them nonplussed. And again, this never bothered Eddie at all. I would go on to do many one-man shows of my own and people not returning for the second half would never be a good thing. Not Eddie though. He argued that it was a good thing. 'If everyone likes my stuff then I must be bland,' he explained. A brave line and one that works only if more people are staying than leaving.

And then finally something happened that was even more revealing and telling for the two careers ahead. I am somewhat embarrassed to recount it here and a little frustrated also. But it did happen and this is an honest book, so here we go. At least at every other show of Eddie's tour, punters would congratulate me and tell me that they had enjoyed my set more than his. This seemed silly to me at the time and it sounds even more ridiculous now, given that Eddie now plays stadia around the world and I concentrate on rural England. I just never believed such things no matter how often I heard it. And with a nod to the self-help books, I realise now that this mind-set has not helped. I put their comments down to people being kind and polite. I never believed that I was as funny as the comics who play the very biggest rooms and I never believed that I would ever play them on my own. And I was right.

A cliché that is often applied to comedy is that 'it is not what you say but how you say it'. There is a lot of truth to this but it helps immeasurably if what you say is funny as well. Take the following joke as an example, which happens to be one of my all-time favourites:

A little boy in the bath, clutching between his legs. He asks his mum if these are his brains. His mum replies, 'Not yet.'

A beautiful joke in every sense: funny, delicate, subtle, witty, economical, simple, gentle, evocative and much else besides. Say these words in this order and they will get a laugh.

Colin Montgomerie explains that young golfers are fearless and that a pro golfer only has so many five-foot putts in him: a quota of 'knee tremblers' and each one that is holed is one gone and a future one missed. It is interesting that the sign of a golfer on the wane is a faltering putting stroke. The shortest shot in the game, over the shortest distance and the shot that everyone agrees is rooted in confidence.

Occasionally, I am asked if I am jealous of Tom and thankfully only by people who don't know me. In truth, bloody right I am. I would love to be Tom Holland if just for a day but as his dad, seeing all that is going on I am a little numbed by it all. I am incredibly admiring of him though. His achievements and how he conducts himself. He has the same intangible quality that Eddie has. He believes in himself and given his life to date, why wouldn't he? The best way that I can demonstrate this is by recounting a true story from his days playing Billy Elliot.

I have tiresome and strict rituals ahead of a show. All the self-help books that I start and rarely finish call these defensive mechanisms and they all agree that they are unhelpful. Mine include needing to be alone. I like to pace. I stop talking to people. I need water. I need a set list of my material in a pocket and I must know where this is. I keep checking for it, as if on stage in the event of me drying I will just pluck it out of my pocket. *Now where was I?*

One day in 2008, I sat with my family in Pizza Express in Victoria, just along from the Victoria Palace Theatre. We were all there except for Tom because that night my twelve-year-old was working, playing one of his very early performances as Billy. Understandably, I was nervous and more interested in Tom than my pizza (Capriccosa with anchovies if you're interested). I did flirt with the salads in Pizza Express for a short time, but was quickly lured back by the melted cheese. But tonight, I was worried about Tom and hoped that he was all right. Suddenly I felt anxious and cross with myself. What the hell were we thinking, putting our little boy through something as stressful as a West End Show? He doesn't need this kind of pressure. No kid does. The restaurant was busy with diners, many of whom were probably heading to the show themselves to watch my little boy perform for them. He would be backstage now, most likely petrified and blocking out his night ahead. No big deal, Tom; just a three-hour show that completely hinges on your performance. I wanted to call him but I figured that he would be busy, all that training and auditioning about to be distilled into one evening in front of a few thousand people. Blimey! One more beer, please?

There was some commotion towards the front of the restaurant, a bunch of kids being loud and exuberant. Most likely, they were going to the show and were excited at the prospect. But on our way out of the restaurant, I was shocked to see that Tom was among them. He looked relaxed and seemingly without a care in the world. Shouldn't he be pacing right now, or running through lines or steps or at the very least, stretching a hamstring rather than eating a dough ball?

I had a quick word with him to wish him well and it felt strange that it was mostly him doing the assuring. It reminded me of my encounter with Elton John and the similar role reversal all those years ago. 'Dad, I'll be fine, don't worry,' and of course, he was. Funny that, how beliefs can become a reality, something we could all keep in mind as we get older. And the key for me in all of this is twofold. For myself, to rediscover this cherished sense of abandon and apply it to my writing and performing, and as a parent, to maintain my boys' sense of buoyancy that they all enjoy and benefit from now. And if I was running a book on this, I like my odds for achieving the latter, which is a good thing I am pleased to say.

Having People...

You will have noticed already that I am frequently wrong about things. I did not expect Tom to be cast as Billy and I certainly did not expect him to land the part in *The Impossible*. And yet I fully expected my own films to get made, which is now a perfect emblem for this book.

With hindsight, it is easy to mould past events to a current narrative and a suitable one at that, but *Eclipsed* has needed no such adaptations. Too many things have conspired too perfectly already for this story not to complete itself.

Calling time on Tom's days as Billy, I worried how he would adjust back to a more normal and certainly more mundane life. Tom had much to miss. The show itself and the thrill of performing to so many people, but the theatre company also. From the Fifth anniversary show and Tom's last performance as Billy, I am incredibly grateful to the fans of the show that have provided us with many stunning photographs. My memory as it is, it is very stressful watching anything that is as pivotal and important as these events were. This is because as much as enjoying the evening and every moment, I am also worrying about trying to savour it all and not allowing the evening to fade. This happened throughout the making and promoting of The Impossible as well. So, to receive such photos has been unbelievably heartening and kind. They are literally invaluable to my family and we are all very grateful, including Tom.

Playing the title role of Billy, Tom had been the centre of a vast performing company, bonded closely together by something as affirming as putting on a show eight times a week. Being part of any musical is a very collaborative and shared experience that most people will never enjoy. Sure, we might work in teams in our careers. We might be part of a sales team or an accounts team and enjoy an annual shindig at a local hotel with a free bar, but it's hardly the same. This unwieldy company of *Billy Elliot the Musical* extends to hundreds of people, all mutually dependent on each other. My family is comparatively large and we all get on. For most the time, it's a happy home. But, nonetheless, family life was going to be a big comedown after *Billy*.

To this end, my plan was to get Tom an agent. Theatrical agent, talent agent, call them what you will; agents are all the same. They are the oil that lubricates the engine of show business. Like being a film producer, being an agent is not really a profession. There are no exams to pass and no formal training, just common sense and on-the-job, pick-it-up-as-you-go-along. In fact, the role of the agent is largely unnecessary, by which I mean that 'the arts' would happily continue without them. Without agents, people would still write books and films and plays and some would find audiences and others wouldn't. And yet the profession of being agent has emerged nonetheless. Principally they broker deals and they also act as a filter. They qualify material for the studios, the broadcasters and the publishers, and the agent is all powerful and here to stay. So rather than buck the trend and freeze to death in show business, we all have agents: comedians, directors, actors, writers, producers, stuntmen, presenters, editors, footballers, golfers and perhaps, worryingly, even politicians. We are all for sale and so we all have agents. And I reasoned that it made sense for Tom to bag himself an agent so that when he left the show, he would still feel a connection to showbiz.

The producers of *Billy Elliot* were a good place to start my search. I knew the agencies but I didn't know individual agents and which company might suit Tom. Plus, I also hoped that the producers might place a call on Tom's behalf.

The casting director at *Billy* was unequivocal in recommending a very well-known agency called Curtis Brown. Google them and you'll see instantly that they are one of London's big players: a famous literary agency looking after a raft of highly successful authors who dominate the bestseller lists, plus the estates of deceased literary giants as well. As such, being represented by Curtis Brown is a qualification? Some years ago, the company added a talent wing. 'Talent' is the ghastly collective noun used for performers and unsurprisingly, the talent wing of Curtis Brown quickly caught a thermal and now boasts a solid list of 'talent'.

Personally, I am very familiar with the agency because in keeping with this story, Curtis Brown, you may recall were once my agents too, another twist and connection between father and son. They are no longer my agents because rather unusually I decided to dispense with their services. I did this because I knew that one day I would write this book and it might offer a good comic slant for the story if I happened to have left the agents who were now being recommended for my son.

Leaving Curtis Brown ranks as one of my poorest strategic decisions and just to add a little more seasoning to this already bubbling pot, since leaving, I have asked them to re-sign me on two separate occasions: once to the film division and then again to the books department. On both occasions, I received the polite rejection letter: a letter where the key word is always 'but', and is something that most writers learn to accept.

So now I was being asked to consider Curtis Brown to represent Tom and I am pleased to report that my personal circumstances were never a factor in my thinking. It might have been embarrassing and even a little humiliating – *We don't want the old man but the son, we like* – but such is life. Plus, I also factored in that should they reject Tom, then I would be in an excellent position to console him. Like father like son, although not as it turned out.

Nikki wasn't exactly sold on the idea of recruiting an agent. We both wanted Tom home and not stuck in the shop window for more work, but I assured her that this wouldn't happen. It would just be a figurative thing. Tom would have an agent and that would be it. Based on my experience of a big talent agency, we would never hear from them again, the lazy bastards! Maybe once or twice a year and even then, only from an assistant because the agent will be too busy working on their hotter clients.

I have a broad theory about the agent/client relationship and it is simply this: there is no such thing as a good agent, not really; there are just hot clients. I say this somewhat facetiously, enjoying the notion that any agent reading this now is probably foaming with rage.

Not that there isn't plenty of scope for agents to delineate themselves of course. Agents can be intelligent, persuasive, connected, kind, financially astute, editorially sharp, organized, effective, ambitious, determined, committed, proactive and responsive and as such, some agents are much better than others. This goes without saying, but what really gives an agent an edge is having hot clients. And agents cannot make clients hot. If they could, then it would follow that all their clients are hot and this is never the case. An actor clutching an Oscar is bound to be delighted with their agent's attentive nature, but rest assured that the same agent will have clients on their list who are fed up and ready to leave. This is the nature of the game. Hot clients create traction for the agent to attract new 'talent'. Hot clients are in demand and get the attention of the agent. Hot clients can be used as leverage for the agent's lesser known stablemates. Hot clients. It's all about having and keeping hot clients.

We are recommended an agent at Curtis Brown. I am told that she is young, up and coming and hungry, and I sigh a little too knowingly. In show business, being young and new is really where it's at. Being at the point of being discovered is the most exciting time and a key skill is to recognize it and when to strike out for fame. There are exceptions to this – the late bloomers like Ricky Gervais and Julian Fellowes – but these are rare. But the 'young and new' window is small and fleeting, and so the quest for stardom needs to be struck for quickly. Life is too short to hang around. Up and coming will soon plateau and there will always be someone newer and younger behind.

I need to coordinate Tom's diary with the prospective agent, so that she can catch one of Tom's last performances as Billy. We agree a date, a Thursday in May, but as Tom has been injured this will be his first performance for almost two weeks and I am mindful that his stamina might have dropped. The resident director, advises us firmly against allowing a prospective agent to attend, but with shows running out Nikki and I agree and the wheels of his next five years are put in motion. We don't tell Tom, though. Why would we?

The prospective agent is pointed out to me in the stalls, already sitting down in front of us. Long dark hair, she is sitting alone and as Act 1 proceeds, I try to establish whether she is enjoying the show and Tom's performance by her head movements alone. This is not an easy thing to discern, even for someone as acutely 'intuitive' as me, but still I try. I think she's enjoying it though and I tell Nikki as much, but she doesn't bother to respond to her silly husband.

I also wonder if she knows that I have been a Curtis Brown client and in my paranoia, I decide that she does. I imagine that the Curtis Brown agents must have weekly meetings to discuss projects and prospective clients. Then I worry how this might impact on how they will consider my son. Damn it, I might be scuppering Tom's chances while he is still in the blocks. I cast such negative thoughts aside. She is here to assess the talents of the boy on stage and not his dad. And Tom is performing as well as ever and she is bound to like him. Right?

As familiar with the show as I am, my mind continues to wander as I study the back of the young lady's head. Maybe she has no idea that I was with Curtis Brown and then even worse, I wonder if she even knows who I am, that I am Dominic Holland, the comedian. But then, why would she? She looks young. The casting director at Billy said she was young or was it just hungry? Going on the thickness of her hair, I'm going with late twenties and this means she probably wasn't around for Dominic Holland the Golden Year. In ten minutes' time, it will be the interval and I will be meeting with her and then I will have my answers. I will know what she thinks of Tom and whether she knows who I am? Show business types are highly sensitised to such feelings and marginally famous people like myself know instinctively when we are recognised or not.

Curtain down and hastily over to the pub across from the stage door, and Nikki and I are formally introduced to Tom's prospective agent. I am more anxious than Nikki. The meeting is rushed with the second act looming. It's an important meeting but we can't keep two thousand people waiting. She is personable and kind about Tom and within moments, I am back in my seat. The meeting was positive, definitely positive. She likes Tom and this is a good thing. In fact, it's the only thing that matters. But I have no idea whether she knows who I am or that I am an ex-client. But so, what? This is about Tom and not me, but I ask Nikki anyway. Do you think she knew who I was? Nikki doesn't answer and I understand. It's all about the boy now.

The show finishes and out of politeness, we wait to bid her goodnight and we both do that awful phone gesture with our hands. But we hear nothing the next day and then again, nothing the day after. This surprises me and by now Nikki starts to worry. She asks me when they might call. I like being asked, but I don't know the answer. I was with Curtis Brown for years and based on my experience, they might never call at all. I don't say this, though. Then, we get the phone call. The agent is smitten and would like to meet us both. Oh, and Tom of course.

By the time, we finally introduced Tom to his agent we had already agreed that he would sign to the agency: an executive decision as it were. At our very first meeting with her (no Tom), she explained that she would be constantly in touch and I nodded knowingly. Afterwards, I explained to Nikki that this was utter bollocks, just standard new agent/client spiel.

I will end this chapter as it began, by reminding readers that I am frequently wrong and particularly so here. As I say, agents are only in touch with their hot clients and as I was about to discover, Tom was already smoking.

You Have No New Messages

This is a phrase that no one wants to hear – 'You have no new messages' – and it debunks the maxim that 'no news is good news'. Having no new messages, texts, tweets, whatsapps, emails... is always a hollow moment and a reason why I resent the pre-eminence of the smart phone. Of course, they are devilishly useful, but they do drain our hopes just as efficiently as they connect us to the internet and to each other. I lament the passing of the old answerphones, which we all relied upon when we were out and incommunicado. They allowed us to imagine what exciting messages were waiting for us at home.

'Hi, Dom, I'm calling from Warner Brothers in Los Angeles. Somehow a script of yours got into my in-tray and I love it, I really do. If you get a moment when you get this, could you call me on...'

Such a sexy message has never been left for me, but this is to miss the point. It was the anticipation of such a message and the hope that the answerphone provided us with. A hope now denied us by the bloody mobile. No need to hurry home to our potential good news, except for the snail-mail, but when was the last time anyone received any good news from a postman? Watch people on a plane as the seatbelt signs go off. Thumbs pressing the ON button. Finally, on the ground and ironically wishing to re-connect with the cloud, desperate and hopeful for that life-affirming beep or vibrate that says we're needed. A feeling which is heightened for anyone who is self-employed and particularly so in the arts, where 'we' are for sale and so a message from our agent (head of sales) is the best message of all.

Early in my career, during my hot phase, (remember, I thought this was a thing and not a phase) I shared an agent with Rupert Everett no less, a fact I was keen to share with him when we met at some function or other. Rupert didn't seem as happy as me to learn that we were stable mates. He is very tall and could do nothing other than look down on me. Added to this his default superiority, he said that he hoped his agent didn't spend too much time on me and I was genuinely shocked and confused. Was he joking? Or was Rupert Everett genuinely threatened by me? Surely not. It was unlikely that we would ever go up for the same parts. *They've passed on tall and handsome Rupert and gone with short and odd-looking Dominic.* Within six months I didn't survive this agent's frequent client culls and I was cut loose. I presume Rupert was kept on though? And it quickly became apparent to me what type of client Tom was to his new agent. He was much more Rupert than Dominic.

Whatever gigs I am doing during the week I always spend a good deal of my day sitting at my computer on my various projects. Most writers are big on procrastination and are easily distracted. My mobile phone ringing is always my preferred distraction. It could be the call to change everything or more realistically, a call with an offer of a gig. Therefore, the name 'Nikki' appearing on my screen is my least favourite call, because it is never an offer of work or at least not a job that excites me. 'Dom, can you take the chicken out of the oven?'

Now though, mostly when my phone rings, it is to do with Tom. I don't act in any official capacity for Tom. I'm not his manager, at least not on his payroll. I'm just his dad, but his agent can't very well call Tom himself because he is at school attempting to be a 'normal' kid again.

Right from the off, his agent has always been in touch. A lot. Before he even left *Billy*, she flagged up a film project called *The Impossible* and I paid it scant attention. It was a lead role in a Hollywood film. He leaves *Billy* and his next job is a leading role in a Hollywood movie? Yeah, right? So, thanks for phoning but if you'll excuse me, I have a novel to finish because I have a family to provide for.

Then she called again to arrange for Tom to meet the casting director of said film. Really, are we still on this? I looked at the diary and quickly spotted that Tom could not make the meeting because it clashed with a meeting he already had in with Britain's Prime Minister. I'm serious by the way.

Gordon Brown was about to go to the country and one of his advisers obviously saw some capital in a cute photo-shoot with the current Billy Elliot's. A chance then to visit Downing Street or a meeting with a casting director? Naturally, I discuss everything with Nikki and most of the stuff with Tom as well and in this instance, we were all unanimous. Tom should go to Downing Street because there was no way he was getting cast in this film.

Back in my office tinkering on my novel, A Man's Life, a project I have been writing continually for too many years when my mobile rings. No prizes for guessing who it is. This time Tom's agent suggests that because Tom can't make the meeting, he should go on tape (record himself) reading a scene from the script. This would need to be filmed at Curtis Brown's London offices and at a time that suits his schedule and presumably mine as well. I check my diary and it's not looking good. It has more windows than a conservatory, but I don't say this obviously. Acts always like to give off the impression that they are snowed under – *If my mobile phone would ever stop ringing I might be able to finish this novel...* I explain that if I move some stuff around then I might be able to create a small window on Wednesday.

Taking Tom into the offices of Curtis Brown to 'go on tape' is potentially traumatic for me. I had taken Tom to their offices before and without incident, but I had a bad feeling about this impending appointment. And rarely for me, on this occasion, I am right.

Into the lift on the ground floor, Tom and I are accompanied by a lady who is familiar to me, but I am confused because she looks very much like the sales director at the publisher of my two novels. I have a vague notion that she has jumped ships to become a literary agent and this is now confirmed.

My publishing experience was the best and then the most miserable experience of my professional life, with the misery far outlasting the joy. It was a two-novel deal, but before my second novel was published, my publisher decided to release me. This created the perverse situation that my second novel selling well would not suit the managers who had fired me. *And we let him go, why?* So, my second novel, *The Ripple Effect*, was always doomed.

I don't think this was a personal decision, although my hopes for my first novel, *Only in America*, were naïve and would have irked any publisher. More so, the decision would have been based on numbers. Publishing is a brutal business. Units sold are all that matters and their decision would have been based on current and projected sales from the sales director I presume? This is conjecture on my part. The lady in the lift with me that day might have fought to retain me; I just don't know and at the time I never got to ask. But in my head at least, I was in an elevator of all places with the person who had halted my career as a novelist and it made for a strained conversation, especially when I explained why I was visiting her agency today. I had failed in selling my fiction and now here I was, trying to flog my offspring.

We were met in reception and Tom was taken off to do his thing while I waited and flapped. Who was going to be next out of the lift? The journalists from *The Scotsman* and *The Herald* who had ruined my Edinburgh in 1994?

The lift doors opened and sure enough I was faced with my ex-agent. The man I had left. He looked more surprised to see me than I did and fair enough, this was his office after all. Another polite but awkward exchange and I sat down again and wished that Tom would hurry up. He needed to get to a rehearsal for the West End show he was starring in that night. And I had a gig to get to, in a room above a pub.

Around this time, Tom's agent called frequently with other parts also. There was a part in an American film, *Extremely Loud and Incredibly Close*, to be directed by Stephen Daldry and starring Sandra Bullock and Tom Hanks. I chuckled at his potential on-screen parents and Googled the name of the writer, Jonathan Safran Foer, who had written the novel also. Depressingly, he was ten years younger than me. Worse, this was only his second novel and furthermore, his second book being turned into a motion picture. I bought the book and quickly read it, but could hardly advise Tom on its merits because I could barely understand the bloody thing. It was more a stream of consciousness than a narrative and it made me feel even more isolated from the world I was trying to enter.

Tom's agent called again to explain that the casting director had now seen the recording that Tom had made. She liked him but was worried about his 'northern' accent, an affectation developed during his time playing Billy. Despite this, she wanted to meet him and hoped that he wasn't having tea with the Queen. And still I didn't bother to do any research on the film because I just did not consider the possibility that Tom would ever get cast. Luckily, Nikki did, however. She had the sense to look it up and she excitedly shared with me what she had discovered. Such illustrious actors already attached to the film, we both imagined and laughed, much like we had done the first time we had seen Billy Elliot. So, when his agent called to say that Naomi Watts and Ewan McGregor were confirmed as the parents in the film I could play it coolly, as if it was no big deal. I gave a masterly performance of understatement and surely, by now, she must have known that I am in the business myself. At this point in time I could never have imagined what was to come.

Tom duly went along to meet the casting director and he said it went well, with his customary sense of cool and confidence.

'What did you have to do?' I asked and he just shrugged.

'Just read this stuff out and answered some questions.'

'And it went okay?'

'Yeah, it went well.'

Then his agent calls again. Tom has done very well indeed and now the director wants to meet him and I wonder for the first time. Maybe, just maybe...

Seriously, it was that Big...

This is a cliché applied to the fisherman, but it really applies to us all. Who doesn't exaggerate? I certainly do. And wouldn't life be duller if we didn't all embellish just a little? Surely, it is a good thing that the fisherman feels the need to add a few pounds and inches – to, in effect, lie. Only, I don't think that exaggerations are lies. Not really. Not in the bad sense of the word anyway. Not like 'I did not kill that woman, Your Honour' or 'She said yes'. Exaggerations do no harm and they add a little colour to life.

But with Tom being cast in *The Impossible*, I cannot possibly exaggerate just how exciting this whole process has been or the impact it has had on my whole family – mostly on Tom, but on his mum and his brothers as well. And on me of course, with this story I must tell.

Tom had been seen a couple of times already and had met the film's director, J.A. Bayona twice, and each time the feedback had been good. But then we the parents were called in for a meeting in London. Naturally, I could make some space in my diary.

It was now down to just four boys to play Lucas and the producers wanted to meet their parents or guardians to explain how demanding the role was and perhaps to assess how committed the parents might be to their cause.

The meeting took place at Spotlight in Leicester Square and I was accompanied by Tom's agent. It was a warm June afternoon and the reception area was hot and a little tense. Eye contact was mostly avoided as we were all there for the same thing.

Eventually, we were called through and I met Sandra Hermida for the first time, the line producer, and Belen Atienza, producer of *The Impossible*, both of whom would become friends in the years to come. Sandra began by congratulating us all on having such talented children, which was kind of her, but it felt hollow because there was only one part in the film and not four. Three sets of parents were bound to end up disappointed. My son nearly being cast as Lucas in *The Impossible* wouldn't be much consolation. Sandra then moved onto the role of Lucas and the extreme demands it would make on the young actor who was cast. None of the parents flinched. We were all still in. Sandra took us through what we already knew; that filming could take as long as six months and take in locations all over Thailand and Spain. Four nods. That's why we're all here, lady. What else? Any down sides?

Belen chipped in that the boy would need to have the full support of his family and as such, all immediate family would be transported and accommodated with siblings educated and tutored as necessary. Naturally, knowing the business as I do, I would have insisted on all of this anyway! Tom couldn't possibly perform at his best without his brothers with him and naturally his parents also and his mentor and spiritual guide, (me), the potentially world class stand-up comedian...

Then they threw the floor open to us, the parents. Any questions? One mother asked about the finance for the film and if it was robust. She did so with a tired air, as if she had been at this stage many times before with her son only for the movie to fall over. I was confident that I could match her disappointments in film and raise her every time, but I was saying nothing and spending most of my energy trying to look like a supportive parent. If the parents were being assessed then I wanted an A-star.

Belen took this question about finance in her stride and I can now see that she must have enjoyed answering it. After all, it is every film producer's dream to be able to explain that her film was fully financed and furthermore, had already been sold to every territory in the world. And with this answer the bar was raised a little higher. Any more questions? I still had none. What the hell do I know about film-making anyway? Then a gentleman piped up. He was keen to hint that his charge already had much experience of being on a film set, perhaps as a volley over the other parent's bows? Sure, pal, but can he run up a wall and nail a pirouette? He went on to say that he had read the script carefully and noted some inconsistencies. This was music to my ears. I hoped he might offer his services to rewrite it. He didn't, but still I figured that he had to be a question mark at least and so possibly the odds had slightly narrowed in Tom's favour. In fact, I had read the script also and thought that it was decidedly average but I kept this to myself and once again, what do I know about film?

To conclude, Sandra explained that all four (three?) boys would need to be seen for one final audition with J.A. Bayona and then the successful boy would need to spend some time with Ewan McGregor and Naomi Watts for a bonding session. This was an exciting prospect and prompted me to ask my one and only question: where? Where would this meeting take place with these two movie stars? 'New York,' Belen said, as though she'd just said Milton Keynes. New York. The Big Apple. Bloody hell. No pressure, Tom, but you absolutely must get this part. I didn't say this of course. In fact, I didn't even tell him that this meeting had taken place. Why would I? He knew what was at stake. Adding the New York trip would only increase the pressure on him. I would later learn that Tom wasn't under any pressure at all for the final audition because he had already been cast, but not knowing this at the time, I reverted to my factory settings of 'worried'.

I read the script again, looking for some nuance and things that I might be able to pass onto Tom for his final audition. In a scene pre-tsunami, the family spend a day on the beach where an impromptu football match takes place.

EXT. BEACH. DAY
The Belon family are playing football, watched by their mum, Maria, who is reading a book. LUCAS scores a goal, beating his dad in the process, and celebrates by leaping boldly and punching the air...

Immediately, I imagined that his scene might have more impact if Lucas were to celebrate with a somersault and backflip and just by chance, Tom would be able to do this easily. He could even run up a palm tree if they wanted. I wondered whether I should suggest this to Tom, that at his next and final audition he might casually drop into conversation that he could celebrate a goal in true Mario Ballotelli style. But I didn't in the end. He had enough on his mind, plus I thought it would make him appear too needy for the part.

Ahead of the final audition, Tom was asked to have a session with an acting coach at Pineapple Studios in Covent Garden, a place Tom was very familiar with already. I can't recall the man's name, but he was very warm and pantomime camp, which might have thrown Tom had he not spent so much time in musical theatre already. I left them to it and returned at the time I was told. The chap had a very serious look and beckoned me aside. Whatever it was, it had to be important. He went on to tell me a little too loudly that Tom was bloody magnificent. He didn't add 'darling' but he might as well have done and Tom certainly heard. I thanked him genuinely and he wished us good luck. Things looked good then.

'Whatever you did in that session, Tom,' I said, 'do that again for J.A. and we'll get to go to New York for a weekend.'

Nikki took Tom along to the final and all-important audition. It was held at the American Church on Tottenham Court Road and I decided that this was not a good omen. I had been to many auditions at this wretched place and never been cast in so much as a Pop Tarts commercial, let alone a movie. But I reminded myself that this wasn't me being considered; this was Tom and he is different.

On the day, I was watching my twins play a school cricket match and my son Sam was next in to bat. I had been feeding him balls for twenty minutes or so to help get his eye in, but still I worried for him as he trundled out to the middle. Some of the boys had their own cricket kit and naturally, it fitted them. My boys had no kit of their own and used the one-size-fits-all-except-for-the-Holland-brothers school equipment. Sam stumbled and tripped his way to the middle more than marched. 'Choose the right ball,' I called out even though I knew he couldn't hear, not with that massive helmet on. 'Eye on the ball,' I called out pointlessly. The first ball was a wide. The second, Sam blocked. The third, he knocked up beautifully at chest height to mid-off. The shitty kid caught it easily. Out! Bollocks! Who'd be a dad? Another bad omen then as I got ready to console my little boy and wondered if I might be doing the same to his older brother later that evening.

Nikki rang after the audition and I asked how it had gone, more as a reflex than a serious enquiry. Nikki would have mooched about Heals while Tom was being put through his paces. One piece of good news though was that Tom had managed to do a backflip in his audition and without any prompting from me. And assuming he landed it, this couldn't hurt. Apparently, there had been a piano in the rehearsal studio at the American Church and during a break, chatting about *Billy Elliot*, Tom casually climbed onto the piano and somersaulted off it as he had done nightly for the last two years in the show. And I recount this now because there is a rather lovely conclusion to this little tale and the effect that *Billy Elliot* has had on Tom's life. Because during the many rewrites of the script, at some point, the leap in the air by the jubilant Lucas was indeed replaced with a somersault and backflip, which made the edit and are now in the film for all to see: an indelible reminder of what opportunities have arisen from his time in the show.

After this audition, there followed a long wait – longer than I expected and certainly too long for comfort. A week passed and then another. Reluctantly, I concluded that the role had gone elsewhere, although I hoped that I was wrong. I realised that the audition tapes of Tom would need to be seen by the various producers and perhaps even the film's investors. His agent was equally in the dark and waiting as well. Finally, we were assured that a decision would be made by the end of the following week. The Friday in question quickly arrived and by 5.00 p.m., with still no word, I had all but given up hope. Is the close of business 5.00 p.m. or 6.00 p.m.? And isn't it even earlier on a Friday?

I was at my twins' school for their last ever sports day at the primary school Tom had attended. Tom was back to watch his brothers and to catch up with old friends and various teachers as well. Both Sam and Harry were doing the high jump and so they were unlikely to remain in the competition long enough to provide a useful distraction. At nearly 6.00 p.m., both boys had bruised shins and were out, and so it seemed was Tom. Nikki was en route with Paddy and still I hadn't heard anything. Business hours are not 6.30 p.m. So, it was over then and I was explaining as much to another mum and friend. I kept checking my phone to make sure that I had a signal. The area wasn't terribly reliable but the signal was fine, so the darned thing just wasn't ringing. Welcome to my world, Tom. Then it rang. It was Tom's agent, but at this late hour I thought that she was just calling out of courtesy. The best I could hope for was that there had been a delay in the decision and once again, I was wrong.

She got straight to it. Tom had the role and she went on to say something else, but by now I had stopped listening. I just needed to get to Tom. My mum-friend got the news by my body language alone and hugged me quickly and like a mind-reader, pointed to where Tom was larking about with his mates. I got to him as his agent was still chatting away and my face alone was all he needed. He smiled broadly and punched the air: an interesting choice of understatement given that he could have back-flipped about the place.

I apologised to his agent and hung up. I had calls to make, first amongst them to Nikki, mindful that she was driving, but I placed the call anyway. By the time Nikki and Paddy arrived, Tom's entire primary school knew. The whole of the twins' year had been to see him play Billy as had many of the staff, and now they were wishing him well for the adventure he was about to embark on. An extraordinary adventure which none of us realised would turn out quite like it has.

Nikki was ecstatic and desperate to call her folks, but there was no need. I had called them already, my folks as well and pretty much everyone else who mattered. In two minutes, flat I crashed through my entire phonebook to share the exciting news.

Later that month in New York, after I had been thrown out of that meeting, I went for dinner one evening with J.A. Bayona and the star of his forthcoming feature film. In truth, I am sure that he would rather have just taken Tom for a meal, but I was hanging around reception like a lost sheep. At dinner, we talked about the auditioning process and how protracted it had been and then all was revealed. J.A. had first seen Tom on YouTube talking about being Billy Elliot. Watching this video now, it strikes me how young he was, and how fleeting life really is. The video is still available at this link. http://www.youtube.com/watch?v=-omDVx5IEI4

It was at the insistence of the casting director, Shaheen Baig that JA watch this youtube clip for which I have since thanked her.

Shaheen had met Tom in London and was excited to share her find with her ultimate boss, the director of the film. But JA was apparently becoming disconsolate with his search for a boy to play Lucas. He was in Thailand on one of his many reconnaissance visits, scouting locations for his film when Shaheen first brought Tom to his attention. He was busy and distracted but Shaheen was insistent. Finally, he relented and fired up his laptop and watched the clip and he was interested enough to fly to London to meet with this kid.

At this first audition/meeting, J.A. Bayona asked Tom to show emotion at the prospect of losing his mum, something like what he had been doing in Billy for the past two years. Whatever Tom did, it was enough because JA had cast him at this stage as his Lucas. But because the film pivoted on the character of Lucas, other producers and financiers needed to be convinced also and so Tom would be seen a further three times.

Pinch Me

Holidays come in all different shapes and sizes. They vary in length, destination and style: camping, hotel, villa, sports, skiing, sailing, all-inclusive, self-catering. In fact, holidays are impossible to really categorise. Is a gap year a holiday? In fact, the one and only thing that is consistent in all holidays is money. A holiday is the only time in our lives when the money we have is not simply money - because it is 'spending' money. And this little prefix is critical. It changes everything.

As the name implies, spending money is to be spent. Spending money is indulgent. It has been saved, set aside and allocated. It is not like ordinary money that needs to be budgeted and accounted for. It is not needed for the mortgage, the rent, tax or even that dreaded ISA date that comes around too soon each year. *Really, I can't invest ten grand? I'd love to if only I had it!*

And now I need to explain a rather extraordinary financial arrangement in show business called per diems. My school did offer Latin, but only to those in the top set and as such I had never come across the term before. It refers to the money given weekly to an actor and his dependents for subsistence during filming. Per diems are paid in cash and they are tax-free. The literal translation of per diems is per day, but I prefer the more heartfelt and realistic – get in, you little beauty.

This extraordinarily generous provision should not have taken me entirely by surprise when we arrived on the first film location in Alicante, Spain. I say this because I had received such payments in New York only a month earlier, but I hadn't considered that this situation might continue and I'm not sure why. Perhaps I thought that the cash payments in New York had been a mistake and some production assistant had got a good telling off once it was discovered. 'What the fuck? You gave the dad cash? Why? What for? We got his plane ticket, his hotel, his breakfast – he had the warmed granola - and you thought he needed more?'

Having just arrived in Spain, on set for the very first time, Sandra Hermida, the line producer, gestured that she needed to see me alone.

The family could go off to explore one of the world's largest water tanks, but Sandra and I had other matters to attend to.

The largest water tank in Europe. Alicante, Spain

By now, you should know just how much I loved this moment. I didn't know what it was that Sandra wanted, but perhaps they had heard that I was a writer. Maybe they'd read one of my novels or even one of my optioned screenplays and they wanted me to give the dialogue on their script a quick polish.

It was nothing quite as romantic as this, but it turned out to be every bit as sexy. A blasting hot day, it was with some relief to get into the relative cool of the air-conditioned production office, which was just a metal Portakabin. I shut the door and was quickly introduced to various people. Names were exchanged but none of them really stuck, transfixed as I was by the photograph on the wall. The wall was completely covered with A4 copies of head-shots, perhaps as many as fifty. Each one was a portrait of the actor playing a character in the film and the wall ended with Tom, Ewan and then Naomi.

It seems a little strange when I recall this now, but it was at this point when it really struck home to me just what Tom was involved in. I already knew of course. I had signed a contract. I had been to New York for heaven's sake and met his famous screen parents who now hung next to him on the wall. But somehow, seeing the whole cast all hanging together really brought it home to me and I was very excited. Over my career, I have spent many hours in production offices on various TV shows with booking charts on the wall. These charts plot the forthcoming shows and what guests will appear and when. They are strictly delineated in categories, starting with the wish-list bookings, the A-list celebrities who validate each show. These names appear with question marks next to them or TBC (to be confirmed) and once such a star is confirmed, an American movie actor or singer, other bookings become less important. Only, this wasn't a TV production office in Teddington for *Des O'Connor Tonight*. This was a movie set and I abandoned my pseudo cool exterior and whipped out my camera.

And then down to film business with Sandra Hermida. She handed me an envelope as a nearby printer spewed out a sheet of A4. As soon as I held the envelope I knew what it was. The weight, the feel, even the shape of it was unmistakeable. It was cash. The envelope was white but it really should have been brown. For over twenty years, every penny I have ever spent has been money that I have earned from gigs. Some hard fought, others easy, but all gigs completed, invoiced and remitted in full, apart from one in Stockton-on-Tess which at the time of writing, is still outstanding. But now a lady was giving me cash for nothing. This hadn't happened to me since I had got pocket money as a kid and it felt bloody marvellous. This day was rapidly becoming one of the best days of my life and I didn't realise at the time that it would quickly be trumped by days, weeks and years ahead, and all due to the endeavours of my children.

Our day had begun in London. A car was picking up our whole family and taking us to a London airport and – do you know what? – I didn't even know which one. I assumed it was Gatwick because we were heading to Spain, Alicante to be exact, and I figured that the driver would know which airport. The film company had sent through an itinerary with a destination address and appropriate web links, but being a natural born follower, I hadn't bothered to read any of them.

Right enough, it was Gatwick. We all had a good laugh at the *Billy Elliot* posters of Tom adorning the South Terminal and we made the short flight south to Spain.

A display at Gatwick airport

Right again, the film people were waiting for us at the other end with an *A-Team*-style bus parked right outside the terminal as other 'lesser' tourists scrambled onto coaches and probably wondered who this illustrious family was. *The dad is familiar. I think I might have been at school with him. Or maybe I've worked with him...*

It was a beautiful day and spirits were high as we were driven the short distance to our apartments, which the film company had entirely taken over for the forthcoming six weeks. Our apartments were called El Plantio Golf Resort and the clue really is in the name. It was a decent drive and a three iron from the airport and so within moments of landing I was amidst the lush fairways of a golf development. Not for the first time in all of this, I muttered to myself, 'Get in.'

Now though, I was on a movie set and being handed free cash by this special and very, very lovely lady. Spending money had just taken on an entirely different meaning. The film world and my son, I salute you both. And even though per diems became a weekly ritual for the entire six months of filming, unsurprisingly, it wasn't something that I ever got used to or bored of. It was always a thrill, like going to a cash point machine with no PIN number needed or a PIN that I could just make up on the spot – free cash with no consequences. I kept thinking they might come to their senses, but they never did. Really? Again?

The only thing that I can liken per diems to is sick pay, which is not something a comedian ever gets to enjoy. Unless a comic gets himself on stage for his slot, he doesn't get paid. In my entire career, I have only ever missed two gigs through illness. And a comic can't really afford too many bad days at the office either, not if he wants to get booked again that is.

Now, if this chapter so far has been grating then I can only apologise, especially since I haven't even got to the ultimate upside yet. Bad reviews of books are inevitable, particularly on the internet. One irate reader of *Only in America* was so incensed by my book that he wrote in his review that he hurled the novel across his bedroom in disgust. With this in mind, I am conscious of readers using expensive e-readers which will fare less well if hurled into a wall. So, you have been warned because this next section could be excruciating, particularly for parents and if so, then I suggest you take a pause. Put your device down and just walk away. Take some deep breaths, but please do come back when you feel ready because I have much more to share. And some further personal hurt which might compensate for what is about to come?

Okay, here we go. I am not normally a fan of bureaucracy and regulation. Year on year, all governments of whatever hue become bigger and less efficient with more and more red tape to wrap their electorate in. However, I can make certain exceptions to this and I must say that I rapidly warmed to and completely embraced the set of laws that govern show business and the strict regulations that apply to minors in entertainment. These state that any child under a certain age should be provided with a guardian always and where a parent cannot be present, then a professional chaperone must be provided. The key word to consider here is professional. A professional by definition is paid for services rendered. When Tom had been Billy, he was chaperoned everywhere and literally all the time. This has safety implications but also legal ramifications in our litigious age. Any company needs to account for the child in their charge as much to protect itself against any accusations of any impropriety and with *Billy*, this was absolute. During Tom's time in the show, it would not have been possible for either of his parents to act as his chaperone. We have other children and we both have jobs, but on *The Impossible*, since we were going to be there on location with him...

Can you see where this is going now? Need I remind you of the word 'professional'?

What this meant was that, in effect, Nikki was going to be paid to be Tom's mum. This is a job that Nikki had done for ages, his whole life in fact, a job she loves doing and certainly doesn't require paying for. Not that we said this, obviously.

So, there we are. At least I warned you. Free cash and a salary for being his parents – sickening, I know. But I urge you to read on if just for the account of my miserable trip to LA on film 'business' which is worth it alone.

In the Words of Bonnie Tyler

Bonnie Tyler screamed at the world, 'I need a hero,' and I can see her point. Don't we all, Bonnie? We all need a hero on occasion but as well as this, we all need to be a hero ourselves from time to time, which brings me neatly to children and parenthood.

Children lead particularly hero-centric lives. Naturally, this begins with action figures and superheroes. This is the dressing-up phase of a child's life, which naturally gives way to sports, pop and rock star heroes. And as romantic as I am, I like to think that parents should be their kids' heroes as well. Immediately, this puts me on slightly shaky ground, given that my boys are now old enough to have comedy heroes of their own, who are often comics I know and have worked with. But leaving comedy aside, I still strive for hero status within my own four walls.

A few examples of this quest are worth recounting here and one that was so spectacularly punctured. Each morning, I take my youngest son, Paddy, to school, something that I love doing. Being able to walk to school is a privilege, or rather I walked and Patrick rides his scooter. The final stretch to the school is a pretty steep and long hill and mostly I must push Patrick up the hill to deliver him safety to school. And then I would walk home, down the hill with the scooter over my shoulder? No, of course I didn't. What self-respecting dad would ever do such a thing? I bombed down the hill at breakneck speed and I enjoyed the infamy that came with it. Mums looked on disapprovingly. They texted Nikki, who rebuked me for being so cavalier (these were not her exact words). I fell off regularly with various scrapes and bruises. But still I continued, mostly because I am a man and enjoyed it, but also because I knew that Patrick liked the idea of his dad being an Action Man. Worth explaining here that he never actually said this but I imagined that he did. And then one morning in July 2012, I fell off the hurtling scooter and almost snapped my left foot off and it was all my fault.

Two weeks in hospital, two operations and unable to work for three months with zero income is a heavy price to pay for trying to be a hero, but it has provided an unlikely upside. The stand-up routine that this calamity inspired is the opening of my very first recorded DVD and so it might yet pay? We'll see. Available at www.domhollandbooks.com

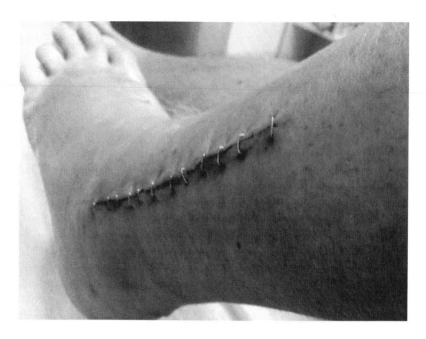

Not my finest hour but it did lead to a good routine

Another area of my quest for hero status in the Holland household is associated with my making my boys a packed lunch each school morning. The system at their school for lunches is a credit system and my boys rapidly depleted their balances on bottles of Oasis and chocolate chip cookies, so we axed it altogether. Step forward an early morning hero, albeit one in pyjamas and without a cape. I give you Sandwich Dad. I took to the role instantly. I think it appealed to my hunter/gatherer instincts, to provide for my little men as they went out to school each morning. As I write this now, I am conscious that taking Paddy to school and now making the sandwiches as well, it might raise the question, and where the hell is the mum? Suffice to say that Nikki is the engine of our family and entirely responsible for the story behind this book, as you already know.

Plus, Sandwich Dad built upon something that I was already doing each morning anyway called 'The Fruit Bowl'. It is really nothing more than fruit juice, and so why the peculiar name, 'The Fruit Bowl'? It stems from how this all began. I used to cut a grapefruit in half, sugar the fruit and break the flesh up into a little bowl of juice. It was the only way I could get my boys to eat them. I called them Fruits Bowls and the name stuck even when I went industrial and bought a machine for juicing all kinds of fruit and vegetables. I've been doing this for years and it inspired a story that became my third novel, *A Man's Life*. A novel that has taken almost a decade to write and finally publish; an unlikely upside to go alongside my boys' good start to the day and regular bowel movements.

And I recall when writing A Man's Life that I could complete my best attempt at becoming a hero-dad. My family was all in Thailand for the making of The Impossible. I was back and forth as and when gigs allowed, but I was home alone in London in the freezing winter of 2010 and I took perverse joy in being able to not heat the house. Nikki is an enormous fan of heat. In her ideal world, a house needs to be heated year-round except for July and August? So, seeing through an entire winter with no heating really appealed to me. I heated my office, where I would spend all day writing my novel, (yet again) but the rest of the house was like an igloo and I walked around clinging on to a hot water bottle. It was madness really but happy madness.

Lying in bed early one morning and most likely shivering when the phone rang. It was way too early for a phone call and despite the cold, I leapt out of bed. I was panicking. No one calls so early. It was 5am and so it had to be Nikki and it had to be bad news.

Knowing me as she does, Nikki allayed my fears as soon as I answered. 'Dom, everything is fine. Nothing to worry about. Don't panic.' The reason for the call was because it was our twins' birthday in a few days' time and wouldn't it be a great idea if I flew out to surprise them? Their birthday is Valentine's Day (another reason then?) plus shooting on the movie was winding down and Saturday night was bound to end up as a party at Memories Bar. So, all told, it was a great idea, but unfortunately out of the question. It was Friday morning and I could cancel some club dates over the weekend, but I was due on stage the following Tuesday for a corporate event in London, which I couldn't afford to cancel. Nikki was disappointed but understanding. She told me to go back to sleep and rang off. Only now I couldn't sleep and I lay there shivering and mulling over scenarios and options. Fly today, arrive when? Time difference? Stay two days? Fly back, go straight to the gig? Are there even flights available? The internet said no, so I phoned Bangkok directly. But such a long flight and for such a short period of time? But the notion of surprising my boys was what clinched it.

When I called Nikki a couple of hours later, she was on the film set of The Impossible in Thailand with the boys and I was in a car on my way to Heathrow. A car, two planes, another car and nearly a day later, I arrived at the Orchid Beach Resort on Saturday without my boys knowing a thing.

Tom was out for the day, scuba diving with members of the crew (as you do) and when he got back to the hotel he jumped on his rip stick, which is a kind of scooter (careful), and he proceeded to explain what he had seen beneath the waves. 'I saw a barracuda and a turtle and a...' Then I stood out from behind a pillar and I think I topped anything that the Indian Ocean had to offer. Thank God then that he hadn't seen a whale shark. A turtle I can handle, but a whale shark is the ocean's largest fish!

Flying back not two days later was a bit grim. I was very tired and over a thousand pounds out of pocket, with The Great Room at The Grosvenor House waiting for me. It is a foreboding room. A room where all comedians have played and all comedians have died. In fact, The Great Room has seen so many comedians perish that they really should erect to a memorial to those who have fallen in the noble pursuit of laughter and cash to provide a crust for their families.

That is a line I have used before. It is from a short story I wrote and published called 'Hobbs's Journey' which was inspired by The Great Room. And The Grosvenor House, is the hotel that is the central backdrop for Milly, my main character in *Only in America*.

And finally, Thailand was the backdrop for another act of my heroism, which went so spectacularly wrong, even more so than breaking my leg. The Thai tranche of filming extended from October 2010 to late February 2011 with a two-week break for Christmas. Most of the crew flew back to Europe, but as stated in chapter fifteen – 'Don't Book it Danno' – the Hollands stayed in Thailand for the holiday of a lifetime. For Christmas itself, I really pushed the boat out and booked three nights at the Holiday Inn on the island of Phi Phi (pronounced Pi Pi). A two-hour transfer by boat and we arrived at our beautiful beach-hugging hotel and immediately I soaked up the rarefied atmosphere.

We were the only English family at the hotel, which was almost completely European, mostly Swedes and Germans, with some Swiss I guess and the odd French, but whatever nationality, the hotel patrons all followed a pattern. The men were mostly tall with business-lunch paunches. Their wives were all skinny and attractive, but a little too over-groomed and their kids were mostly white, blonde, cute and in pairs - a boy and girl. The hotel was stuffed then with very wealthy European families with two kids, plus the Hollands who are not rich. And with four kids, I was very much the silver back of the resort.

What follows is most likely a figment of my imagination, but I need to share it with you all and you can decide for yourselves. As I strutted about the pool with my kids frolicking in and out of the water, I imagined how we, the only English family, must have appeared to the other holidaymakers? The mum is attractive and in good shape for four kids; certainly, more attractive than her odd-looking husband who is obviously loaded, to be able to afford such a destination and with four kids and at high season? However, you and I know that I had only transported my family from Khao Lak and not London as it seemed. I made this booking from my all-expenses-paid, Orchid Beach Resort and I had also inadvertently signed up to the mandatory Christmas Eve banquet. In the excitement of it all, I hadn't given the price of this meal any consideration at all. Now though, sitting in my log cabin at the Holiday Inn, I stared at the invitation to the 'banquet' that had been pushed under our door. Quickly, my mind became more focused. I say 'invitation' but it was in fact more of a reminder to what I had already signed up to. I did the maths again and wondered if I had got the conversion of the currency wrong. But I hadn't. Dinner on Christmas Eve was going to cost six hundred pounds and I panicked. It was a special occasion. I hadn't paid for any flights and I suppose I could get the money from savings. But six hundred quid for some prawns? Nikki agreed that it was too expensive and rather unhelpfully asked why I hadn't spotted this when I booked.

I went to see the manager to ask if there wasn't anything we could do;

you know, come to an arrangement? I was hoping to see him in his office and not by the reception desk as the tall bankers and fund managers of Zurich and Frankfurt could watch me squirm.

The manager wasn't entirely sympathetic. This was the Holiday Inn on Phi Phi at Christmas, where the world's hedge-fund types come to unwind. Such guests do not ask for discounts and the meal was mandatory. I humiliated myself a little more and finally he relented, offering me his 'best price' of four hundred pounds for his magnificent buffet. Whether my claim that my family are all very small had any bearing on his decision (yes, I did say this) I have no idea, but it was something that I would come to regret. This is mainly because my youngest child, Patrick – the child who would go on to break my leg – is a big fan of sushi. And reviewers at the Edinburgh Festival always fixated on calling me middle class. I concede now how right they were and so what?

The buffet was a beautiful representation of all foods Asian, including Japanese of course, and Patrick absolutely gorged himself. All evening he was running to and fro from the buffet with a plate full of sticky rice, while his parents hoped that the hotel manager hadn't noticed. We were supposed to be small people with the appetites of birds. I might have even used this expression. During the day, we had skipped lunch and at the banquet, Patrick was like a gannet, and my other boys were more ostrich than sparrow.

The next morning, complete with my storming headache due to my determination to drink four hundred quid's worth of booze, I was conscious of a fellow diner looking at me curiously. I knew that he was going to engage me in conversation and I prepared myself.

He was German or Swiss and clearly a man of means: a fedora hat, a silk scarf and suede moccasins. No socks of course, and an expensive-looking watch completed his look. He smiled easily as he began to explain that he had delighted in seeing my boys the previous evening. Really, how so? I wondered. 'Yes, especially the little one,' he said. 'He practically ate an entire tuna!' Immediately, I blanched. If this guest had noticed Patrick then the bloke who laid on the spread would have noticed as well and I spent the whole of Christmas Day lying low. My days of flaunting my fictional wealth by the pool were over, but my quest for income via my fiction, non-fiction and stand-up is not – as demonstrated by this rather clawing chapter.

Author Footnote

In this chapter I refer to other novels I have written and I am reminded of how angry I was with myself lying in hospital for two weeks with my broken leg. Lying prostrate I resolved to take advantage of the interminable days ahead by mastering the vagaries of online book selling. My intention being to dominate the Amazon book charts.

Five years on, this remains a pipe dream. Authors are happy to spend hundreds of hours creating their masterpiece but it seems almost no hours trying to sell them. There is something tawdry and unseemly for the 'creative' to be seen selling their wares?

I have learnt a few things however. I understand now that reviews are very important for eBooks and particularly, reviews by key reviewers. One of the exciting things about publishing an eBook is that daily sales can be tracked but sadly for most authors, myself included, this is all too easily done. However, I did enjoy one day, when I got a tiny glimpse in to what it must be like to be Lee Child or JK Rowling?

I used to check my sales data every day, something which I have long stopped doing. One morning, however, by 9am I had already sold ten copies of *Only in America* and from here a steady stream of sales continued. Playing golf with my little brother (another Tom but he isn't that little anymore) I was more excited by my score with Amazon than my score on the course. I ended the day at sales of 150 copies and an income of say $300. Okay, not a King's Ransom but not bad and especially so because all I'd done that day was play golf. And so, wouldn't it be intoxicating to achieve such sales tomorrow and the next day... This would be a royalty income; the Holy Grail of the arts world. Future income for past endeavours. It's what we all strive for.

The sales did not continue and they quickly plummeted back to more normal levels; one or two a day and most often, none. Naturally, I was intrigued by my sales spike and so I did some investigating and it transpired that my novel had been reviewed in America by a heavy hitting on-line reviewer. Amazon replied to my email but despite my polite requests, they would not provide me with either her real name or her email address.

Oh, come on, I pleaded. I only wanted to write to thank her and possibly ask if she might review my other books as well...

But Amazon, the shadowy people in the clouds refused. The bastards refused. Data protection apparently. Bloody lawyers.

Famous People

Famous people are just like the rest of us, only they aren't, not really. To start with, they are famous. This means that wherever they go in the world, the people they encounter know who they are and will have opinions about them, both personally and professionally. We either like them or we don't or we might be ambivalent. This can explain why famous people are often guarded and why they often surround themselves with a closed circle of 'people' that they know and trust.

Equally though, famous people are not treated the same as everyone else. They fly in bigger seats, 'stuff' is organised for them and there is generally a lot more fawning in their lives, whether they ask for it or not. Just recently we have received notification about the Toronto Film Festival where *The Impossible* will be shown to the world for the first time. Tom is needed to be there and so are his parents, thank God. This is less because Tom needs his parents and more because his parents could use a weekend away. Tom is being flown business class, with Nikki and I am slumming it at the back. And fair enough. Tom is working and we are tagging along. For this trip, Tom has been measured by Giorgio Armani who would like to dress him: suit, shirt, socks, underwear and shoes, all emblazoned with the famous eagle. And because Tom is not yet a 'small man', these outfits need to be tailored for him specifically. This is not normal of course and has certainly never happened to me. Incidentally, I will be wearing a suit by St Michael to the world premiere.

Despite my career as an entertainer, leaving aside my hanging out with Janet, Elton and Anne of course, the Hollands are a perfectly normal family. We are completely un-show-business and ahead of Tom making *The Impossible*, the prospect of encountering and working with movie stars was a little daunting.

New York wasn't a great start for me with Naomi. Nervous as I was, my brain imploded and I said something silly about New York. Out for our early morning stroll ahead of Tom's 9.00 a.m. meeting, you may recall that we encountered a lot of men with hoses washing down the sidewalks. I expect that they do this in London as well, but I wouldn't know because I haven't been into town early enough to see it. Anyway, at lunch that day, I found myself sitting opposite Ewan and next to Naomi and they probably aren't aware of it but they are intimidating. What to say to them is the first problem, to not come across as star-struck or even worse, as an idiot. With Naomi, I did the latter.

Firstly, for some God forsaken reason, I had it in my head that Naomi has twins. She doesn't. She has two singletons, but because I thought she had twins, I kept going on about my set of twins and how this connected us. You see, because twins are a bloody nightmare. Even the most robust marriages can be destroyed by one full nappy too far and so parents of twins have a natural empathy with each other and – dare I say it? – a bond. Only, I was getting no empathy from Naomi on the twins front at all. How dispassionate is this woman about having twins? I thought to myself before I got my answer. She doesn't have twins, you idiot. Still I persisted with the twins talk and she must have worried now that I was unhinged. Finally, she said unequivocally that she didn't have twins.

'Really? Oh, my God, sorry, I thought you had twins.'

'No. Why would you think that?' It was a good question and one I couldn't really answer. I don't know; because I'm nervous?

Under pressure now, my small-talk was never going to rescue me as we waited for our starters. I was discussing New York with Naomi and further enlightening her with my scintillating observations.

'So many tall buildings! Have you noticed that?' Who would have thought that I am an observational comedian? That I make my living from noticing the quirky things in life that people say and do? Naomi certainly wasn't laughing. I was boring her rigid and panicking, I decided to plump for a more oblique observation. 'And so, clean,' I said. 'New York is so clean.'

At this, Naomi took a moment, as if to check that she had heard me correctly. She looked at me oddly. 'Clean? You think New York is clean?'

I fumbled a little about men with water hoses early in the morning, but by now the starters arrived and the moment passed. Later that day when the summer temperature was at full tilt, as I wandered around Manhattan, my observation of cleanliness haunted me as clouds of pungent and fermenting decay kept enveloping me wherever I went. As if it was following me about to torment me and remind me of my ridiculous comment. New York is vibrant and exciting but it is hardly clean unless observed by someone arriving from one of the great cities of the third world perhaps? Great, Naomi Watts must think I'm a complete twat. Nice one, Dom.

It wasn't until Spain that I would see Naomi again and to begin with, this was only fleetingly. For the first few weeks, she was rehearsing with Tom in a sound stage at the film studios with J.A. The Holland family was accommodated in the golf complex along with the entire crew, but Naomi and her family were ensconced in a private villa up in the hills, complete with a stretch Audi limo with darkened glass.

For weeks, we waved Tom off each morning and when we did venture onto the film set, Naomi had her own trailer and we never met her. We saw her car but we never saw her, and her mystique grew. But with two very young boys of her own (NOT TWINS!) and the Holland boys kicking around, Tom mentioned one evening after rehearsals that Naomi would like our families to hook up over the weekend. I assured everyone that this was just talk. Naomi was just being polite and I wasn't fooled. Naomi Watts is a movie star and movie stars don't mix. She was travelling with her movie star husband, Liev Schreiber. They would have staff with them: a personal trainer, a battery of nannies and personal assistants and probably a chef as well. This was pure conjecture on my part, but I delivered it with aplomb and total conviction. Nikki seemed convinced, which I appreciated, a bit of marital support and all that. Tom looked less persuaded though. He thought Naomi meant it, but I quickly corrected him. Tom was young and naïve and not wise to the whys and wherefores of life and the show business world. It was a curious conclusion, given that Tom worked very closely with Naomi at this stage and they had already become good friends.

You'll be unsurprised to read that Tom came home on Friday evening with the news that Naomi and her whole family were coming to visit our apartments on Sunday afternoon and they wanted to meet the Holland family. There was no time to dwell on the fact that I spout a load of old nonsense quite a lot of the time. I had much ground to make up then with my own family and with the Watts as well. I needed to prove to Naomi that I am not a moron and Nikki hit the gym, concentrating mainly on her stomach.

Sunday was a boiling hot day and by the time Naomi and her family finally arrived, it is fair to say that the entire complex was on tenterhooks. Even the producers and JA were nervous as Naomi, Liev and her beautiful boys were welcomed into our 'humble communal dwelling'. Undeterred by my earlier wrong call, I had given the boys a crash course in movie star etiquette, concentrating mainly on what not to say or ask. Understandably, the boys were most excited about meeting Liev because he was Victor in one of their favourite films, *Wolverine*. In this film, Liev plays a bad ass who no one messes with and I explained that this was just acting and that he wasn't necessarily a tough guy in real life. Making further assumptions, I decided that he might well be a serious actor, looking for more worthy roles in the future and that he might not appreciate being reminded of *Wolverine*. In fact, the more I thought about this the more I reasoned that I was right. So, I drummed home the mantra to my boys – no one is to mention *Wolverine* – and they all agreed.

Liev is an intimidating man: six foot four, well-muscled, with a voice that could sell coffee. Wearing a vest and shorts, he is immediately at ease as we scuttle about with introductions. Then I spot Paddy and my eyes almost pop out of my head. For those who haven't seen *Wolverine*, all you really need to know is that the characters have normal hands from which enormous curved blades emerge from their knuckles, much like a flick knife. Paddy was obedient in that he wasn't going to mention *Wolverine*, but I hadn't said anything about simulating Wolverine's bladed hands with cocktail sticks. Paddy was well prepared to meet his hero. He had gone around various tables in the restaurant and studiously collected twenty or so little tooth picks and carefully arranged them as spikes in between his clenched fists.

Liev spotted the homage immediately. 'Hey, little buddy, what you got there? Are you Wolverine?' And within moments, Liev was bouncing Paddy on his knee and regaling my three other boys about the film: how it was made, where, and if Liev could beat Spider-Man in a fight? Wrong again, Dad. Our dad's an idiot.

This day in Spain stands out as one of the best and funniest memories in this entire story. Reading about it now I am smiling and certainly pleased that I wrote this book because I would never have been able to remember such stuff and in such detail. And reading this preceding passage now with its reference to Spider-Man took me by surprise and makes me smile even more broadly given what has happened to Tom.

From a worried beginning then, it turns out that Liev and Naomi are not like movie stars at all and this comes as a great relief. After a quick lunch, Liev takes to the pool with all the kids from the apartments in tow for a game of Marco Polo. It's a big pool and there are loads of kids, but for a man with a voice as deep as the diving end, it was no problem and he gave all the parents in the complex an hour off from child care. This guy might just be a real-life superhero. Meanwhile, Nikki and Naomi are chatting and getting on well. My boys are playing with her boys and it seems the months ahead are going to be very convivial indeed.

Per diems or not, I am not a profligate man. I am not mean, but thrift is my default and certainly living within my means. Back in the apartment, noting that the sell-by date on a chicken had elapsed, I sniffed the bird and decided that it passed my test, but that it would certainly need to be cooked and eaten today. Nikki is much more risk-averse than me and would have binned the poultry and so I was careful to dispense with the packaging and made a mental note to give it an extra twenty minutes in the oven. My guilt was heightened because I was heading back to London that night for a week of appearances on *The Wright Stuff*, so the risk was being taken by my family and not me.

There are various things in life that are generally accepted to be very stressful: moving to a new house, public-speaking, divorce, traffic jams and I would add to this list, putting on a dinner party. Cooking for friends comes with different layers of stress, depending on various factors. How well do you know or like your guests? Are they guests who you are trying to impress? Are they very good entertainers themselves, where it all seems so relaxed and causal and from nowhere they rustle up a goat's cheese soufflé? Nikki and I are not great entertainers. People expect me to be funny. Nikki worries about the food and I'd rather take everyone out to dinner and pick up the bill.

I had already left Alicante for London and with Sunday evening fast approaching, Nikki thought about turning in. Our boys needed feeding and so Nikki made her polite excuses and headed to our apartment to see what she could cobble together. She found the roasted chicken on the side covered in foil and probably thought wistfully of her thoughtful husband. She found some pasta and salad and got on with preparing the simple meal. Nikki assumed that the two movie stars and their impossibly attractive boys would be making tracks shortly but out of politeness, she told Tom to ask Naomi if she would like to join the Hollands for dinner. Nikki fully expected them to say no, so it must have come as quite a shock when Tom reappeared in the apartment explaining that they would love to stay.

So, let's quickly run down the checklist of stress then; these are people who Nikki barely knows; they are people she would certainly like to impress; they are rich and as such, they probably have a wonderful home and are great entertainers themselves; oh, and they're movie stars as well, which makes so many firsts for Nikki, and where the hell is Dom when she needs him? On a bloody aeroplane, that's where. A good thing then that Nikki was unaware that the chicken she was about to serve up, according to the shop, was supposed to be eaten days ago.

I met Nikki when I was eighteen and knowing her as well as I do, I know that when Tom reappeared in the apartment with his news, her mind would have imploded. After glugging down a glass of wine, she would have dashed around the apartment, picking up stray garments and wet towels. Suddenly, the jar of mayonnaise was swiped away to be replaced by a saucer of mayo and joined by lemon wedges if we had any, plus olive oil. Whenever in any culinary doubt, always go for olive oil. Olive oil is never wrong. Ever!

And in the end, it all passed off well. Nikki and Naomi had kicked off a relationship where they would become great friends and I was relieved that nobody got ill and I only told Nikki about their dalliance with Mr Salmonella once I knew I was in the clear. This was not a comfortable few days for me.

So, it is true what they say; movie stars are just like the rest of us – normal, like you and me – you just need to get to know them, that's all.

It's Not a Wonderful Life

As I write, Tom has just returned from a ten-day trip to LA, on which Nikki accompanied him. He picked up an award and his American agents, WME, arranged meetings for him during the day. These meetings are with casting directors and producers and are called generals, whereby people just want to meet and get to know Tom, the 'talent'. I have never had a film 'general' in my entire career. Incidentally, for this trip, Tom stayed at The Four Seasons, the hotel where I never met Anne Hathaway.

Los Angeles, California, is the capital of the entertainment world. It is the city where stars are made and dreams come true – occasionally. And like thousands of wannabes the world over, I made my pilgrimage to LA with my film project, *Only in America*. It would have been six years ago now and some years after the rights had reverted to me from BBC Films, who were the first company to buy the film rights to the novel. I had written a new script and attracted a London producer who had in turn put me in touch with an LA producer at Sony and Columbia Pictures. For me, this was all heady stuff. The Faldovian Club days had long passed into the annals of time and I had moved on, west in fact, to Hollywood, where it's at.

My man at Sony already produced a solid roster of films. Not films I had enjoyed, but no matter; he was a player and for the moment, I was on his team. He was a great advocate and we became friendly. Over six months or so, he had helped me to develop a completely new screenplay of *Only in America*. The story being rooted in the LA film world, he was particularly useful, explaining the machinations of Hollywood and writing convincing American characters and dialogue. He was encouraging and kind, but looking back now, I probably forced my trip to LA on him. My fault then? Although, my producer in London was keen that I should go. By now I had written a film adaptation of *The Fruit Bowl*, (A Man's Life) which was also well-received in LA and so I had an agenda and a roster of projects to sell.

Everyone knows that you never go to LA with just one idea or just one script. Everyone knows that you only go to LA armed to the teeth with scripts, plus ideas for ten other movies. Everyone knows that you must be prepared to hear the inevitable, 'No, what else you got?' And when you hear this, you don't fumble around with half-baked stuff. You need to fire back immediately with, 'Fuckin' right I do. How about this motherfucker, and this and this and this?'

I know this now, but sadly I didn't at the time of my ill-fated trip. I quickly found it out for myself, however. My man in LA was going to set up meetings for me. Specific meetings about my current projects and generals also. The goal was to return home with a US agent in place to broker the inevitable interest in my two scripts. Sorry to repeat myself, but I am affectionately naïve and hopelessly deluded.

All debutants arriving in LA are full of hope and fully expect to beat the long odds against them. Unfortunately, my excitement evaporated almost immediately. In every way, my timing for the trip was appalling. Firstly, it was February half-term and Nikki and the boys were driving to France with some friends to go skiing. Tom couldn't go because he was playing Billy and dad couldn't go because he was heading out to LA for film meetings. Only, he wasn't as it transpired.

Paying for the trip myself, everything was done on a budget; so, small plane seat, toilet hotel and the smallest hire car available. I arrived on Sunday, ahead of a national holiday on the Monday, which I had expected to be my first day of meetings of my week-long business trip. I needed to stay a week and include a Saturday night to get an affordable flight, but I figured I would need a week anyway to get through the number of players wanting to meet with me. As such, I was disappointed to lose the Monday and I worried that I might not have enough time in LA to fit everyone in. I needn't have worried.

On Monday, I kicked around the theme park at Paramount Studios and took the studio tour, which was exciting but mostly underwhelming. I hadn't come to LA to see a Hollywood movie theme park. I was in LA to see the real thing. I was in town as a film-maker, not as a film fan. Roll on Tuesday when I could get to work.

On Tuesday morning, I was up early and desperate for the day to begin. With the help of my sat-nav, I drove across the city to the famous Columbia Pictures Studio, absolutely bursting with excitement. The guard checked his list. I was on it and the barrier rose. Of course, I was on the list. I'd come all the way from London.

As usual, I was early and I had time to stroll about the place and soak it all up: a working studio with sound stages all around going about its daily normal business; just like a factory, only this factory turned out movies and not widgets. A steady succession of Limousines cruises through the gates and each drives off purposefully in different directions, no doubt delivering movie stars to different lots. Clooney, perhaps, or Streep? I couldn't tell and I didn't worry because it wouldn't be long before I was meeting such luminaries anyway. It was a warm morning and my miserable Monday was forgotten. The London comedy circuit felt a long way off and I was grateful once again for my cold train trip from Stockton where this journey began some ten years before.

With some minutes to spare, I found my producer's office building. As soon as I entered his office complex, a terrible fear and realisation gripped me. I don't know what I was expecting, probably not the welcome that the prodigal son received, but I was hoping that my man would be pleased to see me. Only, he wasn't and I was a little confused. My name was on the front desk so he knew I was coming. I wasn't that early, a few minutes or so, so why then did he look at me like I was a stranger in his garden?

After a cursory hello, he became increasingly flustered and disappeared back into his office, leaving me in his reception area with his assistant. I had been warned by my producer in London that his assistant was particularly beautiful and that I shouldn't stare. After so many phone calls, I felt I knew her well enough by now to warrant a welcome kiss and embrace and so her cold handshake wasn't much help. She told me to take a seat while she continued to look at her screen. Not even a 'How was your flight'?

Soon enough, I was eventually ushered into his office. I had met him once before in London the previous summer. He is handsome and cool-looking and I like him. But today he looks less cool, more flustered and worried. I didn't ask him what meetings he had set up for me. I daren't because I suspected that there were none and my mind wandered to the snow-capped mountains of France.

The tension didn't ease very much when he explained that he was going to set everything up this morning and that he needed a little more time. So, he suggested that I take the studio tour of the Columbia and Sony lot. It was, apparently, one of LA's most exciting tourist attractions. But I wasn't a tourist. I was in town on business and I didn't mention my previous day on the Paramount Tour.

When I was a kid, I can vividly remember being bog-eyed with excitement when I toured the BBC studios in White City with my school. And later in life, when I worked at BBC Television Centre on various comedy shows, I would frequently encounter similar tours of the building: a place that was no longer exciting to me but had just become a place of work. Similarly, now and particularly in my circumstances, I was never going to enjoy the tour of the Sony lot. We were about twelve in number and I was the only non-American and the only one actively thinking about killing myself. The tour guide wasn't helping my mood either.

He was the gayest man that I had ever encountered, which is a ridiculous thing to say, I know, as pointed out by Michael McIntyre's brilliant routine about the idiocy of varying degrees of gayness. Michael does the routine superbly and I can't do it justice here. YouTube it. It's worth it.

An hour or so in to my excruciating tour, our guide suddenly stops still in his tracks, slaps both his cheeks before jazz-handing them to hold the small of his back and exclaims in true pantomime style, 'Oh my God!'

What? What is it? I thought. What could possibly warrant such a dramatic reaction? Has Spielberg just shown up with a spare five minutes wanting to personally show us around the set of *Indiana Jones*? Or is Harrison Ford about to walk out of a sound stage, complete with whip? Or more likely, was it that he had just remembered leaving his iron on at home?

Luckily, I do not have a jealous nature, which often afflicts comedians and showbiz types more generally. I am not jealous of any comic who is earning more money than our 'world class' football players. If a comic can fill an arena and keep them all entertained, then he or she is worth the dough and good luck to them. However, I am mystified by certain comedy careers, so when our tour guide explained why he was so excited, my spirits plunged to new depths. The building we had all stopped outside was apparently the office of Adam Sandler's production company. Plus, Adam's personal golf buggy was parked outside his building, which meant that Adam was in his office at this very moment. Our guide lowered his voice for extra gravitas. 'So, right now, we are all practically standing next to a real-life movie star. How do you like that?'

I couldn't give a shit. Fuck you, pal. I've toured with Eddie Izzard. Damn it, I've worked with Janet Jackson! Adam who? Do you really think I give a shit if he's in his office dreaming up another crap vehicle to star in?

Sadly, my fellow tour members did not feel the same way as me and it was agreed that we should all linger outside the office for fifteen minutes or so in the hope that Adam might emerge. How far is that bridge in San Francisco? I wondered: the one that people regularly jump off. Adam didn't emerge, which was probably lucky for us both.

Later in the day, I was back where I belonged, in the office of a film producer who was going to help me secure an agent who would in turn get my films made. But his quest for meetings whilst I was waiting to see Adam Sandler had not gone well. Tomorrow was Wednesday and he had nothing for me at all, so he suggested that I take the day off. A day off? From what? I didn't say this, however. That would have been rude. I said nothing and left.

Wednesday arrived and passed too slowly and by Thursday, my man had established something of an itinerary for me. My producer in London was aghast at my lack of meetings and so he hooked me up with an English producer who happened to be visiting LA. Peter was his name. Strictly speaking, he was not a producer. He was a publicist for one of the studios in LA, but had ambitions of becoming a producer. As low as I was, he ticked several my boxes. He was pleasant. He was staying at The Four Seasons Hotel on his studio's tab. He has a nice way with language. He likes to name drop and I am happy to catch them. He mentions some huge movie stars with whom he has flown around the world in the private jets of equally famous producers. Not to mention that he loves my script, *Only in America,* and furthermore, he states unequivocally that it's going to get made. Peter is saying all the right things, including 'Would you like to have lunch with me and two big film hitters here at The Four Seasons?' Anne Hathaway is in the next bar with some friends. You know the rest, right?

Then my man finally came through with a meeting for me with a rather extraordinary chap called Nick. It quickly became obvious that Nick was a mate of my LA man and had taken the meeting as a favour to him. But to be fair to Nick, he had read both of my scripts, which was encouraging until he opened the meeting with, 'So, what else you got?' I floundered a little but years as a stand-up meant that I probably faltered less than the average wannabe writer. He wasn't interested in either of my scripts, which he clearly enjoyed telling me, but he did seem taken with a hastily pitched idea that I had plucked from the recesses of my subconscious mind. I waited while he played the idea in his head for a moment. He liked keeping me waiting, like a Roman Emperor and a decision to make with his thumb. He was enjoying the meeting more than me. I knew that his thumb was going to point down, but it was the manner of how he expressed his decision that surprised me.

'That's a great idea for a movie,' he said. 'I could sell that script like that.' At which point he clicked his fingers for impact. 'But you can't write it. You're not the guy.' And that was it. My meeting was over. Next! Maybe he was being kind by being so honest. In the seven-intervening year's I have not made any progress with this project. But after thanking him and leaving his office, I didn't feel very grateful for his wisdom.

I don't think meetings like this are unusual in the film business. In film, if you're hot, then expect obsequious attention but if you're not, then get the fuck out of my face. And this is not the worst meeting that I would ever have. This honour goes to another American film executive who I would meet in London some years later. Like Batman, he too shall remain nameless and even then, he won't thank me for recounting what he said to me in The Groucho Club.

I have a child with a c***.

These were his exact words and he even repeated himself just to be crystal clear. I was stunned and a little confused. It was said to me during what was supposed to a personal interlude during a meeting that was not going well, again about *Only in America*. I allude to it in a little more detail in the epilogue of this book. Something to look forward to then?

But back then in LA having been bruised by Nick, I got back to my car and plugged in the location of my hotel. It was across town via eight-lane highways with exits on both sides of the carriageway. During my week in LA there were at least a few occasions when I very nearly died navigating the LA highways with exits on the right and left? I managed to stay alive, although as I boarded the plane bound for London, it was such a miserable trip that some of my hope for my film projects had certainly perished. Not that anyone should feel sorry for me though, because I would return to LA again in some years to come, on a BA First Class seat, all expenses paid. I would be met at the airport by a limousine that would ferry me safely for a five-day stay in The Four Seasons Hotel: a trip where I would meet five or six movie stars, have incredibly successful 'generals' and finally end up on a red carpet. So I was destined to make it all along in film as this book bears out.

Author Footnote - October 2016

I have an interesting tale to recount here and to do so, it requires some information that I omitted from the original manuscript of this book. You see, my 'LA man' (you will recall my ill-fated LA trip where I kept ending up on tourist studio tours?) happened to be the brother-in-law of Amy Pascal, who at the time was none other than the studio head of Sony Pictures. I am sure Ms Pascal will understand when I say that she is a heavyweight in the world of film. The sort of executive who can get a movie made – and those of you who have read *Only in America*, or know its storyline, the irony will not be lost on you that I did not seek to exploit my LA man's familial connection.

I am lots of things. Excitable. Delusional. Hopeful. Hard working. Funny? (subjective). Loyal. Sensitive. Determined and as you will know by now and it bears repeating, ever hopeful. But one thing I am not and I have never been is presumptuous or pushy and I can prove this.

My LA man (I don't know why I don't just go ahead and name him now?) and I talked about the issue of getting *Only in America* made and we danced around the reality that he was related to Babs Willenheim, the fictional studio head in my story and screenplay. But he was not keen to involve his sister-in-law and I was fine with that. His reasons were his own and we were getting this movie made anyway and we didn't need Ms Pascal?

Now (2002/3), had anyone told me that in 2016 I would be on a movie set with Amy Pascal for a movie which is set to be one of the biggest film releases of 2017, I would have smiled wryly. I would probably have been a little disappointed by the time it had taken for me to reach such a point, but no matter, because it's a marathon and not a sprint and I had been right all along. I was indeed set to become a movie maker. Back in the day, Nikki had other taller and better looking suitors vying for her attention but like a marathon runner, I had worn her down and she took a punt on the odd looking little guy who could make her laugh. But what a smart move this would turn out to be. Maybe her best move ever?

But of course, in 2016 it is not *Only in America* that Amy Pascal is producing and in keeping with this story, the more astute readers will have already guessed which film it is. It is *Homecoming* of course. The new stand-alone Spider-Man film starring some new over-night success called Tom Holland. A boy who was probably born with a silver spoon in his gob or has famous bloody parents...

On set in Atlanta this summer, it was a peculiar moment indeed to be introduced to Amy Pascal, a lady who I felt that I knew already and of course she didn't have a clue who I was. She gushed about Tom and how lucky they have been to find him and again, I smiled wryly. Ever polite, I thanked her and thought back to my meeting in LA over ten years ago and how her name had been discussed in such hallowed tones. Back in the day, I used to imagine ways of meeting her and people like her and asking them to read my script. And now here I am chatting with her. She even hugged me. And so, I am pleased to report that I didn't mention what I do for a living and certainly not my script or my forays in to film.

One thing against me is that my movie (Only in America) is now out of date. Hinging as it does on a script, an actual printed script, my story has been outdated by the iPad and our digital age. A similar thing happens to stand-up routines. My go-to routine for a few years was my fax machine routine which I did on the Royal Variety Show and is on my website for those who are interested - but imagine the blank faces in an audience if I did such a routine now. What the hell is a fax machine?

But the thing is and this is important; I wouldn't have mentioned my script to Any Pascal even if it was still contemporary and available because I don't ever want to compromise Tom. Writing this book has not been plain sailing. Nikki worried and so did Tom that I was chronicling the Holland family life and/or worse still that I am exploiting my son.

This was never my intention and I hope that it does not read in such a way. With all the arcs and coincidences, I just thought it was a story worth telling without even the Spider-Man climax that has now created such a perfect conclusion. I also hoped that it would make a great memoir of an exciting time and something my boys will enjoy and thank me for later-on in life (assuming they ever bloody well read it that is).

My Dad's Bigger than Your Dad

All little boys boast about and compare the prowess of their dads: how big and strong and powerful they are and ultimately, whose dad can beat up everyone else's dad. It's a sort of pre-programmed default-setting in boys, which hopefully wears out with time. I can remember being terribly proud of my dad when he bought himself a new Fiat 132. It was our first ever new car and I can remember being particularly delighted that it had wider tyres than most other cars of the day. Power steering as well. I was spell-bound by the hiss of the power assistance, not that my dad needed it, as strong as he was? But his new car still came a distant second to a boy called John Old whose old man had a Jaguar XJS and so the hierarchy continued.

And in terms of being cool, I was always going to come a very distant second to Liev Schreiber. As dads go, Liev is a formidable opponent.

Liev and I after 9 holes (which I won, stuffed him, actually)

Perhaps it is just part of the male psyche that dads will always compete amongst one another. Not overtly, like hippos bashing heads together, but still dads do compete in a subtler way – unless a swimming pool is involved, when suddenly it's all out in the open. Trousers down and top off. Let's get it on.

I can't explain it, but there is just something about the combination of water, kids and dads. Even before getting into the water, the competition has already started with physique and strength of the abs to withhold any paunch. Swimming attire can even be scrutinized. How the dad gets into the water is also noteworthy. Does the dad dive straight in for maximum marks or does he use the steps, make high-pitched noises and shout at any kids splashing him for the least marks? But it is in water that the competition really gets going. It begins predictably enough with the dad pretending to be a shark and each dad looking to be the Great White. Broadly, the graduation from shark simulations is as follows: threatening to pull the child's trunks down, pulling the trunks down, gentle dunking, heavy dunking, lifting and throwing the child through the air, dad cupping his hands for the child to use as an impromptu spring board and then finally for the older child, the dad allows himself to be a climbing frame/diving board.

The ultimate acid test I suppose is the dad's swimming race, which is somehow acceptable although I am not sure why. No dad on holiday has ever challenged me to a running race so why swimming? And credit to Liev, he didn't suggest a quick 100-metre breaststroke. My breaststroke is dubious anyway and I couldn't even complete the distance, let alone do so competitively.

I say again, Liev is a formidable opponent: tall, muscle-bound, funny, intelligent, handsome and a movie star. I'm five foot six, on top: thinning, elsewhere: fattening and my well-developed sense of humour counts for little when I'm paddling out on a long board to catch some waves, as occurred when we visited their coastal villa a few weeks later.

My boys were spellbound by the man even more so in my absence when I went returned to London for The Wright Stuff and some gigs. Liev and Naomi have two boys, two and three at the time, with white blonde hair. They had a nanny with them – so I was right – but boys want their dad and Liev cunningly figured that the three unemployed Holland boys might be a good distraction for his boys. With me in London, Liev quickly established a new gang of six with him as the leader, naturally. He had means and a car and together they 'smashed' sports shops and McDonalds and they all had a blast.

Even worse, in my absence, the swimming pool competition was ratcheted up a few more notches. To begin with, my boys standing on Liev's head is always going to be a higher top board than mine. And he pressed home his advantage even more with a new game he invented and which Tom was keen to show me in the pool on my return. I was to duck down onto my haunches under the water and from behind me, Tom would hold my hands and climb onto my shoulders, upon which I would then stand up and emerge with my son aloft. All dads are familiar with this but unfortunately, this was not the end. In terms of summit, we were only halfway there. The next stage was for Tom to transfer his feet from my shoulders onto my upturned hands, whereupon I would extend my arms, locking them straight over my head. In weightlifting, this is known as the clean and jerk, which given my setting is a perfect name for this game too.

Liev could do this over and over, up and down, like repetitions but using Tom as a human dumbbell and I couldn't manage one. The highest I could manage was my ears before my shoulders laid down tools and Tom crashed back into the water, laughing as he went. So, still fun for him I guess?

Tom doing the big brother thing

I had brought several DVDs back from London for the boys to watch, including a movie called *Defiance* starring who else but Liev Schreiber. It was certainly a good choice. It co-stars Jamie Bell, the original Billy Elliot, and none other than Daniel Craig, the actor I have in mind to play the lead in my screenplay, *The Fruit Bowl*. A good chance then for me to see if Craig really is the actor I'm looking for! It also features an actor called George McKay, with whom Tom would go on to make a film called *How I Live Now* and they would become firm friends. It starred the wonderful Saoirse Ronan and this is the three of them in London after filming had finished.

Tom with George and Saoirse

Plus, bringing back Liev's movie demonstrates that I don't feel threatened by him and that deep down; I know that I am still the only true hero to my boys?

This might have been a mistake. My boys promptly announce that *Defiance* is their favourite film ever and that Liev is even cooler than they'd thought. For good measure, Tom adds that he is a brilliant actor. Yeah, sure, but can he write?

Another weekend and Naomi invites the Holland family to her beautiful Spanish villa, overlooking the ocean, for a lazy Sunday afternoon. An infinity pool leaks into the ocean, an enormous open-plan lounge with floor-to-ceiling windows exploits the whole view and my boys' jaws drop. Quickly, I explain that this is not their house. It's just a rental, which backfires spectacularly because my boys suggest that I should rent a similar place.

We potter around the house for a while. Nikki and the boys are already familiar and comfortable in the company of the film stars, but I have been in London and so I have some catching up to do. Naomi has a friend staying with her children, a nice lady called Kate. Kate is six-feet tall, slim with long blonde hair and I casually tell Nikki not to feel intimidated in the way that I feel with Liev.

Making small-talk and trying to appear as if this is a normal Sunday afternoon for the Hollands, it transpires that Kate lives in Notting Hill and for some reason, I lose my mind and announce that I have lots of friends living in Notting Hill. I don't. I don't know anyone who lives in Notting Hill. I just know *of* people who live in Notting Hill. And I know this for two reasons.

Back from my recent trip to London and my stint on *The Wright Stuff* and so Notting Hill and its residents are fresh in my mind. This is because on the way home from the Bayswater studio each morning, my driver gives me an impromptu tour of the Notting Hill's rich and famous. The list includes the humble abodes of Annie Lennox, Simon Cowell, Michael Winner, Richard Branson, Elton John (all more Holland Park) and the houses of Denise O'Donoghue and Jimmy Mulville, the co-founders of Hat Trick Productions, the makers of *Have I Got News for You*. I've done this show a couple of times and used to be the warm-up act for the show, but this was ten years ago and I haven't seen either of them since, so they hardly qualify as mates. Put it this way, we've never been to theirs for dinner or vice versa. And if they are mates then I wonder why they never return any overtures of mine via various agents about reappearing on their bloody show.

I hope that my comment might go unnoticed, but no such luck. Kate's interest is piqued and naturally she wants to know who I know because Notting Hill people all know each other. In my immediate panic, I nearly say Annie bloody Lennox. Kate is waiting now. Who do I know in Notting Hill? I grasp at Henrietta. She owns Princess Productions, the company that makes *The Wright Stuff*. She recently sold her company to Shine, owned by Liz Murdoch, for a few million quid. I don't know how many millions exactly but who cares? In the years that I have done *The Wright Stuff*, I have said hello to her a couple of times, but we have never had a conversation. I don't even know her surname. Henrietta though was enough for identification, even in Notting Hill where you'd think Henriettas are two a penny.

'Oh, Henrietta,' Kate says. 'From Princess? She's a friend of mine. Our kids are at school together.'

I blanche. Of course, I should have known. The Notting Hill set and all that.

'Who else?' Kate asks, which is fair enough because I had said that I know loads of people and so I need to fumble on. Nikki can't look.

'Jimmy Mulville?'

Kate nods. Another friend.

'Do you know Richard?' she asks me and I presume she means Richard Curtis, the man who put Notting Hill on the global map, and I nod. I have met Richard a couple of times but we aren't mates.

'And Tim and Eric?' Kate adds and again, no surnames needed. Bevan and Fellner, respectively: the cofounders and multi-millionaire owners of Working Title Films and *Billy Elliot the Musical*.

No, I've never met either of them, although Working Title have rejected everything I've ever offered them, apart from Tom. They might know of me, I thought. At this point, Kate might have thought me rude because I quickly took myself away before I completely crashed and died in the Notting Hill cul-de-sac I had built for myself. I did, however, hear Kate tell Nikki that she was a film producer and I logged her name as a future contact of mine.

After an hour or so, the whole party leaves the villa for the beach and circumstances are about to conspire against me again. It's a shingle beach but has a bank of sharp shale at the verge of the water, almost like a barrier to keep swimmers from entering. Towels are laid down and wind breaks erected whilst I grapple with the fact that I didn't think to put my trunks on in the villa with all its so-handy toilets. There are no such facilities on the beach and so I am faced with the prospect of changing behind a self-held towel. This is always a nightmare. It is a fact that this manoeuver cannot be done without looking like the very thing that the man is trying to hide – a knob. Humans only have two hands and this is insufficient. Liev is already in his trunks – of course he is – and he crunches barefoot across the shingle and shale with six boys in tow and already the surfing lesson has begun. Meanwhile, I am stood on one foot trying to pull up my trunks. Worse is to come. Much worse.

Suitably attired now and keen to make up for lost ground, I am intending to run towards the sea and what's more, to fling myself into the water. I do not give a shit about how cold it is. But this is not possible and I wonder if I have particularly sensitive feet. I hobble across the pebbles, occasionally hooting in pain but safe in the knowledge that my surfing homeboys can't hear me. They can see me though and suddenly I reach the sharp shingle and it is agony. I practically crash to my knees and I crawl into the sea like a highly vulnerable, newly hatched turtle. I couldn't recall the kids needing to stoop so low and of course, the bare-footed Liev marched across it like it was a meadow of spring grass.

I can't surf either. Have I mentioned that? No need to really. I was born and have lived in London all my life; how would I be able surf? School PE was football or running. There was no surfing at my school. You will also have already guessed correctly that Liev can surf, even though he was born and raised in New York, but this story is called *Eclipsed* and it is perfectly formed. So Liev can surf.

Having dinner later, on the beach, as you do, Kate and I are chatting but now I am better prepared and guarded. I would like to discuss films, but I am too wary. Kate mentions that her husband is also a film producer, but I don't probe and nor do I mention that I am in the film business myself - sort of anyway and she probably knows this anyway. Because my scripts have created waves dude...

Kate is returning to London tomorrow for the unenviable weekend of driving her three children to Wales to visit her sister. She is an actress and is making a film in Cardiff. After my Notting Hill disaster, I studiously don't ask who the sister is. I'm far too cool. Her sister is an actress doing a film; so, what? So is my son. My main concern is that Kate's sister will be an actress that I've never heard of, so it's just best not to ask.

Nikki though, less versed and schooled in the ways of show business and its protocol, stumbles blindly in, asking Kate who her sister is. Doh! Only it turns out that her sister is Minnie Driver. As football fans would say, 'There's only one Minnie Driver.' She was nominated for an Oscar for her role in *Tarzan* and worked opposite my old mucker Eddie Izzard in The Riches; she was nearly Mrs Matt Damon and even nearer almost had Barbara Streisand for a mother-in-law. And as such, this whole day takes on an even more surreal feel for me. This is certainly no ordinary Sunday afternoon for the Holland family – the location, the setting and the company: two movie stars, a glamorous film producer with a famous movie star sister and a young kid on the cusp of possibly becoming a star himself, who, thank God, just happens to be my son.

It was useful that I couldn't afford to have my phone set to roaming; otherwise I might have been tempted to look up Kate's husband and discover that he produced *Casino Royale*. The man produces Bond! Another Daniel Craig connection and I start to fantasize that the whole thing is fate again and meant to be. I make a note of Kate and Andrew Driver as people I should contact later. But only once filming is over so I don't compromise Tom. And why not? I think to myself. My scripts are bloody marvellous and I will be doing them both a favour. Plus, we're friends now, right? Close, personal, show-business friends, much like so many other people I know and love living in and around the Notting Hill area of London.

I Might as well Have Put Oxbridge...

Stereotypes are an important part of everyday parlance. They are a default setting even if they are out of step with modern sensitivities. The liberal elite who terrorize us all - tell us that stereotypes are lazy and even dangerous and are always best avoided. But they are not easy to dispense with because as generalizations go, they are often damn accurate and efficient. And on this I, defer to Malcolm Gladwell again, the esteemed thinker on human behaviour. He explains that humans must generalize to process as much information as our brains are exposed to. And I say all this to forewarn any hyper-sensitized politically correct readers that this chapter is going to use some broad stereotypes.

Having never been to Thailand before, I didn't really know what to expect. The closest I had ever been to Thailand was Hong Kong. I don't know how close this is, but to me it felt close. To start with, it was hot. It involved a long flight. The indigenous people in Hong Kong were Asian and they looked like Thai people, especially around the eyes and in physicality and colouring. I did warn you and please, spare your outrage. It's just the workings of my mind and I am being honest.

But despite having never visited the Kingdom of Thailand before, I did already have a good idea what it might be like based on its reputation alone. Stuff about Thailand just permeates my world. Thai people are small. Bangkok is full of strip clubs and prostitutes. The place is incredibly beautiful and the Thai people are kind. I think it is called the land of smiles. I'm sure I've heard this phrase somewhere and if the people smile a lot, then they are likely to be nice. I went to Bulgaria once and it could never be described as the land of smiles. I also know that Thai food is gorgeous but prohibitively expensive. And finally, and most controversially, I know that Thailand is full of men who look like beautiful women. This is something that I cannot explain, but I know it's a fact. So, Thailand then is a lovely place to visit and the idea that Tom had landed a film being shot in Thailand was good news indeed.

I am not so well-travelled that the prospect of a long-haul flight is a chore. It isn't until I get into the air that I remember just how boring they are. But sitting in the departure lounge, it still feels cool. Throw into the mix that I am bound for Bangkok, or Sin City (see above stereotypes), where I am joining my wife, youngest son and eldest son who is filming a movie and you can get a picture of how excited I am in Heathrow T3. Not even I can imagine how excited my twins, Sam and Harry, must be. Horrid Henry long forgotten.

Being as disorganized as I am, it was lucky that I met Hugh Jocelyn at the airport. Hugh is the father of Samuel Jocelyn, who plays the middle brother in the film and has received excellent notices and well deserved too.

Hugh is a very proper and organized sort of chap and without his knowing it, I quickly installed him as the leader of our party.

It is only relatively recently, in the last ten years or so, that I realized that I am a follower and not a leader. I like to be led. I like to be told what to do and where I am supposed to be. Just tell me a time and a place and I will be there, on time! But there was a time in my life when I genuinely thought that I was a leader. 'Natural leader' was proudly emblazoned on my Curriculum Vitae for years and I genuinely believed it was true. And it wasn't like the other lies on my CV, like tennis, theatre and reading. I believed that I was a leader. A skiing holiday sums up my lack of leadership skills perfectly. Skiing holidays usually involve a group of people and always involve indiscernible white slopes of slightly differing gradients. Add in equipment hire, transport, accommodation and a very real risk of injury and clearly a significant degree of natural leadership is required. This leader takes a piste map and doesn't just stare at it as I do. To me, a piste map is complete and utter nonsense – as confusing to me as the London Underground map is to someone arriving from Mongolia – which is why I don't bother with them, preferring to invest complete confidence in 'our leader' whom I will ski behind and never ski past for the entire week.

And as a committed follower, it follows that I am chronically dis-organized. Gathering the information for my annual tax return every year is always a trauma, even worse than handing over my hard-earned cash. Every year I promise myself that next year will be different, but it never is. My accountant knows this now and starts requesting information earlier and earlier each year.

And so, it was as I headed off for the Asian leg of shooting The Impossible; all I knew, was that it was happening in Thailand and little else. Pathetic really and not something I am very proud of. I did know that the film was being shot in Phuket, a location that required a connecting flight from Bangkok. I have an idea that Phuket is an island, but I am not certain. I figure that when we check in at Heathrow, the clerk will let me know our final destination and also that someone will be at the airport to meet us. Nikki has made it there, so how difficult can it be? Although, she was travelling with Tom and to the film company, he is far more important than the rest of us, even me.

Through immigration and in the lounge, I bump into Hugh and he explains that we are not flying on from Bangkok but staying in the capital for the filming of the aeroplane scene that opens the film. I pretend that I know this already. Hugh produces a copy of an email he received explaining it all, including where he is meeting his family and where he will be staying. I suspect that a similar email is in my inbox and I admonish myself for being such a dick. Luckily, though, we are with Hugh now. Hugh is our leader – the man with the plan and the map – and whatever drag or chairlift he heads for, the Hollands would duly follow.

The Novotel in Bangkok is a rather spectacular hotel: a massive central atrium the size of an aircraft hangar, with bedroom windows exposed and rising before us on all four sides. My twins were exhausted and the hotel was a godsend. It was perfect. Or it would have been if they had a booking for me.

'Sorry, I have nothing for the name of Holland.'

This should have been worrying but somehow it wasn't, not really. Maybe it was the receptionist's smile that comforted me. Not even when Hugh's hotel booking came up did I panic. Or even when another pretty receptionist consulted her screen and agreed that the Holland family was not expected at the Novotel. It all felt quite daring and adventurous, being in Thailand with no information other than Phuket, which by now Hugh had confirmed is an island. It was quite comical. *Hello, I am from London. These are my eleven-year-old twins. I am looking for an island called Phuket.* I even chuckled to myself in the light that I had recently visited Spain and New York in my new professional capacity of being a chaperone.

It transpired that we were booked into the hotel after all, the confusion arising because apparently, my eldest son is already a film star and so the rooms were not booked in our family name!

Later into the filming process, I notice that Naomi and Ewan are often omitted from call sheets with their character names used instead. This is for privacy purposes to avoid press and fans stalking the stars. Likewise, Tom, was booked into the hotel under his character name. A little premature, I thought, but maybe a sign of things to come.

It was very early morning, 6.00 a.m., when we knocked on the door for an exciting family reunion. We quickly caught up with each other's news and then the three travellers hit the sack and promptly fell asleep. I was woken a few hours later to what is every dad's worst nightmare. In front of me was my wife and in front of her was our twins' open suitcase. Sam and Harry both looked innocent enough, like they were way too young to be given the responsibility to pack for a three-month trip. Back in London, both had assured me that they had packed all their shorts and T-shirts because I had done my research and I knew that Thailand is hot. But this now cut little ice with Nikki who had made a small pile of the appropriate clothing that my twins had bothered to pack. There was an obvious lack of shorts. Instantly, I regretted telling Nikki how lucky I was to bump into Hugh and joking about how unprepared I had been.

'Bloody baggage handlers,' I offered, but it was no use. Nikki had married a clown after all. Lucky then that we were in a city famed for its cheap fake T-shirts and everything else besides, plus we get per diems, right?

As a family, we are something of a transport challenge, especially on the rare occasion that we need a taxi. I remember on Tom's last night playing Billy, long after the curtain finally came down, all six of us needed a ride home from Victoria and despite my pleas, no black taxi would agree and I needed to stump up for two taxis home. Ouch! But this is not a problem in Bangkok and even on a tuk-tuk. These vehicles really need to be seen to be believed. Imagine a motorbike pulling a flatbed trailer which has rudimentary seating screwed onto it or possibly even nailed. Oh, and a roof as well. Official seating capacity? As many people who fancy their chances. The lack of regulation and law is as refreshing as it is dangerous.

The driver assured me that he could take all six of us even though there wasn't a seatbelt in sight and there wasn't even a back to the vehicle, so any of my kids could have just fallen out. I insisted on hiring two vehicles to take us all to the MBK, the infamous indoor emporium crammed with fake tat – perfect for us, then.

Another thing that you quickly learn in Thailand is that the tuk-tuk is not like a taxi service in the traditional sense of the word, whereby the taxi takes the passenger to where they want to go. The tuk-tuk driver has a much broader license and often takes the unwitting passenger to where he wishes to take them, namely which ever business pays him the most to do so.

Immediately, my driver explained with the aid of a photograph that he would like to show me somewhere else before we headed for MBK. I tried to protest but he was insistent and produced another laminated printout explaining that he would be awarded a tank of petrol if I bought anything at all from the rival shopping centre that we were now hurtling towards. As excited and happy as I was, I quickly relented. I was in Thailand with my family because my son was making a movie. I could always buy a tub of sun screen or some batteries: something small and inexpensive. He can fill his tank and then we can be on our way to MBK.

I was horrified then when the driver delivered me to a men's tailor shop and before I could even protest, a man was measuring my inside leg. Nikki was sitting in a comfy chair with a can of coke and my boys each had a lollipop. Twenty-nine inches, by the way, which in Thailand is 'long'. Per diems or not, there was no way I was buying a bloody suit and we settled on a black tie, which apparently wasn't enough for my man to get his petrol, so he just drove off and left us.

It might be an economic thing, or possibly political, like in China (which I think and suspect is near to Thailand?), but it seems that Thais do not have many children. This is not based on any study of mine or surveys, just an observation based on my very first day in Bangkok. I say this because the Thai people are completely beguiled by the Holland family, mostly I think because we have four boys. Regularly, women would pat each child on the head as if counting them and then hold up four fingers with their mouths agape. 'Four? You have four?' Yes, I nodded proudly like a great big stag, adding to my already inflated sense of self because in Bangkok, for the first time in my life, I am suddenly borderline tall.

Plus, because one of my twins, Harry, has golden curly hair, he was practically cuddled and passed from stallholder to stallholder.

I have since been told that this attention is partly a sales technique, to make the customer feel happy so that they spend more money and I certainly fell for it. In the MBK, there is no such thing as a price tag. Everything is to be negotiated for and skilful haggling is not in my nature. And we bought more than just T-shirts as well. Birkenstocks, anyone? No, me neither. They are posh sandals and Nikki assured me that they were a steal at eight pounds. Nikki knew all about Birkenstocks and indeed was wearing a real pair herself that she had bought in London for fifty pounds. Suddenly, we were all trying on sandals.

Immediately, Tom and I struggled. I am in between sizes and Tom can't find a pair that is comfortable. Nikki, our sandal expert, explains that Birkenstocks are the most comfortable shoe on the market, so we both persevere. The saving is just too much to forfeit. We can't afford not to find a pair that fits. Finally, I find a pair that is not excruciatingly painful, but I worry how feminine they are. I would describe them as Roman Centurion shoes, but Nikki assures me that they're fine. But they still hurt and so do Tom's. But, at eight pounds, so what? Surely, they'll loosen up. We buy six pairs.

Tom and I decide that we need to start breaking in our shoes immediately, right there in the MBK. Quickly, I start to worry that I have picked a battle that I am going to lose. It sounds ridiculous I know, but now every step for me is almost agony. For Tom, as well. He's in so much pain, he's laughing. In turn, this makes me laugh and the on-looking Thais are now even more perplexed by this strange family from a far-off land. I tell Nikki that I feel like Andy McNab, trekking through Iraq, and she laughs as well.

And then I am suddenly confronted by the other thing that makes Bangkok famous. My youngest son, Patrick, is staring at a very tall, skinny lady who is beaming and posing for him provocatively. 'Dad, what is that?' Patrick asks. This is an indelicate question, which is not easy to answer. His brothers are equally beguiled, but are worldly enough to know the reality. No offense intended, but as pretty as she is and with all the curves in all the right places, this is definitely a man at heart. But how to explain this to a five-year-old?

My situation is made more awkward and comic for the fact that I am wearing feminine sandals myself, which I would have happily swapped for his/her heels. This particular 'lady' is enjoying the attention and when she starts to blow kisses, all of my boy's dissolve into hysterics, which encourages he/r even more. To a kid, this is bound to be funny, but what is interesting is how quickly things become the norm.

The Orchid Beach Resort in Khao Lak would be our home for four months and four of their employees were lady-boys. This label might sound pejorative but it is what they like to be called. Anyway, within weeks, however, they were as normal as everyone else. This is a good thing and is yet another tick in the positive column of Tom landing this role. Becoming more understanding and tolerant of people's differences and proclivities then, to go with learning to surf and dive, not to mention making and getting to see a movie being made.

Not that I didn't make a terrible faux pas, however. The four lady-boys at the Orchid were all lovely, which is a cliché I know, but it happens to be the truth. Perhaps the kindest of them was a lady-boy called Cow. This would not have been his name of course, just how the name was pronounced in English, which was unfortunate given that he was a rotund type and not dissimilar to the shape of a cow. We normally associate Thai lady-boys with ultra-feminine beauty, but what of the boys who don't have the long limbs for this feminine look? Plus, I didn't help matters for Cow either because wanting to appear entirely cool with his choices, I did that over-friendly thing when I first encountered him and I said, 'How are you doing, man?' I couldn't believe I'd said it and instantly I hoped that he didn't have sufficient English to realize.

No such luck. He spoke good English. So, let's recap then; Cow had grown his hair long, shaved his eyebrows, shaved his facial hair with the closest blade currently available, applied make-up, donned a pair of women's shoes and something else? Oh, yes, he had grown himself a pair of breasts and possibly even had his bits removed as well and in my attempt to put him at his ease, I greeted him as 'man'. Comedians are supposed to be quick, articulate and good on their feet, but not all comedians, obviously. Not that Cow seemed to worry and he became a firm favourite of the Holland family during our holiday of a lifetime.

What Price, Memories?

It is difficult to account for all the memories associated with this long story and impossible to put them into any meaningful order. Tom's first night as Billy and the fifth anniversary were certainly special. New York and that first meeting? Taking Tom to see Billy Elliot the Musical on Broadway. The first day of filming? The first screening of the film? None of these events are normal and all of them are difficult to adequately recount, for me at least. But of all the experiences of the last five years, the one that I am most affectionate about is a meal on a Thai beach, which is odd because I was not even there to enjoy it. I should add that it was not a simple meal, far from it. This is the whole point and the extraordinary circumstances of how it all came about. The chef was my mum – Granny Tess to my boys – and the venue was Memories Bar, Khao Lak, Thailand. Where else?

To explain the story adequately and its importance I need to set the scene and its history and introduce my mum in some detail, which will probably embarrass her, but so be it. She will forgive me and it is a story worth telling. Plus, my mum is not a big reader so there is a chance she will never know.

My mum is a formidable woman. From Tipperary in Ireland, she was one of fourteen kids. She came to London and met my dad, qualified as a nurse and has not stopped working since, even when nothing needs doing; she will find some task or other with which to busy herself. There are always windows that need cleaning, a floor that could do with a quick going over or some silver that has seen shinier days. And then there is cooking of course, always cooking. When she visits, she brings homemade bread and when we visit her, we all eat better and more than we do anywhere else. As someone lucky enough to have dined in some top-notch hotels in the world, I can say with some conviction that my mum is indeed a natural and wonderful cook.

You will recall that it was Granny Tess who took Tom to his first *Billy Elliot* audition all those years ago and understandably she wanted to visit Thailand. Thailand is an alluring enough place on its own, never mind the prospect of seeing her first grandson making a movie. My dad couldn't make the long flight, recuperating with his second new hip. Mum was reluctant to leave him and she worried also about such a long journey on her own. It wasn't the flight to Bangkok that worried her. She could read a gate number and get on the correct plane in London, whereupon landing in Bangkok was inevitable, but it was the transfer in Thailand that worried her. And having done it myself, I understood why. Despite my assurances, I could sense her anxiety and so I decided to make a call to Thai Airlines. Nothing new to them, they were familiar with nervous passengers and I didn't bother to explain that this nervous passenger was also fiercely independent as well.

At Heathrow check-in, my mum waited patiently for her boarding card and probably didn't notice the clerk place a phone call. My younger brother, another Tom Holland, and my dad were there to see her off and they were both about to collapse with laughter when a porter arrived with a wheelchair. My mum spent fifty years working in geriatric care and in her retirement, she continues to work as a charitable volunteer. Helping old people is what she does but being helped herself is not, and she was aghast when the man shoved the chair into the back of her legs. She protested of course, but there was little she could do and off she went through to customs as a special passenger.

My mum would have been even more fretful if she knew what awaited her in Thailand, courtesy of her daughter-in-law. Memories Bar on a Saturday had quickly become the place for the entire crew to decamp and relax after a long week of filming. Quite early into filming, one Saturday, as an impromptu thing, Naomi decided that she would bring along a picnic for everyone on the beach that day: some feat, given the numbers (probably twenty or so at least). Naomi prepared food in her beautiful bungalow apartment at the five-star Meridian Hotel. Like I said, Naomi is not like we imagine a movie star to be, delegating chores to her minions. She went to the market herself and bought a load of fruit and other foods, and it was a big success. Cooked meats, fish and even some kind of dessert, the picnic became an instant Saturday tradition and Naomi had set the benchmark high. Because the crew was so international, quickly, different factions started planning for their allotted Saturday. The Italians were quick to pick up the challenge with typical over confidence that comes with all things Italian, but particularly their food. Alessandro Bertolazzi is a hugely admired make-up director and enormous character amongst the crew.

He has worked on movies all over the world and with his team, he assured us that Naomi's standard would be met and surpassed with typical Italian fare: pasta, pizza and for dessert, tiramisu of course. The large Spanish contingent booked in also and then Naomi was happy to take up another weekend, and so it went on, week after week.

The British were probably the second largest contingent after the Spanish and yet it was generally decided that because our cuisine is so hapless, that the Brits would be given a bye. Outrageous, I know and Nikki had other plans. She consulted her diary and worked out when Granny Tess would be arriving and booked a Saturday where everyone on the beach that day would be fed English style. Spain might have won the World Cup and the Italians were, well, just Italians, but Granny Tess was coming and she would whip everyone's ass. Bring it on. Nikki dismissed the disparaging remarks. Her secret weapon was currently being tipped out of a wheelchair at Heathrow onto a plane.

Another thing that characterizes my mum is her competitiveness. It is fierce, but quietly so. Not so you would see it, but it's there. Nikki explained the challenge facing her and Tess protested her disinterest, but instantly rose to the challenge. They said what?

Memories Bar has a separate kitchen hut and by now the self-catering

Saturdays had commandeered this kitchen completely with any lack of food sales more than compensated for by the sale of cold beer and ice teas. Granny Tess looked at the cooking facilities on offer. A few gas stoves, but no oven. And for how many people? Up to 20!

So, what to cook then? And does it have to be English? This is where Tom and his brothers weighed in. From so many meals over the years at my mum's, my boys have a good idea of which meals are their favourites. Tess would have loved the attention and immediately the chosen dish emerged. Chicken Veronique for main course and for pudding, apple crumble and custard, what else? You can see the immediate problems with both dishes. Leaving aside how inappropriate apple crumble and custard is on a Thai Beach and even the fact that there was no oven to roast the chickens or bake the crumble, the real problem was that Chicken Veronique is a French dish and certainly not English. It really needed to be an English dish, but the only possibility was frying and there would be little kudos and no chance of winning with a full English breakfast. Nikki and Tess mulled the conundrum over. Naomi had an oven in her bungalow. And there were no French members of the crew to claim the dish as their own, plus they could always rename it. Chicken Veronica, perhaps?

My mum discovered Chicken Veronique in the Cordon Bleu recipe books, the bastion of French cooking, which she had kept since her nursing days. Very basically, it is chicken roasted in tarragon and served on a bed of julienne potatoes with a white grape sauce poured over the top. It might not sound much but believe me, it's a bit of a show-stopper, delicious to eat and importantly, as impressive to look at. But it is involved and not easy to make. It is time consuming, labour intensive and difficult enough to prepare in a London kitchen and for only six people. Memories Bar, a beach in Thailand for twenty people, is ridiculous.

I hope all readers of this book will want to watch the movie *The Impossible*. If you do, there is scene where Ewan, Naomi and their kids arrive at the Orchid Beach Resort and they walk across the pool terrace to be shown to their fateful accommodation. The scene was rehearsed a few times with Nikki and my mum used as extras to make up background tourists. But, alas, neither my wife nor my mum could be present for when the scene was finally shot because they were both ensconced in Naomi's kitchen preparing the 'best' meal of the entire shoot.

I have already described the long and winding track from the main road to Memories Bar. Roasting six chickens, two enormous crumbles and dozens of potatoes, on the Saturday itself, Nikki had to make the journey back and forth from Memories to Naomi's hotel as many as five times while the sceptical Spaniards and Italians slept off the excesses of their Friday night. Mum and Nikki exhausted themselves but it was worth it.

Mum assumed completed control of the Memories Bar kitchen. Ching and his staff watched with interest and I wonder what bemused them most: the odd meal that was emerging or the lady with the wild red hair who was bossing everyone around? By now the Spanish had arrived, late as was their way, and they were hungry and expectant. The stakes were high. Nikki had told them to expect magic, but no one dared believe it because the English can't cook. And there was a full complement of diners waiting.

Movies are not shot chronologically. They are shot out of sequence to utilize the actors' time and locations most efficiently, which explains why some actors might make the same film without ever meeting. This was the case on *The Impossible*, with only a few occasions when all the key protagonists were in place together. Ewan, for example, was never in Spain where the wave scenes were shot. This Saturday in Thailand though, everyone was present and hungry – Naomi Watts, Liev Schreiber, Ewan McGregor, J.A. Bayona, all the producers, Belen and Sandra, the screenwriter, Sergio, Oscar winners Eugenio Cabarlero and Montse Ribe, plus further crew, families and friends – everyone except me. I was back in London writing my novel, *The Fruit Bowl*, which I was determined to finish

And these unique circumstances – the location, the reason for being there and the illustrious company – all combined to make this a very special meal and it was a raging success. Committed sceptics of English cuisine bowed at the feet of my mum. Chicken Veronica was a complete success. Racist propaganda about our cooking was declared a crime. J.A. Bayona wanted seconds, as did Ewan and Naomi, and there is no quicker way into my mum's affections than asking for more of her food. The crumble was to follow, the knock-out punch for any people still unconvinced. Even the Thais were converted. Granny Tess was a culinary wizard and she swelled with pride as did her grandsons.

In London a few years later, at an early screening of the film, the day that the English kicked the cooking ass of Italy and Spain was brought up by Sergio Sanchez, the writer of the film. Apparently, Tess had promised him the recipe of this great English dish and of course this had never been provided. It is a French dish, but they don't need to know this and the victory remains ours.

The culinary wizards, exhausted but basking in victory

A Regal Holland

August 8th, 2012 was a particularly surreal day in my life and was particularly poignant for this story. Tom finished filming his second feature film, *How I live Now* (*The Impossible* now a distant memory), and Harry, one of my twins, started filming his first feature film, *Caught in Flight*. The film of Princess Diana's life which would eventually be entitled *Diana* and become one of the biggest turkey's in the history of cinema. But no matter, on a single day, No matter, one Holland boy finishes a film, another Holland boy starts a film, whilst I am unable to work because of my badly broken leg, which was caused by another Holland boy. This is a perfect day for my story, but less so for my self-esteem.

Harry being cast in this film is another fluke occurrence and I feel a pressing need to explain how this transpired. In this new film, Harry is playing Prince Harry. His mum, Princess Diana, is being played by Naomi Watts. Harry's middle name is Robert, giving him the initials HRH. He has red wavy hair just like the real life prince and he looks a lot like him as well.

A shoe-in for the role then. At a fitting, Harry was kitted out in the famous Eton uniform, the only way he would get to wear such a thing.

Three years ago, *The Impossible* was just a distant possibility. So, imagine how I would have reacted if now, that the same seer had turned up again, the one who ruined my celebrations after *The Royal Variety Show* with news of village halls. But this time he had good news, that Tom would land the role of Lucas in *The Impossible* and then three years later, Naomi Watts would play the mother of my son Harry in another feature film. I just wouldn't have believed such nonsense. Me play village halls? No chance. Even more fanciful than two of my boys being in movies with Naomi Watts.

Film sets are a strange place to be. Initially, they are always exciting but stressful as well because of unfamiliar faces and protocol. Where to stand? What to say? Can I use my phone? Can I talk to that actor or to that person? Which one is the director? Why does it all take so long? A movie set is a hive of activity, full of people with lots of things to do, fussing about the place urgently. Mostly, important people wear headsets and everyone's default is to look busy and at least as busy as the next person. Parents on the set have absolutely nothing to do. We are present only as a legal requirement. In having and rearing the child who is cast, really, our work is done. With nothing to do, the tedium can be crushing.

On set with Harry in my professional capacity as his chaperone, I am further undermined by my broken leg and my need of a wheelchair.

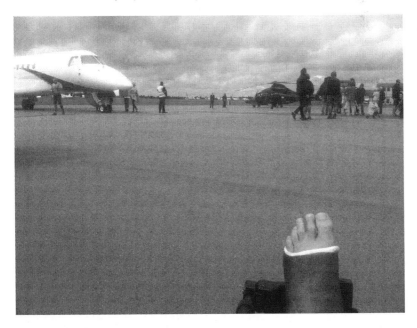

Me on set of Diana

If the hierarchy on a movie is denoted by movement and appearing to be busy, then on this set I am the very lowest of all. Filming on day one (he only has two days scheduled) is at a private airfield in Oxford. The scene is Princess Diana returning to Blighty from somewhere far flung in a private jet with her boys. They alight the jet where a royal helicopter is waiting for the two young princes with a few Jaguar cars, with plenty of police and men in suits with dark glasses and bulging breast pockets. Harry has little to do – nothing almost – just walk from a plane, kiss and hug his mum goodbye and get in the chopper. But as I watch him I still think he does all this with aplomb. Maybe he too could become an actor?

On set, I am aware of the gaze of a certain individual. He looks important and I suspect he is one of the producers. His gaze is not warm, more of a scowl, and he obviously wants to know who I am. It's the wheelchair and the cast. He doesn't know who I am and even though he is some distance away, I can sense what he is saying. 'Just who the hell is that bloke? The bloke on my film set drinking my coffee?' When someone close by explained who I was, I expect he was dismissive. Just a bloody dad.

Naomi was on set and I hadn't yet caught up with her, mindful as I was to keep my distance. But at the first break in filming, she came bounding over and gave me a great big hug. It was great to see her and doubly satisfying because no doubt it freaked out the bloke scowling at me earlier on. '...just who the hell is this dad?' No doubt he would have wanted to know. It's too long a story. Perhaps, I will send him this book.

Harry loved his day. What kid wouldn't? He was picked up in a Limousine Audi. He had his own trailer for the day, complete with a fridge and a telly. At home, we have both electrical appliances but somehow, they are more exciting in a trailer. He also had a polite young man (with a headset) at his beck and call. 'Can I get you anything, Harry?' Out of a private jet and into a helicopter and then Nikki arrived on set with his brothers. Not Tom, though. He was working, remember. Harry was pleased to see his twin, Sam, and little brother, Paddy. He showed them his trailer and they all ate some fruit just for the sake of it. Because it was there. But then reality struck hard when filming was wrapped for the day. Harry had been treated like a prince all day. He had arrived in an Audi and went home in our beaten-up old Fiat. Prince had been dropped. He was just plain Harry again.

Before we fired up the Fiat, Naomi joked that she was now targeting roles for my other boys and given how this story has developed so far, nothing would surprise me. Naomi was joking of course and so was Nikki when she said, 'Never mind the boys; how about getting a role for Dom?' Naomi laughed at this preposterous notion. Perhaps a little too hard. Naomi joked that I couldn't play her son, so I suggested that I could play her love interest and at this Nikki and Naomi both laughed their socks off. And luckily, so did I.

Author Footnote

Reading this book, something else occurs to me very prominently and further explains the 'perfection' of this story. I alluded to it earlier when I mention that such a story would not work as well if it was written by an equally successful dad.

Mick Jagger. Sting. Simon Le Bon. Marco Pierre White. Paul McCartney.

David Beckham. Edward Fox. George Best. Steve Tyler. Goldie Hawn. Don Jonson. Martin Sheen. Clint Eastwood. Francis Coppola...

This list is practically endless and is of course, celebrities and their famous offspring.

As a rule, I find the offspring of famous people almost always grating. Therefore, it suits my sensitivities that I am not a famous person and that Tom won't ever have to battle with the notion that his success is not his own.

That said, given that I am still busy trying to become successful (or famous) it is not lost on me that Tom's 'stardom' might even shine brightly on his old man. And if this does occur, then how will this sit with my views on nepotism?

Bring it on, I say, albeit with my apologies in advance and with a contrite nod to my good bloody fortune.

The Red Carpet

There are not many places on earth where a red carpet is appropriate. On the way into a movie theatre for a premiere or an awards ceremony? The head offices of DHL or Virgin Atlantic? And not anywhere else.

Anyone who is involved with the film business will imagine their personal moment on the red carpet and probably never forget their first experience on it. I certainly have and unsurprisingly, my first experience of the red shag pile came courtesy of Tom. It happened in Toronto at the Toronto International Film Festival in September 2012, where *The Impossible* had its world premiere. Naturally, Tom was needed to attend, and Summit Entertainment, the Hollywood Studio, was kind enough to invite his parents along as well. It was touch and go whether I would be able to make it with my broken leg and the deep vein thrombosis I had developed in my calf. There was some debate amongst my doctors about whether I should fly or not. They explained the risks to me, with death being the worst-case scenario. But ultimately, it was my decision and as such, it was no decision at all. Wild horses could not keep me from getting on that plane, darling. I am one of life's great adventurers. I had broken my leg being a maverick and a risk-taker, a man who laughs at danger, and so it was fitting that my leg and blocked vein should add an element of danger to me completing this story.

Nikki and I parted company with Tom at Heathrow, sat in different compartments of the same plane and met up again in Toronto, and very grateful we were too. We were to be accommodated at The Trump Hotel in Toronto. I had never been to a Trump Hotel before, but knowing the proprietor by reputation, I had an idea that his hotel would be on the opulent side. And not having gigged for twelve weeks after my embarrassing scooter accident, I was short on income and worried that living in Donald's gaff for a week might be something of a stretch. I warned Nikki that we might even need to eat elsewhere, but let's wait and see.

When we checked in at the hotel, the receptionist explained that all charges to our room were being met by the studio except for the spa. I needed to hear this again. 'All charges, really?'

'Yes, sir, that is correct.'

'You mean, all food and drink in this hotel is being picked up?'

'Yes, sir.'

I looked about at the marble palace and still I needed some clarity. 'Even the mini bar and the room service?'

The receptionist was now a little bored with me and checked his screen again. 'Yes, sir! Everything.'

I could barely contain myself. Understandably, Nikki and I were thrilled and funnily enough, almost instantly hungry and thirsty as well. No spa treatments, though? This might be a good thing because I could step in and offer my wife any number of back rubs and massages that she needed. I made this generous offer and added that this was an open offer and available twenty-four hours a day. Nikki laughed. A good sign?

Our luggage had already been whisked away and now the receptionist with our key cards was ready to lead us to our rooms. He needn't have done this and I would have preferred it if he hadn't. I'm not being flash, but I was confident that I could find our bedroom on my own. I've stayed in enough hotels to know that room 729 is going to be on the seventh floor and that room 729 would be situated numerically. He led us to the elevators. He pushed the button and we all waited. I made a mental note of everything so far because presumably he would only show us to our room once, and afterwards we would be on our own. The elevator arrived, he got in first and held his arm over the threshold, the way that people used to do on the London Underground before they fitted doors that can slice through bone. Safely inside, he pushed a button with the number 7 on it. I knew it. From the elevator and in to room 729, he could have shown me the main features of the room – bed, toilet, basin and TV – but he didn't bother, which I appreciated. This is where you empty your bladder? This is where you sleep and bother your wife... For all of his efforts, I wasn't overwhelmed at the prospect of handing him a twenty-dollar bill for his trouble. This was the lowest denomination note I had and even with the news that our sustenance was being picked up, twenty dollars for showing me how to use an elevator and count – come on!

And now I was panicking because our bags had yet to be delivered. I was hoping that the bell boys might have got to our room ahead of us, but why would they do this? This is North America, the land of the tip. This is a five-star hotel in film festival week. Ka-ching! There was a knock at the door and I knew it was the bellboys, whereupon I did something about which I am not proud. I hid. Yes, I'm afraid so. Broken leg and skint as I was, I hid in the toilet to avoid doling out another twenty bucks.

The day of the premiere is fun. First off, Tom is whisked off to a press junket for *Variety Magazine*, who will be interviewing a range of actors from various movies being screened at the festival. The interviews are being held in a downtown department store where at the same venue Elton John is also appearing to launch his new range of candles of all things. I wonder if Tom might be able to catch up with Elton, but unfortunately their schedules clash. 'Another time, darling. Call me.'

J.A. arrives and he and Tom are delighted to see each other. On offer is lots of free stuff for the celebs. Tom's picture is taken and he chooses himself a free New Era hat. (Long since lost.)

My photograph is not taken and even though I am offered a hat, I decline. I am forty-five. I am not a film director or a professional golfer; so strictly speaking, I have no reason to ever wear a hat.

I am worried about meeting Ewan McGregor who is due any moment. I don't really know why; perhaps because I just haven't seen him for two years. He was lovely during filming, but I worry that this might just have been an on-the-set thing. Now he might play the A-list card and pretend he doesn't remember who I am. This is not my real concern. What is troubling me is my blog, *Eclipsed* - the precursor to this book. Let's be clear, writing a blog is not terribly cool. Too often, people write blogs when they can't get a more legitimate and official outlet for their work. People write columns in newspapers. People without columns write blogs. I tried to secure a column for this story with all the major newspapers it ended up as a blog. Add into the mix the personal nature of my blog and I feel even more vulnerable and compromised. Before I began writing, I sought the permission of the film's production company, Naomi and Ewan. They all agreed but I wonder what they all think about it and again I worry. Because they must read it, surely?

Then Ewan arrives. He looks groomed. The sonofabitch gets more handsome every time I see him. Tom jumps at him and they embrace. I hover. Julian Clary and Vic Reeves are on my mind; they have both done the 'do I know you', underling thing to me, but not Ewan McGregor. He has way too much class and self-assurance. He spots me, smiles broadly and gives Nikki and me a communal hug. He even remembers my name. The guy is a blinking star.

Then Johnny Depp arrives and a flutter of excitement spreads through the room. I am excited too, but I manage to conceal it. I'm in the film business myself you know? Plus, Johnny is just a regular Joe, right?

Just a bloke like you and I, and a bloody scruffy one at that. Furthermore, I have yet to forgive him for *Charlie and the Chocolate Factory*, which ranks as a crime against Roald Dahl and cinema more generally. He looks over in my direction and smiles at me and all is forgiven. It was Tim Burton's fault, obviously. I am in the same room as Johnny 'cheekbones' Depp, so he too can be added to my list of colleagues, above even, Anne?

At a party in the afternoon, we arrive with Tom, but immediately he is wrestled away from us by a man who we later discover is a Hollywood 'manager'. He 'manages' many clients, including some of the biggest stars in the world. He explains to Nikki that he would like to manage Tom. This is a little awkward for Nikki because she knows that there is currently no vacancy. Tom's dad is scratching around for a career at present and even though I have yet to formally apply for the role, I am confident of landing the job. Like I said earlier in this book, nepotism is only irksome until it conspires for you.

Tom is taken around the room from player to player, some I recognize – Helen Hunt, Ben Affleck and Woody Harrelson – and others I don't, mainly actors from Glee. Nikki and I sit aside and look on. Naturally, I would like to join Tom on these informal meetings, but I know not to. With a blog as huge as mine, the stars are likely to clam up anyway.

Later that evening, we are all set for the premiere. In Tom's itinerary, his 'people' have allowed a full forty-five minutes for his make-up and a further forty-five minutes for him to get dressed. This is a little excessive. He is sixteen years old. He has a made-to-measure suit from Giorgio Armani, complete with GA shirt and shoes. His make-up for post-tsunami scenes in the movie didn't take forty-five minutes and so with so much time to spare, he joined me in helping to zip up Nikki's dress, which must have shrunk on the plane? It turns out that there is a hidden cost to free food at The Trump Hotel after all.

Whilst Mrs Holland bought a brand-new outfit for this evening, I have given scant regard to what I am going to wear. I have brought with me a suit from Marks and Spencer with a shirt by whoever and no tie. And yet I am confident that my look will be completely unique on the red carpet because I am splitting my footwear between a formal shoe and an orthopaedic air boot. My look is completed by two crutches but in a moment of inspiration, I decide to drop a crutch and just go with the one – more casual.

We ride to the theatre in an enormous Audi. I don't know which model, but Audi 'Fuck You' seems about right. On the way to the Prince of Wales theatre, I can sense that Tom is nervous. Who wouldn't be? It has been organized that Ewan and Naomi will arrive at the theatre after Tom because, whatever crowds and press have gathered, it is Naomi and Ewan they are waiting to see. In fact, I wonder if anyone will even know who Tom is. No one will have seen the film at this stage, so he will just look like a spoilt, well-dressed kid getting out of a flash car – the kid of a producer perhaps or even a famous UK comic? Tom asks me what we can expect and for once in my showbiz life, I am honest. Sorry, Tom, no idea mate, this is a first for me as well.

Clayton, our ultra-polite limo driver, tells us that we are one minute away. I look ahead and there are indeed crowds: big crowds and all cordoned off behind ropes. The car stops and we get ready to exit. It is busy and congested and it appears that my decision to drop a crutch is an inspired one and is more than just a fashion statement. Tom gets out first and instantly people cheer. He smiles and instinctively waves and then people start calling out his name.

Tom at Toronto Film Festival

At first I am bemused. How the hell do they know who he is? And then it dawns on me. It's my blog of course. It's massive you know...

These two photos from the premiere in Toronto are particularly appropriate for this story and I considered them both as potential book covers. I like both images of Tom but I like the photographs more so because of how I feature in them.

An unflattering photo of me – but I'm okay with it

From here, Tom proceeds down and along the red carpet, speaking to anyone with a microphone. He seems to be very at ease and in control. He smiles easily and takes it all in. People remark to me that he's a natural and I smile inwardly. Chip off the old block eh?

Tom takes to the stage with Ewan, Naomi and JA to introduce the film.

On stage interviews at the world premiere, Toronto

The first time I have seen Tom on stage since Billy which is surreal enough and then the movie plays and I watch it for the third time, and the first time on a very big screen. The venue is a beautiful Victorian theatre much like the Victoria Palace where I have seen Tom perform many times and yet this experience is even more overwhelming. I enjoy the film much more than I did when I first saw it in London. Then I was too nervous to really take it in. But now in Toronto, with such a massive audience and knowing what to expect, I can relax and fully enjoy it. I sit next to Tom and throughout the film, I grab at his knee and squeeze. It is a squeeze that he understands completely, telling him how proud I am without having to say anything.

But this screening felt special for another couple of reasons. Firstly, the whole occasion of this being a world premiere. This film had become a massive part of our family life for over two years. We had seen it being made in Thailand and Spain, and had forged some great friendships along the way. The whole film-making experience had been a privilege for us, and now there we were in Toronto enjoying the limelight and the film itself. It had been a holiday of a lifetime and now a holiday 'video' to trump all others. *The Impossible* – the project that just keeps on giving.

The other reason why this screening was special was because the

Belon family was present also. The film is based on their remarkable story and despite some occasional notices that are flat wrong, the film is an accurate depiction of what happened to them on that fateful day. The family was present for much of the filming and was crucial to the film's authenticity.

And on this, just a quick riposte to some of the film's detractors; regarding the absence of Thai people in the film and the over-dramatization of Maria's injuries. All the characters in the film are based on real encounters. They are not fictional. Maria and Lucas did rescue a small blonde Swedish boy called Daniel who they hope to meet again once the film is released. Lucas did repatriate a Swedish father called Benstrom with his son in hospital. Henry was helped to look for his children by a German tourist with an injured leg. Khao Lak is a holiday destination and the indiscriminate tsunami brushed and mixed up all before it. Some survived, many did not, but who the Belon family encountered was not an editorial decision by the film-makers. As for Maria's injuries, she is a remarkable lady. Some reviewers have noted the 'fuss and tears' that her character sheds in the film, which is a particularly asinine observation. The last scene of the movie is Maria and her family on board a hospital plane from Thailand, bound for Singapore. This is the point where their story and the film end, but the nightmare for Maria and her family has a long way to run. In Singapore, Maria spent four months in hospital. She had some eighteen operations and was read the last rights on two occasions. The carnage and injury associated with a tsunami are obvious, but less apparent is the silent killer of infection that engulfs people and wreaks havoc after the waters have receded. The ground is pulverized by the water and what is churned up and ingested by people poisons them. Maria was heavily infected and medics worked frantically to save her life as her family looked on. Different cocktails of drugs were used on survivors all over the world as holiday-makers were repatriated home. And when a cure was found for the strain of infection pertinent to Thailand, the information was shared by medics worldwide and who knows how many other lives were saved as result.

In Toronto, at the end of the screening, a spotlight was shone onto the Belon family and they were embraced by the actors and the crew who had brought their story to the screen: a remarkable family both off and on screen represented brilliantly by J.A Bayona and his team who had been working on this project for more than five years. In the theatre that night, the whole auditorium stood up and cheered when the spotlight picked out the real family.

I suspect that the general audience did not realize who exactly it was they were cheering. No announcement was made, so they wouldn't have known that it was the real family, but nonetheless the audience understood that a special moment was taking place in the stalls. I whipped out my camera and began an impromptu recording, not sure if I would get anything. I just pointed and hoped and I can remember being frustrated that I could not see Tom in the melee. And then, as if J.A. could hear me, he shot off in search of something and quickly re-emerged from the crowd with Tom. He held his hand aloft and the whole theatre cheered their appreciation. It was an extraordinary moment for Nikki and I, and I imagine for Tom as well.

Tom loves J.A. Bayona and they have become truly great friends.

This picture was taken by Nikki on set and captures the bond between the two of them. Tom had never been on a film set before and this was only JA Bayona's second feature film and his first in English. They needed to trust each other and this image represents this perfectly. JA Bayona has had an extraordinary impact on Tom.

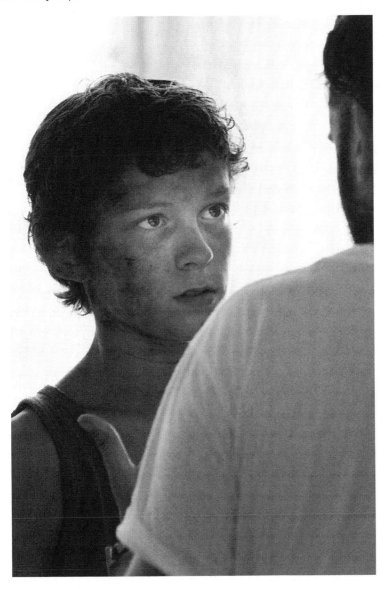

My favourite picture. Tom with JA, taken by his mum

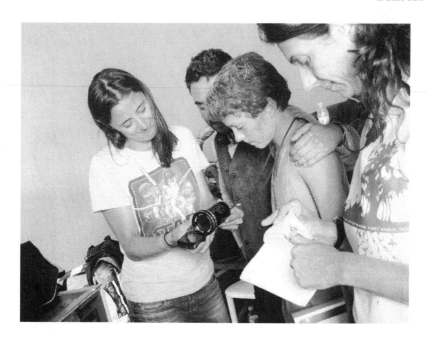

The final shooting day on The Impossible

This shot was taken on the final day's shooting in Madrid, when Tom was presented by JA with the lens he had used to shoot The Orphanage.

Many people have such an influence on Tom's career and life. Stephen Daldry with his eerie eye, Ben Perkins, Nick Evans and Juan Antonio Bayona of course. JA.'s impact on Tom is really immeasurable. With the notices and accolades that Tom is now receiving, it is fair to say that JA has changed his life.

Receiving a Hollywood Spotlight Award, Tom said the following: 'I would like to thank Juan Antonio Bayona, my director and my friend...' and this sums it all up really.

Ewan and Naomi also were the perfect screen parents that Tom could ever have wished for. They are both parents themselves and have been so kind to Tom and indeed to my whole family. A good thing for boys to have male role models growing up and Tom couldn't do much better than Ewan McGregor.

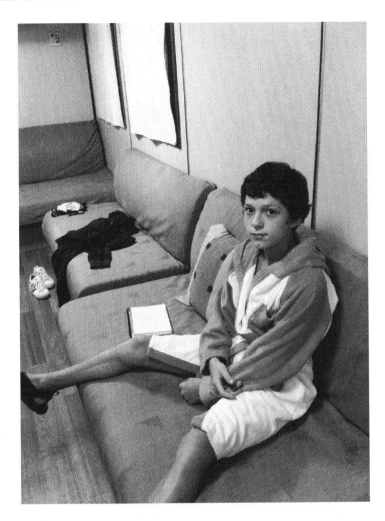

The very first day of who knows what?

This shot was taken in Tom's trailer on the very first day of shooting on location in Thailand. It is about 5am. What strikes me is how young and vulnerable he looks. And now with the benefit of hindsight and knowing what lies ahead for him, I like this photo even more.

As Tom's dad, I feel very blessed that the film was so long in post-production.

Such a long post-production has allowed Tom to have two years away from any of the attention he is experiencing now. He's done a lot of growing in this time and is much better able to cope with whoever and whatever he encounters.

The after-show party took place in the Toronto Soho House, part of the London chain of private clubs where I have sat many times for meetings about very little.

The party was busy and loud, and conversations needed to be snatched. And with my sore leg (Patrick's fault), I spied a quiet table and sat down alone, happy to reflect on the evening's events and to observe the goings on around me. Nikki joined me and quickly Ewan ambled over with his agent, publicist and his lawyer. It all seemed comic to me. To be in this strange city, in a private club, having just sat through my son's film and now chilling with a movie star and his 'people'.

The whole experience had been thrilling and could not be topped seeing Lake Erie emptying itself into Lake Ontario – better known as Niagara Falls – which we visited just ahead of flying home.

The Blinding and Very Happy Eclipse

I am delighted to be finally eclipsed and I hope that feeling has come over in the preceding pages.

I always envisaged and hoped that this story should end in Hollywood at the premiere of *The Impossible*. But this was becoming unlikely because at first, the US premiere was going to be in New York, then the Toronto Film Festival was going to suffice, but then finally an LA premiere was inked in, as I hoped it always would be. A Hollywood premiere was always going to happen if just for me to complete this book. Just as night follows day, the red carpet in tinsel town was going to get rolled out for me and my story. Because this is *Eclipsed* and it is fated.

The date was confirmed as December 10th, 2012 and I was excited to be accompanying Tom. This would-be Tom's third trip to the West Coast in little over a month and my first trip since my ill-fated visit some seven years earlier. Let's call it the Anne Hathaway or Adam Sandler trip; take your pick. This trip, though, would be entirely different. My first LA trip, I went as a substitute with little chance of any game-time, but now I am travelling with the captain to a Hollywood premiere and the end of *Eclipsed*, a blog I had started nearly two years earlier and a book I have spent more time writing than I care to admit.

Flying first class is one of the great barometers of success, the preserve of the rich and the famous. Never mind the decent meal that is provided. Most of us can afford some nice nosh from time to time, but a seat on a plane that turns into a bed is a luxury beyond almost all of us. In effect, a first-class airline ticket is the most expensive bed on earth or more accurately, just off it.

As well as comfort, it strikes me that a large part of the first-class 'offer' is keeping its patrons away from the normal people who are also flying about the globe. Same terminal, but different check-ins and airport lounges and on board, a separate cabin of course with that all-important curtain that is snapped shut.

Tom is at an advantage having done all of this twice already, and I am quick on the uptake plus I know the general form anyway. One of the cardinal rules is not to stare at any famous people who might be sharing the first-class airport lounge with you. Staring is what the people in the main airport do, the people who we are segregated from – dare I say it? – The plebs. Staring is not done and so on my 'who's who?' general sweep of the first-class lounge, I clock Gwyneth (no surname needed) and I breeze quickly on. Nothing to see here. There is no one else present of any note, but hers is a big scalp and I am excited when I sit back down. I tell Tom who she is and then pointlessly I tell him not to look over. Naturally, he looks over. I roll my eyes and we both laugh. I recall how nervous and excited I was back in New York when I first met Tom's screen parents and how they became friends and 'normal' in the process. I signed off Chapter Twenty-Five with the words, 'Movie stars are just like the rest of us – normal, like you and I – you just have to get to know them, that's all.' This is true and perfectly demonstrated here because I don't know Gwyneth Paltrow at all and so I am excited all over again. Silly really, but there we are. The price of fame? In the making and writing of this book, I have met many illustrious people, but not yet so many that sharing their presence loses its allure.

Angelina Jolie or 'Ange' (as I know her) - seen here in heels!

On this subject, a funny incident took place in Toronto earlier in the year. Dustin Hoffman was sitting in the hotel having breakfast and again, I enjoyed pointing him out to Tom. Tom was less impressed, however, because he didn't know who he was.

'Dad, which one? The little guy?'

I quickly ran through Hoffman's canon: *Rain Man, Kramer vs. Kramer, The Graduate, All the President's Men, The Marathon Man, Outbreak, Tootsie?* Tom shook his head to these and we had to finally settle on *Meet the Fockers.* Tom was now duly impressed and all was well.

As we leave the lounge, Gwyneth is leaving too. She kisses a scruffy looking bloke goodbye, who I later realize must have been Chris Martin and if not, then I had just missed a major scoop. Now though, we are in the main airport, which is busy with normal people everywhere: the people who fly in seats that barely recline and eat what they are given and when they are told. Gwyneth really picks up the pace now. She is tall and has a long and purposeful stride, and the very attractive lady from BA accompanying her is practically running to keep up. The star has her 'game' face fixed forward and makes no eye contact with anything or anyone. I'm interested in how people react to her as they pass. Some people recognize her and look, but most people do not and no one dares to approach. Her body language is unmistakable. Looking at me is fine. Talking to me is not. Touching? Are you freaking insane?

We take a train to the plane: a short ride and a brief mingle with those passengers who will have more chance of surviving a plane crash because they will occupy the rear of the aircraft, but this is a risk I am willing to take. We get checked through a marginally quicker channel and finally we board the plane, and yes, I enjoy my alleluia moment of turning left. We are escorted to our seats, which is not necessary, but I say thank you, nonetheless. Gwyneth is already on board and right at the very front, which is a surprise because we lost her en route. Is there a faster train she took? Who knows? Who cares? Tom and I are 'slumming' it at the back of the first-class cabin, just like kids on the bus. So, there is a hierarchy it seems even within first class.

We settle down for the long flight ahead – or Tom does whilst I am busy fiddling with all kinds of buttons and just exploring my sense of space. Our cabin has probably twenty seats or so. A handsome man is sorting himself out just ahead of us. Tom recognizes him before I do and I add Eddie Redmayne to my archive. I already know all about Eddie: Eton, Cambridge, male model. Our Eddie was at the front of the queue when it came to picking up life chances and good for him. He seems like a nice bloke and I like him. Then we are joined by Tom Hooper, the film director responsible for *The King's Speech* and now *Les Miserables*. He and Gwyneth strike up a conversation immediately and Eddie is drawn in also. They might already know each other but I suspect that they don't and that this is a fame thing I have mentioned already.

Deep into the twelve-hour flight, I am aware of someone talking to Tom. It is Tom Hooper. The director has introduced himself and I wonder how the hell he knows who Tom is. Has he seen a screening of The Impossible? Or possibly read my blog? I recall a Friday afternoon in my car some years ago. He was a guest on BBC 5 live, basking in the enormous success of *The King's Speech*, which had seemingly taken him by surprise as well. He was being feted by all and found himself at a dinner at the White House, where President Obama referenced his film during his speech. As I drove along, I had tried to imagine what it must be like to have the film world at your beck and call. And now here he is, this vaunted director, introducing himself to Tom, and I smile inwardly before it finally dawns on me. He must have seen that Tom was reading a script ahead of his meeting in LA next week with Drew Barrymore.

Now Eddie joins the conversation also and I smile again at the incredulity of the whole thing and the trajectory that Tom finds himself on. Literally on cloud nine, I should imagine. People often ask me what it is like seeing my son do such things and I can't really answer. Surreal and sometimes numbing is the best I can offer, which never feels adequate or satisfactory.

Tom is becoming famous. How famous and for how long is an unknown. Through all this madness, Nikki and I have always been mindful and keen to keep a sense of normality in our son's life. And key to this strategy is for Tom to remain at school for his sixth form: arguably the best and most formative time of a kid's life, just on the cusp of adulthood.

But his childhood has been nothing close to normal and it becomes more unusual with each trip and each passing week. I have not recounted in this book all of what is going on in Tom's life and career for reasons already explained. A new routine in my daily life nowadays is to check my email first thing when I wake up because LA is eight hours behind us, and often, there will be some news from America overnight: an interview request or a script or something that requires my attention on behalf of my unusual eldest son.

Tom's family life is completely normal. At home, he is just Tom and his brothers don't defer to him or give him an inch, and quite right too. During a recent trip to LA accompanied by his mum, we skyped each other a lot and one evening during a meal with my boys at home, we set my laptop up and all six of us had dinner together.

Technology working for me? A rare thing

For his sixth form, Tom joined a theatrical school where no one knew anything about him. During a theatre class one day, the teacher required the students to perform some rudimentary ballet moves and naturally, Tom looked different to his peers. Suitably impressed and probably a little surprised, his teacher enquired if he had ever taken ballet classes and she suggested that he could be a Billy Elliot. On another occasion, a friend of his who was studying production was instructed to study the work of the prestigious make-up artist, Alessandro Bertolazzi, the man who had made Tom up every day for sixth months on *The Impossible*. His friend wondered how he might go about studying Alessandro and Tom offered to give him a ring.

One of my abiding memories at school was when our chemistry and sports teacher, a priest called Father Young, explained to our cricket team that I would make fielding in cricket bearable by making everyone laugh. This is a tiny thing I know, just an innocuous comment, but one which I enjoyed and has always stuck with me. Maybe because I wanted to be a comedian and I liked and rated this man, whatever; it ranks as one of my adolescent memories. I can't imagine then how Tom must feel walking into school at present with a huge billboard shadowing the gates from where his face stares down. One of my twins, Sam came home from school recently. 'Had a great day at school today dad. I got on a bus with Tom on it.'

At LAX for the premiere, Tom and I go through security together. I have filled out a form on the plane for immigration purposes and I tick the box 'Business' for the reason for my visit. Now, a huge immigration officer is scrutinising us both and the form that I have completed.

'Mr Holland, what is the nature of your business here in the US? What brings you to LA?'

The answer is fatherhood and this kid standing on my right. I'm with Tom is the answer. Tom is the business.

The beginnings of a paunch? (On me I mean)

But don't underestimate my role. As his dad, I figure that I am still key and that I am still more important than many of the illustrious people he is about to meet.

We check into The Four Seasons, where else and I take great delight in showing Tom where Anne sat and where I passed through. For this whole trip, every time we passed through this lounge, I turned and waved at the imaginary film star and it was funny every time.

We attended a reception one night at the ultra-cool Chateau Marmont. It is one of LA's oldest hotels at nearly eighty years old and like many of the LA residents of a similar age, no expense is spared in keeping the place looking fresh. Jack Black is hosting a screening of *The Impossible* to be followed by a meal.

Mr Holland and Mr Black

This is a photo of the two them during a previous trip. At such events, I tend to let Tom run free. He doesn't want his dad next to him and understandably people want to chat to the kid and not his old man. I see Tom on the balcony chatting with Dustin Hoffman and I fully expect that Tom has learnt from our earlier conversation and has jettisoned *Meet the Fockers* for *The Marathon Man*. I gesture for Tom to come inside when he can. There is someone else I know he would like to meet. Inside, I have been sitting within earshot of Reese Witherspoon and I know that she is very taken with the film.

'How was Dustin Hoffman? Did you mention *Meet the Fockers?*'

'No, I went with *Marathon Man*.' I smile. Tom just gets it. He's practically a pro and being able to bullshit about a film he hasn't seen is a skill he gets directly from me. I point Tom to a lady across the room in the dress with her back to us. It is Reese Witherspoon and without skipping a beat, Tom is off to introduce himself to one of the world's highest paid actresses. Another poignant moment for me to reflect on then? When I was his age, I spent a large proportion of my waking day thinking about girls. But the images of hippos crashing heads reappeared to terrorize me and unlike Tom, approaching any girl, let alone a movie star, was pretty much beyond me. Mind you, I didn't have a movie as my calling card, which is a pretty safe conversation opener. No matter; Tom is nothing like I was at the same age and this is a good thing.

At another reception, I am seated between Jackie Collins and a beautiful actress whom I shall refer to only as Susan. She had been one of the first supermodels in the sixties. The Christie Brinkley of her day. I have met Jackie before and I am excited to see if she remembers me.

Ms Collins has written more books than I have sold

I suspect she won't because it was over fifteen years ago and she only said three words to me: 'You're so funny.' Without embarrassing her, I gave her the chance to recall our encounter, which she didn't, and my subtle prompts were no help either. We had met in the greenroom of *The Clive James Show*. I was the guest on before Jackie and she must have watched my interview on a monitor. During dinner we discussed books, as you would expect, both of us being such giant novelists.

Chatting with 'Susan' on my other side, something truly awful happened, which only ever seems to happen to me. Susan is one of the most beautiful and chic people I have ever met. She is perfectly preserved and doesn't look as though a doctor, a scalpel or a needle has ever been near her. This is not relevant to the story but since this is Hollywood, I mention it anyway. Susan had just seen the film and was particularly taken with Tom and his performance, and was delighted to meet us both ahead of sitting down for dinner. During the meal, though, something happened. Susan must have become confused and somehow decided that I was in fact not the father of the boy acting in the film, but the actual real-life dad on whom the story is based. This slowly occurred to me over a lingering period with certain turns of phrase and comments.

'It must have been awful that tsunami?'

'Yes, it was.'

'Terrible! And yet here you are?'

'Erm...'

This meant I now faced a decision. The sensible thing to do at this point would be to politely correct her and explain that I was Tom's dad and that Tom is just an actor. But I didn't and please don't ask me to explain. Perhaps it was because I did not want to embarrass her and so I let it go. It did no harm if she happened to think that I was Henrique Belon, survivor of the tsunami and real life father of Lucas. Immediately I regretted it. But once committed, I had to fully commit. Playing heavy on my mind was the fact that the real-life Henrique was in the room and sitting at the very next table, with people who no doubt, Susan knew. What was I thinking? What happens if they chat later about their lunch?

'I sat with the real-life father.'

'No, you didn't; I did.'

But I was less worried about this for the moment, as I now fielded questions that came at me thick and fast. As you can imagine, I was desperate to change the subject.

'Isn't this risotto lovely?'

'Yes, but never mind that. How long were you under the water for?'

Bloody hell! I don't know. I can barely swim.

'Er, three minutes.' What the hell was I thinking?

'And what about injuries? Were you injured?'

'Er...' How is it that I get in to situations like this?

'Just bruises,' I said. And then my ruse completely collapsed. Susan stopped talking for a moment as if something suddenly occurred to her. She now looked at me oddly. She was confused. 'But I thought that the real family was Spanish?'

At this I blanched and wondered what my options were now. I speak remarkably fluent English for a Spaniard and even stranger, I speak no Spanish at all, outside, hello, please, thank you and beer? And yet for a split second, I even thought I might still be able to pull this off. Thank God, I didn't and finally I decided to come clean. It was a little awkward and Susan was as embarrassed as me. It was good timing as well because a split second later, an individual gave an impromptu speech and invited the real Maria and Henrique Belon to stand up to receive everyone's applause. I was so relieved. I had just narrowly missed my Spartacus moment, where I would have had to lean in to Susan and claim, 'that bloke is deluded. I'm Henrique.'

At the end of the lunch, saying goodbye to Jackie, I told her that she has written more books than I have managed to sell and she laughed and repeated what she had said to me when we last met, at which we both laughed.

The LA premiere was, if anything, a little bit flat, but only because of what had preceded it. Toronto was the first and then there was Madrid. London had been exciting with so many friends and family present to see the film for the first time.

On the red carpet in LA we also knew that the incredibly long adventure of *The Impossible* was finally ending, which was sad in many respects, as kind as it has been to Tom and my whole family. On the final red carpet, Ewan and Naomi were available to hold Tom's hand as they had both done now for nearly two years. At a meal afterwards, I sat with Ewan and I regaled him with my tsunami survival story from earlier in the day.

The red carpet in London and that paunch again

'Why did you go along with it?' he asked me. Good question and one I couldn't answer, but it was a story I couldn't wait to tell Nikki.

We were heading back to London the next day and I sensed that Tom was so tired that he wasn't going to stay at the post-premiere party for very long. I asked Ewan if he had ever made a film like this before: a film that took six months to film and two years in post-production during which time such strong friendships amongst cast and crew had formed. He thought for a moment and shook his head. More proof then about just how lucky Tom and my whole family have been.

So, my enormous thanks to so many people who made this story possible. To Tom of course for his hard work and being in the right place at the right time, and for crucially doing and saying the right things as well. To my other boys who have all flirted with eclipsing me and I am sure they will do so yet and I promise them not to write about their endeavours. And lastly to Nikki who is without question the main reason behind this book. Had it not been for his mum, he would never have accomplished all this stuff and I would not have been able to write this book, which has been a great privilege.

Author Footnote - Oct 2016

You will recall the BBC Radio 4 show in which I didn't make the edit - the two 'funny' and true stories that I used for the recording were breaking my leg by falling off Paddy's scooter and my encounter at the LA restaurant when for half an hour I pretended that I had survived a tsunami.

Reading this last chapter, I am interested to read my words - 'Tom is becoming famous. How famous and for how long is an unknown'. In truth, we always hoped that Tom's good fortune might continue but realistically we expected that it wouldn't. All good things fade and we worried about his future and his education. Now with hindsight, we worried too much. Today as I write (10th Jan 2017) he is in London making a film with some bloke called Benedict Cumberbatch and he's just been nominated for a BAFTA in the category of breakthrough artist.

But expecting the roles to dry up and because Nikki's dad and her brothers are all brilliantly practical; her two brothers are carpenters and her dad is a self-taught tradesman who can turn his hand to anything. (He is bloody annoying if I am honest and has put a considerable strain on my married life since I specialize in bodging jobs ahead of getting professionals in to salvage matters for my exasperated wife.)

And so, Nikki decided that Tom should acquire a trade too to go alongside his ability to act. Having finished *In the Heart of the Sea*, directed by the peerless Ron Howard and with no further work on the horizon, we booked Tom on to a residential woodworking course in Cardiff.

Nikki took him down the M4 and dropped him at his digs; a local family in need of some cash. Tom was not recognized and naturally we didn't explain who he was nor what he had done. He was just any old eighteen-year-old. The course was full of the people who you might expect. Kids who had not fared too well at school and might have been excluded and lots of older people retraining. Squaddies from Iraq and Afghanistan with stories to tell and others recovering from rehab and spells inside. I am sure in the six weeks or so that Tom attended, that he learnt as much about life as he did about joinery.

Our logic was that should his luck run dry and the film roles dwindle, then he can always put up shelves but as things currently stand, these skills might be needed to shelve his glassware that people keep chucking his way.

Epilogue

"Eclipsed" is a shameless piece of opportunism written by a man who missed the fame boat and is now clawing his fingers bloody raw at the edifice of his son's stardom." Dominic Holland, 2013

I can't disagree with much of this statement. But I suppose that tone and context is important and having read the book, my readers can decide whether I am guilty of anything or not? Refuting the allegations that we are pushy parents is a good enough reason alone to have written this book. But there are other reasons besides. Not least that it filled many thousands of spare hours of my time while I waited for my phone to ring.

Whilst I am literary enough to understand that clichés are best avoided, I do need to use them if I am to adequately explain what I have learnt from writing this book. For nearly one hundred thousand words, I have avoided the dreaded word 'journey' but no longer. WARNING : My writing limits are about to be breached.

Life might well be a 'journey', but I better understand now that life should not be lived as such. Life is not like a vacation where we suffer the flight to get to the beach. Life is a journey that needs to be lived at every moment. We are deluding ourselves if we sit and wait for some ultimate outcome or destination. The only absolute destination is the inevitable one that awaits us all.

Not that we shouldn't be ambitious, though. I don't regret any of my efforts in the film world because as I have already said, endeavour is always worth it. With it comes hope and hope is essential for us all whoever we are.

Do not ever feel sorry or worried for this man

I have frequently mentioned luck in this book and specifically the role that good fortune plays in the life of any successful person, myself included. Writing this book, has been a useful reminder of just how fortunate I have been.

And I don't mean in my health – something which we all take for granted - but lucky in my on-going career and now with this book. It was having such lofty ambitions as a writer (coupled with a confidence crisis) that allowed this story to emerge, not to mention having a son like Tom to complete it. But equally, I am lucky that I can write this book at all. Having failed English Language O-level (grade E at my first attempt), it would have been a brave teacher who predicted me having any career as a writer.

More indulgently, *Eclipsed* is a very long-winded answer to the two questions I am most frequently asked when I encounter people who recognize me. They aren't easy questions to answer and writing this book is preferable to attempting a response on a busy tube train or elsewhere. The questions then? 'How come you aren't on telly anymore?' Followed by, 'So, what have you been up to then?' The answers to both questions are really the same: trying to get on just like everyone else in the world. Because life is a series of struggles and our success is a factor of how we cope with them and I mean in all areas of life: as a comedian, a writer, dad, friend, brother, husband, golfer and son. But I don't say this in a mawkish sense and certainly not to garner any sympathy. I use struggle in an affirmative sense of the word, because having written this book, I understand much better now that life is meant to be a challenge and that with challenge must come struggle.

And finally, there is another reason that I wrote this book – the most important reason of all in fact. I haven't mentioned it yet, possibly because it doesn't cast me in a particularly good light. But remaining honest until the bitter end, I leave it to the penultimate paragraph of the epilogue to finally come clean.

You will recall that by law Tom requires a chaperone and therefore he was always going to need to be accompanied to LA for the premiere of 'The Impossible'. I have long dreamt of attending an LA premiere ever since I sat on that freezing cold train out of Stockton-On-Tees in 1995. You can see my thinking now? Clearly, Nikki is equally well-qualified to accompany Tom, but is she as deserving? Sure, she spotted that Tom could dance but this blog and this book has been a monumental effort. Well over a million words...

I hope it shows, but this book has a Herculean effort. Ernest Hemingway once said - "A man has got to take a lot of punishment to write a really funny book." How funny this book is, is not for me to say but it is as funny as I can write it be and it has certainly metered out some punishment.

And fittingly, I will finish in the world of film and muse about what might happen next to Tom and to me. Maybe things will continue for Tom but enough about the kid - what about the dad I hear you cry?

Tom no longer travels like the rest of us

Well, the glass is half full and I can't stop myself from dreaming. Forget all that self-help, navel-gazing guff I have just espoused above, about enjoying the bloody journey and living in the moment? There is a destination alright, let me tell you and it's Hollywood?

And to finish, I need to revisit my most hideous meeting in the world of film. You will recall that it was in a private members club in London. The Groucho Club on Dean Street. The man I was meeting was a very angry and very self-important American film executive, in effect, a bully and a complete and utter knob. He had flown in for the day and he obviously enjoyed beating up on a writer and showing off to his colleague. You may recall that he referred to having a child with a c***. To this, I didn't know how to respond and I probably just stared at him wide eyed. Does he mean that he has a daughter and if so, then what a way to describe her?

In fact, he was referring to his wife. He has a child with his wife, who happens to be a c***. Like I say, what a knob. We were meeting about my screenplay, *Only in America* and having completely trashed it and my ability as a writer – "*... reading your script, I'm not getting that you're a comedian... Seriously, I'm not getting that you're a funny guy.*' I should have walked out then but typically I didn't. Only having sons, I wanted to tell him that I didn't have any kids with c**** but I didn't. I did tell him though about the exploits of my eldest son and that I was writing a blog with plans for a book called *Eclipsed*. His eyes widened and suddenly he slammed his fists onto the desk and shouted, 'Right there! That's it! Write that! That's the movie you should write. That's a hit fucking movie.'

Can you see it? *Eclipsed the Movie*?

And wouldn't this be the greatest and most delicious irony of all, that *Eclipsed*, borne out of my miserable experiences in film, should go onto become my breakthrough after all?

Sure, this is hopelessly romantic, I know, but it excites me nonetheless. For crying out loud, it's a funny story with a cute kid and a happy ending! What's not to like? And do you know what? The more I think about it, the more I can see it...

At this, Nikki sighs heavily and looks to the heavens. Why can't her deluded husband just let it go; especially now that the eclipse is complete?

Why don't we listen to the doctors when they tell us to stay in the shade because it is safer? I don't apologise thinking this way because I can't help it. Not really. It's all about endeavour you see and life in the Holland household goes on pretty much as before.

The man who introduced me to Rural Arts, Richard Bucknell gave me some great advice when I came to writing this book. And given its personal content and sensitivities, it is a book that has been written and rewritten many tens of times. Richard warned me that I must not write a book with any rancour or sadness. Even if my career parabola flattened earlier than I would have liked. To the reading public, I am still Dominic Holland and a lucky sod, compared to what most people do for a living. Richard summed it up nicely, saying that the book needed to be written by a cool dad about his cooler son. And too many rewrites later, I hope I have struck this balance. This picture was taken at the premiere of *The Impossible* in London, do I look like a man who wants people to feel sorry for me?

I welcome correspondence from my readers and viewers unless it is abusive to which you should not expect a response.

@domholland

Domholland1@gmail.com

Other books
by
Dominic Holland

Author's note

A question I am commonly asked; of all the things that I do, which of them do I most enjoy?

The answer to this is writing. Sure, doing 'great' stand-up is exhilarating but for this to happen, I need everything to be just so. I need my head to feel right. The audience have a big role to play plus there are further conditions and nuances required for a great gig.

Writing however is largely independent of circumstances. There is not a bad sound system to blame, a drunk heckler or a lifeless audience to contend with. Writers all have the same laptops and software packages; the only variable being our imaginations, our skill and the time that we put in.

And no matter that I am not a literary writer, nor a wordsmith but I do love to write; in the way that I imagine musicians must feel when they play.

But this is not to say that writing alone is enough. By its nature, writing is a solitary pursuit, but all writers tap away in the hope that their work will be found and read and enjoyed.

The cliché states that everyone has a novel in them and with the advent of eBooks allowing authors to circumvent the gatekeepers, many more people will get their novel out there. And most of these will fail, practically all of them in fact - but so what, because what value, hope eh?

But that said, anyone brave enough to put themselves up for public consumption had better get used to disappointment.

Which helps to explain how important it is to receive positive feedback from readers. Stinker reviews aside (something which all authors need to live with) I would like to thank all the people who have come to my books and particularly those of you who have taken the time to review them. In my despondent moments, I sometimes read a snapshot of these reviews and they remind me that I must continue tapping away.

Below are a range of these reviews for all my books...

Only in America

It all began with this novel. The story of Only in America was inspired from my experiences with my first ever screenplay, The Faldovian Club. This story became my first novel and this whole film and book experience underpins the story of my only work of non-fiction, Eclipsed.

*

"This book is so charming and funny. A genuine page turner, I read it on holiday and missed big chunks of Venice"
Sandi Toksvig

"A fine stand-up comic has turned in to a first class, laugh out loud novelist. Read and enjoy"
Barry Cryer

"The only book I have ever read in one sitting. Of all the books by comedians turning their hands to novel writing - this is the funniest, most enjoyable and satisfying"
Nottingham Post

"As soon as you pick it up, you forget about everything that you have you to do, and you read it from cover to cover and you laugh out loud and love it."
Jenny Hanley

"Witty and charming. Astonishingly good. Quite irritating in fact."
Angus Deayton

"...of all the comedians turning their hands to novel writing – including Stephen Fry – this is the funniest, most enjoyable and satisfying."
Nottingham Post

"Holland's novel is witty, warm, enjoyable, addictive, captivating and hilariously funny. Laughing out loud on your own can be an unnerving experience, but laugh uncontrollably I did."
Oxford Mail

Open Links

This book was written for the Anthony Nolan Trust - the largest bone barrow register in the world. Anthony Nolan saves many hundreds of lives each year. All monies from this book go to this charity in the hope that somewhere, sometime, someone with blood cancer will be tissue matched and their life will be saved. By buying Open Links, you will be helping to make this happen. Thank you.

*

"From the first page I was gripped, and delighted to be reading a 'can't put this down' book. The story was funny and inspiring, the warm characters formed clear pictures in my head and the writing flowed effortlessly without a dull moment. There were several laugh out loud moments, and I have to admit an occasional tear fell on my cheek"

"This is a seriously good read... making it very hard to put down and it was always a case of "Just one more chapter...""

"Mr Holland will take you on the most entertaining and heart-tugging "round" of your life"

"Like the best underdog tales, this builds momentum beautifully and has a heart of gold"

"This is a genuinely touching story that had me thinking "just one more hole" each time I picked it up. A great read and an even better cause"

"Genuinely one of the funniest and most heart-warming books I have read in years"

"This story has it all, and caught me where it counts in the "big picture" department. A great story with an even greater cause. Books like this are written from a deep place to do true good in the world. What more can you say?"

A Man's Life

This novel began its life as a screenplay called The Fruit Bowl and played an integral role in the story that you have just read, Eclipsed. I did manage to sell this screenplay and it was nearly set up as a film on two occasions before it eventually perished and why I decided to write the novel. It is available only as an eBook (at present) and even though I did have it professionally copy edited, I am weary of being scolded for its typos. I have given it another pass but I suspect that some remain - so my apologies.

*

"Within 3 chapters I was hooked and distraught as the story unfolded and then intrigued as we moved into the plot. I couldn't put it down, really wanted to know how it ended and am a little bereft now I've finished it"

"Quite simply one of the best books I have read! Very much in the John O'Farrell mould - only better - how on earth someone hasn't turned this into a film I just don't know. I have re-read the final couple of chapters a few times as they are simply wonderful"

"What an enjoyable book. I am sitting here a 1.30am feeling a little lost because I have finished this book. You know that sad empty feeling when something great is over"

"Having read his two previous books, The Ripple Effect and Only in America (both of which I'd strongly urge you to check out and buy as well), over the last few years I always kept an eye out on Amazon for his next offering. Finally I managed to find A Man's Life and bought it without hesitation. I wasn't disappointed"

"It is extremely rare that I write a review of a book but on this occasion, I feel that it is necessary and hope that it will help to spread the word of this excellent author and comedian"

"Equally as good as The Ripple Effect and Only in America (both of which I would also recommend)"

The Ripple Effect

Currently, available as an eBook only. Or not available in any good book shops!

I do have plans to create a print book version.

A joyous romp - The Ripple Effect is an Ealing comedy for the 21st Century
Alan Coren

Only in America was a step in the right direction, but The Ripple Effect heralds Holland's emergence in to the literary big time.
The Sunday Times

Proof that Holland is a master of comedy
Northern Echo

'A belter of a novel. This could be the book of the season.'
Danny Baker

Funny, gripping and hard to put down – what more do you want from a novel?'
The Sunday Times

'An infectious, warm-hearted tale about real people pulling together.'
The Mirror

'Not every stand-up comedian manages to be as funny in print as they are on stage. Dominic Holland is one of the few who is.'
Liverpool Daily Post

'Proof that Holland is a master of comedy.'
Yorkshire Evening Press

Eclipsed

"One might think this is a selfish attempt to gain fame and fortune at the expense of his son. This is the not the case. Eclipsed is written with more brutal honesty and self-deprecating humour than can be expected from anyone with selfish intentions"

"Dominic Holland bravely exposes his hopes and disappointments, his talents and his frailties in a story which is ultimately redemptive in its fearless honesty and open-hearted spirit. 'Eclipsed' is a bitter-sweet tale of great liveliness and warmth; above all, it is profoundly human"

"Dominic Holland doesn't claim 'superior genes', 'unique talent' or 'fate' for his son Tom, but gives credit to his hard work, application and a high degree of natural talent. This is a truly remarkable, balanced perspective given the dizzy heights to which Tom's career has already achieved and which have so far eluded his old man"

"Whilst the context for Eclipsed is unique, the themes of parental love, pride, self-esteem versus self-doubt and the sense of handing the baton on to the next generation are universal. For any parent who has ever let their child beat them in a running race to encourage them when they were young, only to have them sail past you leaving you panting in their wake once they come of age, this book will resonate strongly. It is funny, fast-paced, moving and uplifting in equal measure. And at the heart of the story is the belief that hope will triumph over most things"

"I loved this book as it's funny, honest and heartfelt. My kind of book. Any parent could relate to this and at times it felt like I was reading the script of a movie. I hope you enjoy it, I did"

"Dominic's style is funny, candid, engaging and honest. The way he describes the scenes and events is hilarious and at times I sat on the train laughing out loud. I recommend it to all twenty first century parents"

Available as an eBook and hard copy via Anthonynolan.com

Made in the USA
Middletown, DE
26 July 2019